LYNCHING TO BELONG

NUMBER 106:

Centennial Series of the Association of Former Students,
Texas A&M University

Lynching TO BELONG

CLAIMING WHITENESS THROUGH RACIAL VIOLENCE

Cynthia Skove Nevels

TEXAS A&M UNIVERSITY PRESS
College Station

The paper used in this book meets the minimum requirements
of the American National Standard for Permanence
of Paper for Printed Library Materials, z39.48-1984.
Binding materials have been chosen for durability.

Library of Congress Cataloging-in-Publication Data

Nevels, Cynthia Skove, 1955–
Lynching to belong : claiming Whiteness through racial violence /
Cynthia Skove Nevels. — 1st ed.
p.   cm. — (Centennial series of the Association of Former Students,
Texas A&M University ; no. 106)
Includes bibliographical references and index.
ISBN-13: 978-1-58544-589-9 (cloth : alk. paper)
ISBN-10: 1-58544-589-4 (cloth : alk. paper)
1. Brazos County (Tex.)—Race relations—History—19th century.   2. Brazos
County (Tex.)—Race relations—History—20th century.   3. Whites—Race
identity—Texas—Brazos County—History.   4. European Americans—Race
identity—Texas—Brazos County—History.   5. Immigrants—Texas—Brazos
County—Social conditions.   6. Immigrants—Texas—Brazos County—Attitudes—
History.   7. Racism—Texas—Brazos County—History.   8. African Americans—
Crimes against—Texas—Brazos County—History.   9. Lynching—Texas—Brazos
County—History.   10. Violence—Texas—Brazos County—History.   I. Title.
F392.B84N485   2007
305.8009764′242—dc22
2007007624

TO BOB

CONTENTS

ILLUSTRATIONS

ACKNOWLEDGMENTS

I owe thanks beyond measure to Walter Buenger, and to David Vaught and Sylvia Grider at Texas A&M University, where the idea for this project first germinated. Their enthusiastic support, helpful advice, and research knowledge made this undertaking possible. Dr. Buenger, who served as my committee chair, allowed me to pursue this project according to my own instincts and on my own timetable, and for that freedom I am grateful indeed. Without his continuing help and counsel, this project would not have reached book form. Dr. Vaught's ardent belief in the value of good writing challenged me to let no sentence slide by without examining it for greater clarity. To Dr. Grider I owe a new appreciation of the value of tangible resources; cemeteries are now among my favorite places in which to conduct research.

My great regret is that Robert Calvert, whose knowledge of Texas history never failed to astonish me, did not live long enough to see this research completed. As the graduate adviser at the time I started my academic studies, he was a superb cheerleader, and without his welcoming encouragement I would never have begun. Thanks are also due to Walter Kamphoefner for helpful discussions about Germans in Texas. I am grateful to Dale Baum, who probably knows more than anyone else living about Brazos Valley history and politics, for reading and commenting on an early version of a chapter. Sarah Alpern deserves special acknowledgment. Her infectious interest in women's history, and her enthusiastic response to a graduate paper I wrote for her on ladies and lynching laid the groundwork for what eventually became this book. Carol Higham provided early encouragement and direction, and her ability to find humor in the most macabre history offered both relief and inspiration. I am also deeply grateful for the careful attention James SoRelle and William D. Carrigan gave to earlier versions of the manuscript and for the important suggestions they made for its improvement.

It is impossible to adequately thank Bill Page at the Texas A&M University Library, whose research collections and encyclopedic knowledge of Brazos County history shaved off years of research time for me. But for him

I would still be hunched over microfilm machines, and I would certainly have missed many important tidbits of information that proved critical to the book. His interest in this project and good humor often helped to revive my flagging energy. I must also thank the staff of the Carnegie Center of Brazos Valley History—Nancy Ross, Shirley Ferguson, Diane Smith, and Sandra Simoneaux—for their cheerful assistance in finding critical documents related to the county's history, despite the sometimes terrible subject of my research. David Ely at the Carnegie Center provided critical help in obtaining photographs.

I am grateful also for the assistance of Vincent J. Palazzo Sr., Andrew C. Ramirez, Vincent J. Palazzo Jr., and David Wayne Marino, who were willing to share with me what they knew of their Italian forebears. I am thankful also to Ernie Wentrcek for helpful conversation about the Czech community and to Cosmo and Antoinette Guido for insight into Brazos Varisco. Zane Anderson provided valuable assistance in telling me about the Parker-Astin store. I also owe thanks to George Hamilton, whose early research into Brazos County's lawmen and outlaws proved extremely helpful, and to Louise Hamilton for her assistance in digging out old documents that turned out to be useful indeed. I am also grateful for the Hamiltons' willingness to lend important photographs for use in this book.

Much of the genesis of this book can be traced to early conversations about race and history with Mell Pruitt, Ronnie Jackson, Sunny Nash, and Rev. Maurice Green. Their honesty and thoughtful reflection taught me more than any graduate seminar, and I am deeply obligated to them.

To Christel Brymer I owe a special debt. Her unflagging curiosity about the fate of Fannie Palazzo kept mine alive, and she proved to be a most valuable research assistant. If Sylvia Grider convinced me that research treasure lay hidden in cemeteries, Beth Stus and Bernean Deeter enabled me to gather such treasure in particularly healthful ways. As fellow explorers of Brazos County geography, they never tired of listening to my dreadful stories about the county's past on our bicycling expeditions to old cemeteries scattered across Brazos County. Thanks to them, I am a much better cyclist, not to mention a better reader of tombstones. Without the encouragement of Jane Bolin and Shelby Jaedicke, and the support of Deborah Simpson, Cathy Littleton, Sunny O'Neal, and Susan Haven, this project would have come to a standstill long ago.

My parents, Jim and Flo Skove, are indefatigable clippers of newspapers, and they never doubted the viability of this project, thus providing more encouragement than they could realize. Dave Skove and Jamie Skove were most helpful readers of an early version of the manuscript. Katie and Robby Nevels showed more patience than I had any right to expect, and grew up believing that researching gruesome historical murders was a normal thing for a mother to do. And to the one who never stopped believing in the value of this project, and never stopped asking questions about my daily progress, I owe an immeasurable debt of gratitude: my husband, Bob Nevels.

LYNCHING TO BELONG

INTRODUCTION

Our fellow citizens of foreign birth will, like all good citizens, vote intel-ligently, freely and conscientiously in the primary, and will stick to the ticket like a man. Of course, there are certain matters about which they are very peculiar . . .

BRYAN EAGLE, 26 June 1890

There was something unconventional about the reasons why five black men died in Brazos County, Texas, around the turn of the twentieth century. The victims died in a series of violent racial eruptions, but they were by no means the only black men in Brazos County to die a violent death at the hands of angry whites. At least sixteen were killed by various means in the last decades of the nineteenth century, a time when the lives of black men throughout the South were particularly vulnerable to brutal endings. And at first glance, nothing seemed exceptional about the deaths of these five. The causes were unremarkable. An alleged rape of a white woman or an attack on a respected public official sparked each of the three episodes. There was nothing extraordinary about the resulting lynchings and legal ex-ecution. They were closely similar to other such events occurring regularly across Texas and the rest of the South. At least on the surface, anyway, they all seemed to follow a standard script.[1]

But there was an intriguing aspect, a curious twist, to these deaths. In each case, European immigrants of different nationalities—first Italian, then Irish, and finally Bohemian, or Czech—played crucial roles at the be-ginning of each story and helped to launch a series of events that culminated in death. The first two incidents, in 1896 and 1897, were mob-led lynchings. The third, a complex court case that stretched from 1900 to 1901, ended in an execution that was characteristic in some respects of a legal lynching. Why were these Europeans present in what were essentially southern racial affairs, and what did they stand to gain?

Answers to these questions begin with an understanding of life in Brazos County during the late nineteenth century. Texas, with its seemingly unbounded opportunities in unsettled land, had attracted tens of thousands of new residents in the aftermath of the Civil War, and many of these sojourners had made their way to the state's central region. The well-watered valleys of the Trinity, Colorado, and Brazos Rivers had already drawn thousands of settlers before the war, an inflow that accelerated afterward into explosive growth. As was the case elsewhere in east-central Texas, the patchwork of prairie, timber, and fertile floodplain that made up Brazos County lured hundreds of newcomers each year. But such population growth, and the constant changes it produced, did not make for a peaceful social climate. Historians have noted the violence of southern society compared with other regions in the United States, and Brazos County was most southern in this respect. Vengeful feuds, mysterious shootings, arson attacks, mob-led lynchings, and racial brutality of every sort marked the county's history well into the twentieth century, as was the case in most of central Texas.

What contemporaries called a race riot convulsed Brazos County during the tumultuous years of Reconstruction. The county also numbered at least sixteen lynch victims over the next sixty years, making it one of the state's top counties for racial violence. Texas as a whole was prone to lynching, earning the unfortunate ranking of number three in the nation for lynch victims, after Mississippi and Georgia. And the most lynch-prone part of Texas was the same area that had attracted so many new settlers before and after the war: the south-central and Gulf plain river valleys of the Trinity, Brazos, and Colorado. In fact, Brazos County is dead center in the area where the heaviest concentration of lynchings took place—the eleven counties along the Brazos River between Waco and the Gulf of Mexico.[2]

Such racial brutality perhaps is not surprising, given the history and demographic makeup of the region. The state's most prosperous slave plantations before the Civil War were located along the Brazos River, where many of the state's African Americans continued to live after the war. Cotton and sugar production formed the economic base of the area, and both required significant numbers of laborers. As a result, most of the counties in this area had high proportions of African American residents, from one-third to three-quarters of the population. Lynching was one of several tools that whites could use to maintain control over this labor force, while eliminating any threat of political competition and ensuring white supremacy.[3]

Lynching has become a much-studied topic in southern history in recent decades, as historians have increasingly recognized the significance of this most deadly form of racial domination. Historians, sociologists, and literary critics have been pondering a host of explanations for such widespread and public brutality, which resulted in the gruesome deaths of thousands of Americans in the South, West, and Midwest between 1880 and 1930. In the South, the vast majority of victims were African American. No single explanation has dominated; lynching is a question that seems to give a different answer depending on who is asking and why they are asking the question. Lynching was about economics. It had strong political overtones. There were psychosexual aspects, social repercussions, cultural meanings. It had religious significance, and it was about gender. And always, the immediate reason behind any single lynching was simple contingency: a lethal combination of specific social, political, economic, or religious factors that on a particular day in a particular place exploded into horrific violence.[4]

In Brazos County, one of those contingencies was the presence of a significant number of eastern and southern European immigrants, a small part of new immigration then entering the nation. Scores of historians have examined the nature and impact of such immigration, but nearly all of their work has focused on the northern and western regions of the United States. European immigration to the South has not been widely explored. Noticing a high number of foreign-born laborers who entered the South in the early part of the nineteenth century, historians Ira Berlin and Herbert G. Gutman in 1983 issued a call for greater attention to the impact of this immigration on urban areas of the antebellum South. Complaining that too many historians had ignored the heavy presence of foreign-born workers in skilled urban occupations, Berlin and Gutman labeled the immigrant "the South's invisible man." Hearing no answer almost a decade later, Dennis C. Rousey repeated the call for closer scrutiny of the diverse ethnic backgrounds of antebellum southerners. Rousey clearly demonstrated that urban populations had as much, if not more, ethnic and cultural diversity as northern cities of the same period.[5]

Rousey, however, conceded that foreign immigration to the South tapered off considerably after the Civil War, becoming a mere trickle compared to the gush of new arrivals that seemed to swamp major cities of the North. "The depressed economic conditions and endemic political and racial violence of the region held little allure for potential immigrants," Rousey noted, thus implying that historians were justified in ignoring immigration to the postwar South as inconsequential. Indeed, beginning with Walter Fleming's analysis in 1905, historians have routinely noted the tiny percentages of foreign-born people in the New South and gone no further.

C. Vann Woodward gave immigration no more than a few paragraphs in his classic *Origins of the New South* (1951), and Edward Ayers never mentioned it in his 1992 survey of the region, *The Promise of the New South*.[6]

But if overall percentages look puny when considering the South as a region, they gain significance when one examines particular patterns of immigration settlement, as Berlin and Gutman had argued in reference to antebellum cities. In certain areas of the postwar South, foreign immigration was by no means insubstantial. Thousands of Italians poured into southern Louisiana in the 1880s and 1890s, causing intense anxiety among Democrats who were trying to disenfranchise black voters and felt threatened by the Italians' indeterminate racial status. Meanwhile, in Florida, Tampa was experiencing explosive growth as the cigar industry attracted tens of thousands of Cuban and Spanish workers, causing the city's establishment elite to resort to intimidating violence in order to break strikes and defuse political threats. By the 1920s in Texas—the most multiethnic of southern states even in its earliest history—hundreds of thousands of Mexican-born and Mexican American farm laborers were struggling to gain a foothold in the state's cotton kingdom.[7]

Texas immigrants have hardly been ignored, but even here much work remains to be done. Historians have written about each of the major immigrant groups that arrived in Texas in the nineteenth century, but most of these works examine immigrant groups as discrete units, with little reference to the larger social and racial climate of Texas and the South. The exceptions are works focusing on Mexicans, whose life prospects were deeply marked by racial prejudice from the dominant Anglo population. Neil Foley argued that the Mexicans' swelling numbers after 1910 created a complex, three-way racial dynamic involving Mexicans, African Americans, and Anglos. As a result of the racial tensions and class conflict that ensued, Foley argued that "'whiteness' itself fissured along race and class lines," with poor whites descending nearly to the social level of blacks. Foley noted that eventually middle-class Texas Mexicans moved out of what he called the "ethnoracial borderlands between blackness and whiteness"—an area still inhabited by countless Mexican laborers—in order to construct identities as white Americans. Meanwhile, the bottom-rung ethnic and racial position of African Americans did not change.[8]

Foley's book is one of a growing number of "whiteness" studies that have formed a subgenre of works on American racialism by focusing on the historical construction of white identity. Whatever its value in explaining American social and cultural history, whiteness as a category of analysis seems to be salient in the highly racialized South. Texas offers especially fertile territory for such analysis, as an ethnic and racial borderland where the three components of Foley's triad—American-born Anglos, African Americans, and Mexicans—vied for privilege and power, and where European immigrants also entered the mix. Complaining about the overly generalized nature of many whiteness studies, historian Peter Kolchin called for future whiteness studies to "include greater attention to historical and geographical context" and "more sustained treatment of actual lived relations."[9]

As if in response to Kolchin's call, historians Michael Phillips and Stephanie Cole have each closely examined such "lived relations" in the complex history of Dallas. Cole examined the difficulties experienced by Dallasites as they attempted to fit various "outsiders," such as Jews and Chinese immigrants, into racial boxes. Phillips investigated the city's various power struggles between the white elite and the African American, Mexican American, and Jewish communities. Phillips argued that racial identity and the quest for white status proved too divisive for Mexican American and Jewish communities to combine forces with African Americans in order to combat the power monopoly of the white elite. As a result, African Americans were largely excluded from power. Meanwhile, through varying strategies of accommodation and assimilation, Mexican American and Jewish groups each achieved a limited degree of political strength.[10]

Brazos County, about 185 miles south of Dallas, also offers abundant opportunity to examine the geographical and historical context of racial struggle, in which white identity determined power and privilege. On the face of it, Brazos County seemed typical of rural communities in the Jim Crow South at the end of the nineteenth century. Heavily dependent on cotton production, the county was also burdened with memories of slavery and plantation agriculture, and the loss and upheaval of war. But much had changed since the end of the Civil War. By the 1890s the population of Brazos County had grown dramatically. In terms of racial percentages, it was about evenly divided between black and white. As was the case throughout the South, many of the county's families, white or black, were watching their dreams of landownership slowly erode as more and more were forced to make their living by sharecropping and tenant farming on land owned by wealthy whites. Meanwhile, members of the white elite were busy erecting new and elegant homes—largely with the profits from cotton—in the burgeoning railroad town of Bryan, which also served as the county seat. By the end of the nineteenth century, wealthy whites were well along toward their goal of solidifying their power not only over the economic life of the county, but also in its political arena. After some decades of uncertainty and political flux, Democratic leaders, most of whom lived in Bryan, finally were on the verge of controlling troublesome and rebellious political movements, both local and regional.

But then an unexpected change took place. Just as the county's white elite began to congratulate themselves for achieving control over what they called a "white man's country," a large and unfamiliar group of newcomers showed up. Into this southern racial dyad of white and black were thrust new and initially unclassifiable elements: hundreds of eastern and southern European immigrants. Were they white, or black, or something in between?[11] By legal definition, and according to U.S. naturalization requirements, they were white. But elsewhere in the nation, many Americans were increasingly questioning such status. In northeastern cities thousands of these new immigrants were arriving daily, to the growing consternation of nativists, whose strident calls for immigration restriction pointed to the new arrivals' degenerate character and low racial characteristics. Especially troublesome to nativists in the North were newcomers from eastern and southern Europe. Fearful nativists theorized about racial tendencies of these Europeans toward indolence and crime, and questioned these newcomers' innate abilities, or fitness, for self-government.[12]

In the South, where only two racial categories existed by the 1890s—white or black—the status of such immigrants was a puzzle indeed. Very few Mexicans or Mexican Americans lived in Brazos County at this point, so there had been no challenge to the racially bifurcated society since its inception in the 1820s. Substantial numbers of Mexicans would not move into Brazos County until well after the turn of the twentieth century. Now, at the end of the nineteenth century, the question loomed large: just where did these new European immigrants fit into Brazos County's southern racial hierarchy, social structure, and cultural landscape?

White, native-born southerners of Brazos County could not answer such a question definitively, at least not at first. In the end, the immigrants and their children helped to answer the question themselves. What aided them considerably as they answered that question were raging political conflicts that erupted in the 1890s. White Democrats fought for power at the local county level throughout the Brazos Valley by finally and permanently demolishing black Republican political strength and obliterating other non-Democratic opposition. Such political turbulence contributed to brutal racial violence, and this in turn provided an opportunity for immigrants to resolve their own racial ambiguities. By the time they arrived in Brazos

County, some of the immigrants—namely, the Sicilian Italians—had already experienced the South's highly racialized environment during a troubled sojourn in Louisiana. Within a few years, many came to realize the social and economic advantages of white skin. By the turn of the century, when they were arriving in Brazos County in droves, the county's foreign-born immigrants began claiming whiteness with a vengeance. They did so by taking advantage of, or even participating in, the South's most brutal form of racial domination: the lynching of black men. For each of the immigrant groups caught up in the violence—Italians, Irish, and Bohemians—the deaths of black men helped to resolve the immigrants' ambiguous racial identity and to bestow the privileges of whiteness.

This study does not examine in any depth the presence of Mexicans and Mexican Americans in Brazos County in the 1890s, despite their similar status as "in-between southerners," which in many ways continues to this day. The reason for their absence from this study is that Mexicans were largely absent from Brazos County during the time period under investigation. Most Mexicans and Mexican Americans lived farther south in Texas, in regions closer to the border with Mexico. Census records show few residents of Mexican birth in Brazos County before the turn of the twentieth century, and they made only rare appearances in the local newspapers. Such evidence suggests that the limited presence of Mexicans did not register as a problematic issue in the minds of the white, native-born southerners of Brazos County nearly to the degree that newly arriving Europeans did. That situation would change in later decades, as more and more Mexicans and their descendants began to move into Brazos County during the twentieth century to take jobs as laborers and farm workers. By the 1920s Mexicans and Mexican Americans were becoming visible indeed, just as the number of newly arriving Europeans sharply tapered off in the wake of restrictive national immigration legislation. But that is the subject of another study; this study instead focuses on the degree to which lynching and racial oppression aimed at African Americans enabled European immigrants to assimilate into southern white society as the nineteenth century drew to a close.[13]

Chapter 1 presents a historical overview of Brazos County's development in the nineteenth century, focusing on the violence and racial turmoil that characterized the area. Chapter 2 examines the ongoing political turbulence that county residents experienced in the decades after Reconstruction, which culminated in several bitter local elections in the 1890s. It was in the midst of this electoral agitation that fresh outbreaks of racial violence occurred. The next three chapters examine, in order, the county's Italian, Irish, and Bohemian communities and the degree to which they participated in lethal violence against African Americans. In addition to the three lynching incidents studied here, other, smaller episodes of conflict in Brazos County during the same time period also offer insight into the shifting racial terrain of nineteenth-century Texas. Such conflict, especially as it spilled into the courtroom, revealed much about the varying and unstable social position of Brazos County's immigrants, which fluctuated according to national origin, language, perceived racial identity, class, age, and gender.

The final chapter discusses the degree to which these immigrant groups eventually were assimilated into Brazos County's white society. As the years passed, eastern and southern European immigrants, while at first politically and socially marginalized by native-born whites, in turn helped to further marginalize the county's African Americans, though not always intentionally. Their in-between racial status enabled these immigrants initially to acquire property and wealth that was generally denied to blacks. And as they did so, they were offered membership in white society, thus achieving an insider status that black residents of Brazos County would not reach for a very long time to come, if ever. Such membership enabled these immigrants to vote and eventually exercise some degree of political power. As historian Charles L. Flynn noted, "The equation of whiteness with membership in society was inseparable from the implicit equation of black labor with agricultural labor as a whole and of whiteness with capital. . . . White equaled property, equaled capital, equaled society. Black equaled poverty, equaled labor, equaled something somehow alien."[14]

White also equaled domination, and the ability to insist on a certain level of justice in criminal affairs—in both legal and extralegal arenas—that was denied to blacks. One of the fastest ways to establish whiteness was through violent racial oppression, a method that a number of immigrants did not shun. It is perhaps not coincidental that racial violence somewhat subsided in Brazos County after the turn of the twentieth century, when these new immigrants became an established part of the county's social scene. As the twentieth century wore on, it became apparent that the real outsiders in Brazos County were not the foreign-born, but those who had always been on the outside, the African Americans.

Chapter 1

THE BANNER COUNTY

*Brazos is the banner county of the State in growth and prosperity. . . .
During the last decade of years, town and cities have sprung into existence, lands have trebled and quadrupled in value.*

DAILY STATE JOURNAL (Austin), 27 November 1870

*It would be criminal in us to bring up our children in such a place. . . .
Drinking, swearing, Sabbath breaking, and every other vice is practiced
by the majority of the people and the others smile at it, instead of frown-
ing it down . . . drinking, gambling, stealing, shooting, and horse racing
fill up the picture.*

Letter from Sarah Dodson in Bryan
to relatives in Alabama, 21 November 1866[1]

Perhaps Brazos County was no more violent than other counties in
nineteenth-century Texas, but it certainly had its share of bloodlust and
brutal death. By the time sizeable numbers of European immigrants were
calling Brazos County their home in the 1890s, the county's culture of violence and racial oppression was already well established, and had been so for
decades. Lynchings were not uncommon events. They came early and often
in the county's history, and they were a significant feature of the southern
culture that these immigrants encountered, and into which they eventually
became assimilated. Historian William Carrigan has underscored the importance of examining the historical development of a culture of collective
violence in order to understand how and why lynchings took place. Carrigan was deeply interested in the historical memory of violence in central
Texas—that is, the ingrained habits of reprisal and retribution that shaped
the culture of this region. Carrigan's purpose, among other things, was to
trace the decades-long, death-strewn road that led to the very public torture
and burning of Jesse Washington before a crowd of 15,000 spectators in

Waco in 1916. "Lynching and mob violence, in short, had been praised for generations," he noted.[2]

Similarly, to understand the culture of violence in Brazos County more clearly, a look back at the county's early history is essential. Three ingredients were important in the creation of Brazos County's nineteenth-century cultural character. First of all, the early if short-lived dominance of the town of Millican gave birth to a high degree of violence and a love of vengeance, especially during the Civil War and Reconstruction era. Second, a continuing stream of newcomers—including foreigners, African Americans, and white southerners—resulted in explosive growth and political instability in the decades after the Civil War, which in turn sparked further violence. Third, an intractable southern racial social order that began with slavery later culminated in the Jim Crow era at the close of the nineteenth century, creating an environment of violence and oppression aimed specifically at African Americans. By the turn of the twentieth century, it was all in place. An exclusionary, hierarchical, and racialized regime maintained by vengeful lynchings and brutality had triumphed. And that, of course, would prove to be of immeasurable benefit to the county's new European immigrants.

At the time of its first white settlement in the 1820s, what would one day be known as Brazos County was part of Stephen F. Austin's colony, the northernmost reach of the empresario's territory granted to him by first the Spanish, then the Mexican government. Austin's territory stretched northward from the Gulf, fanning out into the central area of the state and ending near the Old San Antonio Road, which would be the northern border of Brazos County, about 150 miles from the Gulf coast. Only a handful of Austin's "Old Three Hundred" settlers ended up living in this area, however, as it would be another half-century before the advantages of Brazos County became widely evident. Most of Austin's colonists preferred to be closer to the Gulf, where the bottomlands of the Brazos and Colorado Rivers were easier to clear and settle, and the rivers themselves more navigable. Before the Anglos, the Spanish had virtually ignored the area, merely traveling past occasionally on the Old San Antonio Road on their way from San Antonio to outposts in East Texas and back. And before the Spanish, the Indians apparently did not consider the place worth settling. Groups of Tonkawa drifted through on hunting excursions, and possibly Apaches and Comanches occasionally hunted buffalo here, but there is little evidence that any of these groups decided to set up permanent settlements.[3]

So it remained for Robert Millican, a seventy-four-year-old farmer of Irish descent who hailed from Spartanburg County, South Carolina, to arrive as the first permanent white settler of the south-central area of Texas that would become Brazos County. He came in 1824 with a large and extended family in tow—a wife, eleven children, at least eight grandchildren, and an assortment of servants and slaves. Several of Millican's adult children also received land grants from Stephen F. Austin, and they all set up homes near each other in a fertile area at the southern tip of the county, near where the Navasota River flowed into the Brazos. His two married sons also brought slaves along with their families, thus establishing slavery at the start of the county's settlement as an important labor source and economic mainstay.[4]

Millican's sojourn in Texas lasted only about twelve years. At age eighty-six, he died of pneumonia and measles on the banks of the Trinity River during the panicked exodus of 1836 known as the "Runaway Scrape" in the midst of the Texas Revolution. But his sons lived on, some of them fighting in the revolution against Mexico, which earned them still more land. Before long, they had enough to donate some for a town site bearing the family name in 1859. As a town of importance, Millican had a short but happy life, though its demise was long and painful. It was established just in time for the arrival of the Houston & Texas Central Railroad, one of the very few railway lines in the state in the 1850s that extended northward out from Houston. Railroad construction began in 1856, and the line reached Millican in 1860.[5]

The new town, located about 80 miles north of Houston, boomed immediately. The advent of the Civil War prevented the railway from extending any farther north, and as the railway's northern terminus, Millican became a major transportation hub for the state. With no rail connections north of Millican, nearly all of central and northern Texas depended on Millican as the trade and transportation gateway to the Gulf ports. By 1864, it was home to 3,000 souls, and another 5,000 Confederate troops were housed in nearby training camps, giving the county a closer connection to the war than it might have had otherwise. Prosperity seemed to break out on all sides: hotels, livery stables, stores, saloons, churches, and schools sprouted quickly.[6]

But the next year the war was over, and so were Millican's good times. In the year following, the town began its downward climb to what would one day be virtual oblivion. The H&TC Railway resumed its northward trek, sucking away Millican's economic life and transplanting it to the new town of Bryan a few miles north in 1867. Widespread crop failure hit in 1867, and next came a yellow fever epidemic that wiped out a substantial part of what remained of the population the same year. And the year after,

1868, saw a racial confrontation that cost still more lives and engendered further turmoil.[7]

Clearly, Brazos County's future was not in Millican. Nevertheless, certain characteristics of the community—a substantial reliance on slavery, its close connection with the Confederacy, brutal racial repression in the aftermath of war, family feuding, and random violence of every sort—would mark the rest of the county for decades to come. By the time Millican began its precipitous decline, the county as a whole was poised for an enormous growth spurt that eventually would propel it far past its neighboring counties in population and economic strength. But Brazos County would always retain something of Millican's racial and cultural heritage. Indeed, one could argue that it was Millican—today no more than a shadow of a community at a quiet country crossroads, immediately evident only by the presence of a historical marker and a post office—that gave Brazos County its cultural and social character.

Brazos County became known as such in 1842, after going through several name and boundary changes. It settled at 588 square miles that offered a richly textured landscape from which would emerge a variegated agriculture. Unevenly divided by a ridge that runs north-south, which the railroad would later follow, the county ranged from rolling upland pastures best suited for cattle grazing on the east, to fertile river bottomlands amenable to cotton plantations on the west. The county forms a sort of triangle between the Navasota River on the east, the Brazos River on the west, and the historic Old San Antonio Road—known also as El Camino Real—on the north. Now considered part of south-central Texas, it is also in the middle of the eastern portion of Texas that contained the majority of the state's population through most of the nineteenth century. Eventually the county became part of the northern end of the larger Brazos River Valley agricultural sector, and was also part of a fertile, riverine, cotton-producing corridor known as the Brazos Bottom. Indeed, cotton would become vitally important to Brazos County's growth, particularly at the turn of the twentieth century, though the county as a whole would never become part of the state's prime cotton-growing region because of its soil. The county lies just outside the edge of the Blackland Prairie, which curves away on the northwest, and which became the state's major cotton-producing area in the early twentieth century.[8]

In 1842, at about the same time the county was finally established as Brazos County, a group of five men, including one of Robert Millican's sons, picked a spot in the north-central area of the county for its official seat.

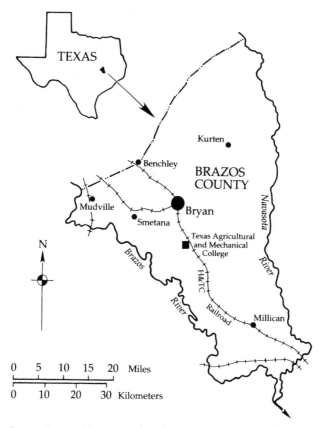

Brazos County, Texas. Map by John V. Cotter

They named it Boonville, possibly after a group member's illustrious uncle, Daniel Boone. Like the town of Millican, Boonville was not destined to thrive in the long term, and it never reached anything like Millican's heady, war-borne heyday. To begin with, only two families wanted to live there. Everyone else—about forty-five families at that point—preferred various settlements or isolated farmsteads that were scattered around the county and located next to larger rivers and creeks. Carter Creek, Boonville's water source, offered meager attractions compared to the alluvial soil near the Brazos River on the west, or the creeks nearer the flood-prone Navasota on the east. Until the last decades of the nineteenth century, most of the county's farmers preferred the eastern side of the county, nearer the Navasota, for raising crops, especially corn, and mostly left the fertile bottomlands of the Brazos for later generations.[9]

At first, county growth was slow. By 1850, 614 people were living in the county, of whom 148 were enslaved. About one-third of white families owned slaves, a somewhat higher proportion than in the state as a whole. Having joined the nation as a new state five years earlier, Texas was attracting a steady stream of newcomers, who were pushing into previously unsettled areas along the state's western frontier. Brazos County was not on the list of most attractive destinations at this point, probably because it was so far inland from the Gulf. Its rivers were not easily navigated, and it was perhaps a little too near territory inhabited by Comanches and other Indian groups to the north. It was one of the state's smallest populated counties at the time. Areas with better river access, such as Grimes County to the southeast, and regions farther west along the Colorado River, were attracting thousands more of the state's newcomers.[10]

By 1850, Brazos County farmers had managed to clear only 2,000 acres for crops. They concentrated mostly on growing corn, planting only a few fields of cotton here and there. Their total output was 142 bales of cotton, a mere pittance compared with the thousands of bales that more populated areas, such as neighboring Grimes and Washington Counties, were producing. Not coincidentally, the largest slaveholder in the county in 1850 was John Millican, Robert Millican's oldest son, whose twenty-seven slaves worked prime cotton land near the county's most accessible part of the Brazos River. Because getting crops to market was such a problem for everyone else, subsistence farming predominated elsewhere in the county. Nearly all of the other slaveholding families owned fewer than ten slaves.[11]

Ten years later, on the eve of the Civil War, the county had changed dramatically. By 1860 the population had more than quadrupled, largely spurred by the arrival of the Houston & Texas Central Railroad in the lower end of the county in Millican, and by the certain prospect that the railroad would continue to build northward through the county and beyond. But even before the railroad arrived, Brazos County farmers, joined by a steady stream of newcomers, had been busy. By the time the war began, they had broken up the rolling prairie and cleared away trees from more than 14,000 acres, and were producing an annual total of more than 2,000 bales of cotton. However, only a handful of Brazos County's farmers had sizeable plantations; only one had increased his slaveholding to more than one hundred slaves; and twenty-eight had more than ten slaves. The rest of the slaveholders (about 70 percent) continued to work small farms with fewer than ten slaves, a proportion close to what prevailed across the South at the time.[12]

Even so, slavery was clearly the economic basis of the county by now, as could be seen in the 1860 census. Slaves numbered more than 1,000 at this point and made up about 40 percent of the county residents. More important, a slaveholding ethos now permeated the farms, plantations, and settlements stretching between the Navasota and Brazos Rivers. Like a prevailing wind, the origins of southern-born whites had shifted, which proved to be a critical change. At first, most of those who had managed to set up homesteads in Brazos County were from states such as Tennessee, with the upper South predominating as a place of origin. Now, the majority of white immigrants to the county were sweeping in from the lower South, bringing with them plantation agriculture and a greater interest in cotton production. Like the rest of the eastern half of Texas, the culture and economy of Brazos County was becoming more and more like the plantation South. Hundreds of white families were rumbling in on oxcarts and wagons from Louisiana, Mississippi, Alabama, South Carolina, and Georgia, and they were bringing with them their slaves.[13]

The change had vast implications for the future. This culture—which included the ideology of white supremacy and the total domination of blacks—would remain firmly in place through the end of the Civil War and far beyond. It would be virtually unaffected by the arrival in later decades of significant numbers of Europeans, who accepted the southern white value system as they assimilated into Brazos County society and became racialized themselves. It would last out the nineteenth century and endure well into the twentieth, and it would survive economic depression and bustling growth, political upheaval and social change, flood, drought, and storms of every kind. By 1860 the county was intimately tied to the lower South, and would remain so.[14]

By 1860 the proportion of foreign-born residents stood at about 8 percent, though doubtless their presence was more noticeable than their numbers would indicate. Brazos County's growing communities and settlements needed people with specialized talents and skills, and many of these foreigners fit the bill. They included a schoolteacher, several merchants, and skilled craftsmen such as carpenters and blacksmiths. At this point, though, nearly everyone in Brazos County was an immigrant of one sort or another. Few of the county's residents had been born in the county; less than half of them had even been born in Texas. The prevalence of newcomers and people born outside the county would persist throughout the nineteenth and twentieth centuries, keeping the local social hierarchy somewhat loose and permeable. County residents were forced to adjust to a constantly shifting population, saying hello and goodbye—especially hello—nearly continually. Judging from the social news and tidbits published by the local newspaper in the

1890s, social prominence and political power seemed to depend far more on what one owned than on the reputation of one's family. In most cases, one's family members were unknowable because they lived out of state, or even out of the country. But of course, it added immense prestige to have arrived in what later became known nostalgically as the time of "Old Brazos"—the antebellum years, when the county was new, and verdant with possibility, and ripe for anyone, especially slaveholders, to prosper.[15]

Possibly because of the obvious and unavoidable presence of foreign-born residents, the county showed a somewhat contrarian political bent in the 1850s, despite the high influx of lower South slaveholders who elsewhere tended to be Democrat party supporters. This, too, was a trend that would continue long after the war; rebellious political movements would give Democratic leaders headaches for decades to come. During the 1850s Brazos County voters had strongly supported the anti-immigration Know-Nothing party in 1855 and 1856 in opposition to the Democrats. They voted for unionist candidates such as Sam Houston in 1857 and 1859. But by the time war neared, the county fell into line with most of the rest of the state by heartily endorsing secession in a 215–44 vote in 1861.[16]

Support for the Confederacy remained high. As the war went on, various groups of Brazos County men formed companies or parts of companies, perhaps the best known of which was Company 1 of the 21st Texas Cavalry Regiment, which served in Louisiana and Arkansas and suffered one of the county's few combat fatalities. The county may have lost only two men in the Civil War. Undoubtedly the county's greatest asset for the war effort—and its closest connection, in literal terms—was the H&TC railhead at Millican, which became one of the state's two training camps for newly recruited Confederate soldiers. The railroad brought home the war's immediacy as thousands of troops passed through the county on their way to various battlefronts, and as livestock, foodstuffs, and other provisions were collected from the central Texas area and shipped to Confederate armies. In future years, such connections helped to undergird the county's emotional attachment to the Lost Cause, which surged at the end of the nineteenth century with the formation of a United Daughters of the Confederacy chapter and regular reunions of Confederate soldiers and their families.[17]

When the war ended, the county had survived in comparatively good shape. Despite the chaos of a shattered economy, the area enjoyed distinct advantages over much of the rest of the South, and even Texas, most of which had little or no rail service. Very few of Brazos County's men had died during the war, land and livestock had not been ransacked, and the railroad still offered daily train service between Millican and Houston. Brazos County's worst turmoil occurred when the war was over, in the aftermath of emancipation and the further extension of the railroad. In June 1865 Gen. Gordon Granger arrived in Galveston and declared all slaves in Texas free, and soon after, federal troops arrived in Millican. Along with the troops came a series of agents working for the Freedman's Bureau, the federal agency created to help newly freed black slaves and their white former masters adjust to the new social order. As county residents struggled to reorient themselves to a wholly new economic and social world, racial violence in the form of lynchings and assaults erupted throughout the county. Most of it was centered in Millican, where the county's largest concentrations of former slaves lived.[18]

One problem was that local slaveholders were extremely reluctant to embrace or even acknowledge the unwelcome news that their former slaves were now free. A Union soldier posted to Millican in the days immediately after the war's end recalled how it took some time and effort for federal army officers to get the word out to the local black population that slavery had ended. "The trouble was that the negroes had been kept in great ignorance as to the result of the war, so far as they were concerned, and some planters, even to the time of our arrival in the vicinity, told them they were not free, and threatened to shoot them if they left, and in a few instances did so," wrote the soldier in a memoir of his war experiences. "The result was that many of the colored people could not be quieted until they had actually met 'Massa' Lincoln's officers, and heard from them that they were free, and could go where they pleased to work."[19]

Without question Millican had more than its fair share of problems to deal with. Along with the rest of Texas and the South, Millican was faced with a large population of newly freed African Americans and the psychological trauma of living under the authority of an occupying army. But it had other difficulties that were uniquely its own, including a massive loss of population through desertion and disease. With the end of the war, railroad construction in the state started up again in earnest, and the Houston & Central Texas Railroad began to fulfill its earlier promise of building northward. During the 1850s railroad officials had surveyed and platted a new town along the railroad's right of way, some miles north of Millican. But development of the new town was slow because of the interruption of war. A few streets had been laid out and named, and some 300 white residents had drifted in to what was then no more than a village, waiting expectantly for the end of the war and the coming of the railroad. Once railroad construction resumed, all sorts of enterprising newcomers with a sharp eye to the future began to buy up lots and erect stores and homes, and it was not long before a building boom was under way.[20]

The new town was named for Stephen F. Austin's nephew, William Joel Bryan, who had sold or donated part of his county land grant for a town site along the new railroad. Bryan never lived in the county, preferring like others of Austin's colonists to be near the Gulf. Six months after the end of the war, county residents voted to move the county seat a few miles west from Boonville to the brand-new town of Bryan. As a railroad town, Bryan offered far greater advantages as a county seat than Boonville, which had never attracted more than a dozen families at the height of its growth. As soon as the vote was taken, most of Boonville packed up and moved west. And it took Millican's hopeful and ambitious residents about as much time as the Boonvillians to see where the future was headed. Before the first H&TC train engine steamed into Bryan in August 1867, most of Millican's businessmen, merchants, and civic leaders had already dismantled their shops, hotels, homes, and even churches, and had moved themselves—lumber and all—to the new county seat, leaving Millican literally in the dust.

But that was only the beginning of Millican's woes. Next came a widespread crop failure brought on by extremely wet weather, which only added to the financial erosion begun by the departure of many of the town's businesses. Then, a month after the first train steamed in Bryan, a yellow fever epidemic broke out in Millican, causing remaining residents to stampede toward Bryan. "All sort of vehicles were pressed into service, and men, women and children, pots, pans and skillets, dogs, beds and mattresses, promiscuously mixed up, evacuated the town in great disorder," reported a Galveston newspaper in September. "Tar was burning before the doors, asafoetida suspended beneath the noses of those remaining behind." By early October the death rate was still high. "The fever is very bad at Millican, and very fatal. . . . There are now not enough left to bury the dead," the Galveston newspaper gloomily reported. "The Post Office at Millican is now discontinued. The postmaster has fled to the woods, and the telegraph operator is dead."

Such disasters clearly must have left the remaining residents of Millican tense and uncertain about the future. The state as a whole had been flooded by a tidal wave of racial and political turmoil at this point, and Millican was swamped. In March 1867, just as railroad workers were laying down the lines into Bryan, congressional Reconstruction took effect with the arrival of Gen. Philip Sheridan as commander of the new military district of Texas. One of Sheridan's first acts was to appoint a three-man board of registrars for each county to supervise the voter registration of newly freed blacks and to bar the registration of nearly every white voter and local official who had actively supported the Confederacy. As in many counties, one of the newly appointed registrars in Brazos County was a former slave; in this case a local pastor named George Brooks. Like his counterparts across the state, Brooks began his duties in July, just as the H&TC Railroad was finishing its line to Bryan and many of Millican's citizens were packing up to leave.[21]

More political changes were afoot. In the fall of 1867—as Millican was reeling from the massive exodus spurred by the railroad and the yellow fever epidemic—Sheridan authorized the removal of hundreds of state and local officials who had just been elected the year before. As former Confederates and secessionists, many were judged, probably correctly, to be disloyal to the new regime and to be less than willing to ensure that former slaves were accorded their civil rights. A new state constitutional convention and elections were to take place in 1868, but in the meantime, federal military commanders appointed Republicans, some of whom were black, and white unionists to fill local offices. Those who were summarily kicked out of office included all of Millican's and Brazos County's leaders. The only political survivor was the county coroner, who for some reason—possibly because of his expertise—was allowed to keep his job.[22]

Millican's whites were now trying to make sense of a life that had been completely upended multiple times by natural and manmade disasters. Life was hardly better for Millican's African Americans. These newly freed slaves found their first attempts to live autonomously of white domination frustrated at every turn. The Freedman's Bureau posted an agent first in Millican, then in Bryan as the population moved north. Records show a typical assortment of complaints by blacks of ill-treatment, fraud, and intimidation from whites, and complaints by whites who were trying to settle labor contract disputes with blacks. In such a context of desertion, disease, resentment, and chaos of every kind, it is not hard to understand why racial tension in Millican would have soared, finally erupting in armed confrontation. What became known later as a "race riot" occurred there in July 1868, at the end of a monthlong series of tense and occasionally violent racial encounters.[23]

It began on a Sunday morning in June, when the Ku Klux Klan made its first recorded appearance in the county by marching past a church where Millican blacks were attempting to hold worship services. African

Americans undoubtedly saw the act as a highly threatening challenge to their first efforts to hold organized gatherings without white interference. Under slavery, white masters had closely monitored worship services, and across the South, often the first institutions that freed slaves created for themselves were their own churches. These churches held far more than religious meaning. They offered entertainment and emotional relief, provided food and succor for desperate congregants, and—most ominously from the viewpoint of whites—they frequently also were centers for political training.

Significantly, while the Klan was marching in Millican, a new Republican-majority constitutional convention was meeting in Austin to draft a new state constitution. Among other things, this new constitution promised African American men the right to hold office, serve on juries, and testify against whites in court. All of these rights had been specifically denied by the Democrat-controlled state legislature only the year before. As a result of the new convention, these rights were embedded in what became the Constitution of 1869, a document that conservative Democrats and former Confederates throughout Texas universally reviled. The threat of constitutionally guaranteed political and civil rights for blacks, which loomed especially large during that summer of 1868, must surely have galled many of the whites living in Millican, home to a sizeable percentage of Brazos County's black population. Moreover, Democrats throughout the state, including Brazos County, were resorting to violent intimidation at that point to keep African Americans and white Republicans from supporting the Republican party in upcoming fall elections.

A number of black churchgoers in Millican reacted to the Klan parade by opening fire. Fifteen sheeted marchers took to their heels, some leaving behind parts of their costumes on the ground. That churchgoers had taken weapons with them to worship services and were thus ready to open fire on the Klan suggests a high level of preparedness and a strong anticipation of armed confrontation. Indeed, the church pastor, George Brooks, who was also serving as the new voter registrar, subsequently organized a black militia. He led drills every Saturday for several weeks after the aborted Klan rally. Brooks was clearly the community leader for Millican's freed slaves. In addition to working as voter registrar and impromptu militia leader, he directed the local Loyal League, an organization formed in many communities across Texas to help newly freed slaves learn about the political process and generally how to improve their lives. Brooks's new military company was made up of perhaps 200 volunteers, and they performed their drills regularly in the sight of whites, who were becoming more anxious and agitated with each passing day by the unsettling vision of armed black men marching in formation.

The Freedman's Bureau agent acted as negotiator, informing Millican's white leadership that the black militia would disband only when the Klan quit harassing the black community. After weeks of negotiations and tension, a series of armed confrontations erupted in July when Millican's freedmen heard rumors that a black member of the Loyal League had been lynched in the Brazos Bottom. A group of the black militiamen, directed by Brooks, marched to the home of a white landowner, a member of a formerly large slaveholding family, whom they suspected of the killing. Along the way the militia members met up with a large party of armed whites, some of whom had raced down from Bryan and the northern end of the county by train to join the action. Shootings in various places ensued, and the confrontations were sensationalized in Houston and Galveston press reports as a "riot" that supposedly left fifty to sixty blacks dead, with hundreds of combatants on both sides. The San Antonio Express elevated the confrontation to "the Millican war." When peace tentatively settled a few days later, the dead numbered at least six blacks, although the actual casualties were probably much higher. Among the dead was George Brooks, the militia leader. Brooks, already a marked man through his work as voter registrar and leader of the Loyal League, was killed in mysterious circumstances at an unknown point during the confrontation. When his body was discovered a week later, he could only be identified by an odd physical characteristic, a missing finger on his right hand. Federal troops—who had left the county the previous year—were on their way back for a second occupation. They remained for about another year.

By all accounts, Millican as a whole remained violent and disaster-prone for whites as well as blacks through the decades following the war. Shootouts occurred regularly, and murderous feuds and arson attacks erupted yearly. Shortly after the Millican "race riot," the county sheriff, John H. Neill, reportedly resigned from his job because of the chaotic state of affairs in Millican, complaining "he could not discharge his duties in that ruffian community." In 1865 a federal infantryman in a letter home had said of Millican, "It is a miserable cut throat hole. Every one carries a large bowie knife and revolver strapped to him." This depressing assessment was echoed more than twenty years later in a Houston newspaper. "The midnight assassin so often heard of in this town, is again to the front," the paper noted, in an account of yet another outbreak of a feud that left a well-known stockman dead on the ground next to a saloon, about 50 yards from where his father had been killed in a similar shootout ten years earlier.[24]

Members of the extended Millican family were involved with most of these feuds and shootings. An apocryphal story told in the 1960s by Brazos County judge J. W. Barron traced the propensity of the Millican family to land in trouble back to the very first day of their arrival in Brazos County, when they got into a "shooting scrape" with another family named Holland. Stephen F. Austin had to intervene, according to the story, and assigned the Millicans to the west side of the Navasota, which became the Millican community, and the Hollands to the east, which later became Washington County. No documentation exists to corroborate the story, although there was a family of Hollands over in Grimes County, near Millican, who arrived there about the time the Millican family arrived in Brazos County. The story in any case has the flavor of a story of creation, of origins—a tale to explain the later tendency of Millican family members to become embroiled in lawsuits that took years to sort out, and feuds that left themselves and many other Brazos County residents dead.[25]

Some of these feuds, especially after the Civil War, had strong political as well as racial overtones. One feud that broke out in 1870 eventually ended with the death of three men: the Democratic deputy sheriff; his brother, who replaced him as deputy sheriff; and the Republican justice of the peace. What became known as Radical Reconstruction was still under way in the state, led by the Republican governor, Edmund J. Davis, who took office in January 1870. The Republican-controlled state legislature had generated fierce resentment among Democrats and moderate Republicans by, among other things, raising taxes to pay for new schools and road improvements, and by creating a state police force that employed black officers. Davis's opponents fought back in the next election in 1871, when the Democrats won all four of the state's congressional seats. By 1872 the Democrats also recaptured the statehouse, and the next year Davis lost the governorship. But in Brazos County, Republicans remained a strong force for decades after the Democrats had regained control of the state, and around 1872 they sent an African American, John Mitchell, to the statehouse as the county's representative. At this point, most of the county's fiercest political rivalries played out in Millican, which was the stronghold of the county's Republican party. In the early 1870s the town government was dominated by Republicans, including several African Americans who served as town aldermen.[26]

According to newspaper and other accounts, problems in Millican began anew in early February 1870, about a month after Governor Davis took office. The deputy sheriff was a Democrat named William H. Millican. He had arrested several white men charged with serious offenses, and a black man accused of petty larceny. When a mob showed up at the jail one night, Millican apparently decided to look the other way while the mob set the white prisoners free and then hanged the black man. Shortly afterward, a feisty newcomer named Robert C. Myers demanded an investigation. Myers, a white man, had arrived in the town of Millican just after the war and had opened a general store and saloon. He was also active in the Republican party, and thus was a political enemy of William Millican.[27]

Myers was born in a slaveholding family in South Carolina. As an adult with slaves of his own, he had moved to Alabama and then on to Louisiana in search of better farming opportunities. Louisiana proved to be less than ideal. Myers settled on swampy land near the Mississippi River and was forced to spend a great deal of time and effort draining the land and protecting it from flooding. But no sooner had he gotten things more or less in order than war came, and Yankees were in the neighborhood. Some of his slaves escaped across the lines to federal forces. Fearing he would lose the rest, Myers packed up his family and possessions, slaves and all, and headed for Texas.[28]

After a long and arduous trip across East Texas, Myers settled in Robertson County, north of Brazos County, just in time for the end of the war. Wiped out financially by emancipation and the complete loss of his farm labor, Myers then moved to Millican to start over once more, this time as a general merchant and saloon keeper. Within a year he was active in the Republican party, quickly achieving a leadership position, which his son, J. Allen Myers, later maintained well into the twentieth century. In his unpublished autobiography, J. Allen Myers said his father had been a Union sympathizer who joined the Republicans after the war because "he thought the Southern people should control the Negroes and keep the Carpet Baggers from poisoning the minds of the ignorant slave. He advocated attending the Loyal league . . . for this he was called a Negro lover and his family were ostracized from society." In the eyes of local Democrats, the elder Myers's sins were many. He had supported the appointment of several blacks as town aldermen and entertained federal soldiers in his home. And he had voiced objections when he saw freedmen being mistreated—or lynched, as in the case when Deputy Sheriff William Millican let a murderous mob clean out the jail.[29]

Denouncing Myers as a "damned old Radical," William Millican's friends threatened him with death. But Millican decided to settle the

issue himself, and walked into Myers's store on February 6 with a pistol in
his hand. Millican ended up shot dead, and Robert Myers, his oldest son
David, and his nephew, G. W. Hardy, were convicted of his murder and
sentenced to six years of hard labor in the state penitentiary. Fellow Republican Governor Davis, however, pardoned the trio in July on the grounds
that they had acted in self-defense.[30]

Back home again, Myers proceeded to open up his saloon, offer free
drinks to blacks, and call for a political meeting at the African Methodist Church, where he asked to be nominated justice of the peace. It is clear
where Myers's support lay. Thirty-four people were present at the meeting;
thirty-two of them were black. "The Negroes were drunk and boisterous
during Friday and Saturday, one of them firing his pistol off in the air, and
another firing his into the store of Mr. Swann. These two were later arrested
by the citizens and put into the jail until they sobered off. We suppose, as a
legitimate consequence, that R. C. Myers will be Justice for that precinct.
It is unnecessary for us to say what respectable citizens think of such conduct," sniffed the Galveston newspaper.[31]

Myers was duly appointed justice of the peace. Meanwhile John E.
Millican, William's surviving brother, was made constable by the county
commissioners. Trouble was bound to erupt again, which it did the following summer. In June 1871 John Millican apparently assaulted a black man
inside Myers's saloon, and Myers retaliated by insisting on Millican's arrest.
Out on a $200 bond, Millican waited for Myers to walk home one evening,
and promptly assassinated him. Millican was indicted for murder, but before the trial could take place, he in turn was shot dead—supposedly while
coming home from a temperance meeting. Dying in his home, he named
as his killers Myers's second-oldest son and oldest daughter—J. Allen Myers, then seventeen, and his sister, Nonnie Boldridge, whose husband was
another active leader of the county Republican party.[32]

It took four years for the case finally to come to trial under the direction
of a specially appointed district judge, Spencer Ford, a lawyer and "lifelong
Democrat." Ford would later become a prominent member of Bryan's elite
and a close friend of the Myers family, despite their differences in political affiliation. The Galveston newspaper covered the trial, reporting: "Col.
Ford specially submitted to the jury a clear and comprehensive charge, em-
bracing the full law of the case, and adjourned the case till half past two.
During the forenoon session the courthouse was crowded with ladies and
citizens. Soon after the reassembling of the court, the jury brought in a verdict of 'not guilty,' which seemed to meet with general approbation."[33]

The positive reaction to the verdict could be interpreted several ways. The community by then may have had enough of the Millican family's antics. Or J. Allen Myers, orphaned at seventeen by an act of vengeance, may have attracted sympathy. The Republican party may have had sufficient strength to sway community approval toward one of its members, or conversely, the Democrats may not have enjoyed overwhelming support in the county. Probably a mixture of all of these accounted for the verdict and its widespread approval, but the last supposition—that the Democrats did not have a lock hold on the county's political support—would prove highly accurate in the coming decades.

In any case, J. Allen Myers was now a free man. After a series of jobs with the H&TC Railroad, Myers settled in Bryan where eventually he prospered as a successful hardware store merchant. Later he was elected county clerk in 1886 and 1888, and also became the town's postmaster off and on between 1882 and 1915, serving under six Republican presidential administrations.[34]

No doubt J. Allen Myers remained a Republican because of the political job opportunity in the postal service, and because of intense respect for his father, which was evident in the autobiography he wrote many years later. Despite the ostracism his family had experienced in Millican, Myers went on to achieve social prominence in the county, particularly in Bryan. He and his family were frequently noted with approval in the social news of the local newspaper—this despite Myers's continued leadership of a nearly all-black local Republican party. Such prominence suggests that Democratic political affiliation was not necessarily a defining qualification for membership in the county's elite society, perhaps because the political scene was such a hodgepodge of loyalties and factions for most of the nineteenth century. And quite possibly the wealth he generated through his hardware store and post office job earned him a certain respect in Bryan, where successful businessmen were held in high esteem.

When federal troops returned to Brazos County following the "race riot" in October 1868, they were garrisoned this time in the new town of Bryan, signifying the shift in importance from Millican to Bryan. Life in Bryan at that point was hardly less chaotic than in Millican, and probably more so, though without Millican's dark uncertainty. The new town was less than five years old, had been the county seat for two, and slightly more than a year earlier had experienced the festive excitement of the railroad's arrival. Federal soldiers patrolled the streets of the town for only about a year before moving on to other postings, but before they left, other newcomers were pouring into town and settling on farmsteads throughout the county. By the time of the 1870 census the county population had tripled since 1860 and now numbered 9,205.[35]

Among the thousands of new arrivals were Wesley and Sarah Dodson and their two children, who left Alabama just after the war to make a fresh start in Texas. Other family members had already settled in or near Bryan, and the Dodsons joined them late in 1866. It is evident from their correspondence that Bryan was in the throes of an ungainly and unruly boom, and that it would be some years before the place settled into a somewhat stable town. Much of the disorderly character of Millican seemed to have been directly transferred to Bryan. Wesley Dodson apparently arrived first in order to settle their living arrangements, but he had some difficulty finding a suitable place for his family to live. "I have been trying to get a boarding house for us, but so far have not found one that I would carry my family to," he complained in a letter to his wife. "The society here is bad, and I have not met with a religious man in the place. Their drunkenness and profaneness is the reason I would not board with them. . . . No church, no society, nor anything, but Groceries, swearers, drunkards, and gamblers, these are nine tenths of Bryan." A few months later, his wife Sarah echoed her husband's complaints in a letter to relatives back home in Alabama. "The children where I have been grow up like weeds, without a particle of culture. . . . The moral atmosphere is bad here."[36]

Meanwhile, other change was taking place in the northwestern corner of the county, near the Brazos River. Besides the large number of African Americans who lived in Millican, another large concentration of blacks lived in this northwestern section, in a wide, flat area that lay along the Brazos River north of Millican and due west of Bryan. This was Mudville, later also known sometimes as Steele's Store. The area earned the colorful name of Mudville because of frequent flooding of the Little Brazos River, a tributary of the Brazos that flows from Robertson County and cuts diagonally across the northwestern corner of Brazos County. A handful of settlers arrived there in the 1840s, and by the 1850s Mudville was home to the county's largest slaveholders listed on the 1860 census, Thomas Wilson and Mary Wilson, whose combined labor force totaled more than 200 slaves.[37]

After the war Thomas Wilson retained his large landholdings, though another man took precedence in the area: Henry B. Steele. By the 1870s Steele was undeniably the community leader. He ran a general store, which included space for a physician's office and a saloon and served as sort of community center. Steele gradually accumulated more land, and eventually

Main Street, Bryan, around 1870. Many of the town's buildings were haphazard wooden structures through the 1870s. In the coming decades, they were slowly replaced by multi-story brick buildings. Photo courtesy J. D. Conlee

owned a considerable portion of Mudville, employing laborers and share-croppers to work his land. The overwhelming majority of these workers were black. In 1878 Steele formally requested the establishment of a post office in the community, noting that the population of the area was about 75 percent African American. The land was prime Brazos bottomland, broad and fer-tile and perfect for cotton farming. But because of frequent flooding, many prospective landowners had shied away, and much of it still remained to be cleared and settled.[38]

Like Millican, the Mudville area had its share of violence and death. What may have been Brazos County's largest-scale lynching began near there in 1874, when a group of ten black men were reported to have robbed and shot a white store owner named Mr. Leak, and then gang-raped his wife. Four of the men were arrested the next day and lodged in the Bryan jail. What happened next was predictable: "A mob of white men last night called on the Sheriff and demanded the jail keys, but the jailor happened to have them, and could not be found; whereupon they went to the jail and broke it open by force," reported the *Galveston Daily News*. Two were lynched that night near Bryan; the next day the mob hanged three more near the Brazos Bottom, and then finished the episode that night by killing another two, for a total body count of seven.[39]

More violence erupted a few years later, concluding in one of the county's few public executions. This legal hanging took place in Bryan in 1879, when a black man named Ezekiel Bradley was put to death for murdering another black man at Henry Steele's saloon. While it was highly unusual for a black man to receive the death penalty for killing another black, Bradley had a long history of criminal convictions for assaults and theft in the Mudville area, most of them committed against prominent whites who lived there. Thus Bradley's murder conviction likely provided a convenient excuse for ridding the community of an offender who had repeatedly threatened white authority.[40]

But that white authority was about to be shaken by a very different source than the African American population. The very definition of white, and who qualified as white, was about to be seriously questioned. By the time Steele asked for the post office, all sorts of strange-speaking newcomers were beginning to show up in the area, and they were neither southern-born whites nor African Americans. First came a trickle of Czech-speaking Bohemians in the 1870s, and a small but growing number of Italians joined them during the 1880s. By the 1890s large numbers of Italians and Bohemian Czechs were moving into the county en masse, and most of them were renting and even buying land in or near the Mudville area, in the northwestern corner of the county. Smaller communities of Italians and Bohemians were also being established in the northeastern area of the county, but by far the largest concentrations were near the Brazos River.

These newcomers were not black, but they were not exactly white, either—or at least, not the kind of white that had already settled in the rest of the county. Small groups of Moravian Czechs were already established to the south in the College Station and Wellborn area. Germans had been living in the Kurten and Tabor communities in the northeastern area of the county since before the Civil War. Irish railroad workers had already come, and many had gone.[41]

These newcomers were different. There were more of them, they lived in more concentrated communities, and their arrival rate showed no sign of tapering off. Their numbers were increasing every year. They maintained a life somewhat apart from the rest of the county. They had their own fraternal and mutual aid associations, and one group—the Italians—had their own church, while another—the Bohemians—had their own newspaper.

Their voting strength and preferences were difficult to gauge and thus posed a mystery to Democrats, who were struggling at that point to consolidate their power after years of being on the losing end of various political campaigns. The *Bryan Eagle* made little comment about their presence, except to note it once in 1890, during the height of a campaign by the Democrats to wrest power from Republicans, African Americans, and independent voters. Evidently some Democrats must have expressed some anxiety about how, or even whether, these newcomers would vote. Particularly worrisome, it seemed, was the question of whether the "foreign vote" could be manipulated or bought as easily as whites believed the black vote could be. What seemed to be on the minds of these perplexed onlookers, in other words, was whether these immigrants would behave like blacks—would they undermine the best efforts of Democrats to take control of the county? Not to worry, the *Eagle* opined: these newcomers were sure to vote like true and faithful whites—that is, like Democrats.

"There is in reality no 'foreign vote' in our county," the *Eagle* responded reassuringly. "We have in our midst a large number of naturalized citizens, it is true; but when it comes to voting, most of them are just as independent, and free from being 'controlled' as the very best class of our citizens. . . . Our fellow citizens of foreign birth will, like all good citizens, vote intelligently, freely, and conscientiously in the primary, and will stick to the [Democratic] ticket like a man." But then the newspaper added an afterthought, as if to acknowledge the anxiety that these newcomers were raising among the county's native-born whites: "Of course, there are certain matters about which they are very peculiar . . ."[42]

The *Eagle* did not explain just what the peculiarity was, but part of the immigrants' strangeness undoubtedly included their racial status, which was by no means easy to determine in such a southern, race-conscious society as Brazos County. For most of the nineteenth century, there had been only two racial categories in the county that held any significant meaning: white or black. After white southerners began to settle in the area, Native Americans were never present in any large numbers, and they only made brief appearances in the northern end, near Robertson County, during the 1830s and early 1840s. Very few, if any, Mexicans lived in the area until the 1880s, and those tiny numbers did not increase until well into the twentieth century. So at the close of the nineteenth century it was a puzzle to determine in just what racial box these newcomers belonged. By the 1890s Brazos County's binary classification system was being challenged in the same way as in many northeastern cities such as Chicago, New York, and Philadelphia, where thousands of northern and southern European immigrants were arriving daily. Up north, "race was marked by language, nationality, religion, and social status, as well as by color," as historian Matthew Pratt Guterl noted in his study of the complex and shifting understandings of race in turn-of-the-century and early twentieth century America. But such markers were also present, if more muted, in the South, and they were especially visible in places such as Brazos County. Immigrants such as Bohemians and Italians may have had lighter skin than African Americans, but they spoke strange languages, they were poor, at least at first, and they brought very different cultural habits from what southerners—white or black—were accustomed to seeing.[43] As will be shown in subsequent chapters, the immigrants, whether Italian, Bohemian, or even Irish, were aware of these differences and especially of their indeterminate racial status. The Italians perhaps had the most difficult task in resolving their racial ambiguity. All of these immigrants, these in-between southerners, were helped in no small way by the racial and political turmoil that engulfed Brazos County and the surrounding region during the 1890s.

Chapter 2

A WHITE MAN'S TOWN

We can't afford to have any more divisions among the white people, to result in any more such representatives as Elias Mays, or other negroes.
BRYAN EAGLE, 13 February 1890

Perhaps it came as no surprise when a lynch mob killed three black men one night in June 1896, on a country road leading out of Bryan. As spring eased into summer that year, widespread disquiet and simmering tension permeated the county, creating festering sores that finally erupted in a brutal and cathartic killing. Judging from editorial comment in the Bryan newspaper, unease could be found at every level, among every social class, whether black or white, tenant farmer or planter, merchant or craftsman.[1] The land itself seemed to bear witness to the stress. Corn and cotton fields already were beginning to parch, and farmers waited for rains that came only sporadically and were never enough. By early summer county farmers began to give up on their corn crop, cutting it early to salvage what little they had for fodder. Merchants also waited in uncertainty. Cotton markets had been slow for at least three years now and continued to languish, with meager profits mirroring the scant harvest that now seemed likely.[2]

Economic malaise had soaked deep into the county, but it was only part of what ailed Bryan and the many small rural communities that radiated across the countryside. Seething political unrest also was widening the fissures that had formed years earlier, ulcerating old lesions that decades of rivalries and resentments had never allowed to heal. A presidential election was looming in the fall, and alongside the race for the nation's highest office were local races that pitted one area of the county against another. Such political contests highlighted the conflicts between social classes and set racial tension at the breaking point.

The 1896 lynching was a complicated affair by any measure. On one level it was an outburst of invidious political jealousies that found conve-

nient scapegoats in the form of several African American farm workers. But
on a deeper stratum, less obvious but equally deadly forces were at work,
though from a different direction and involving different people. This deeper
source of strife involved racial identity, and it caught up the growing community of Italian immigrants. Thus, this lynching can be probed from two
different vantage points. The racial milieu of the Italians and their involvement in the events leading up to the lynching are discussed in chapter 3,
where a fuller picture of the lynching episode will be drawn. Here the
political landscape in which the murders took place will be explored, because it is important to understand the violence and political culture that
served as a backdrop for Brazos County's European immigrants and their
attempts to join the dominant white society. As will be seen, this was a
rough terrain, full of unpredictable features, and like much of Texas politics
at this time, it was hard to tame.

It was June 1896, and down the road at the A. and M. College a few
miles south of Bryan, week-long commencement exercises were under way,
along with all manner of banquets and receptions for the graduating students. The school had opened in 1876, and a small but active community
known as "College" or sometimes as "College Station," largely made up of
professors, administrators, various staff members and their families, had
grown up near the railroad stop that served the school. More than 300
cadets were now enrolled in the institution, and the state governor himself, Charles A. Culberson, graced the campus that year by speaking at the
graduation ceremonies. The social events in the campus community always
made news up in Bryan, where town leaders were beginning to recognize
the rising importance of the school to the county's economy and general
prestige. Early summer seemed a particularly sociable time of year throughout the county, and numerous festivities were lighting up the social scene
in Bryan as well. The well-heeled white youth of Bryan who had been away
attending schools and colleges were now home for the summer, and as the
Eagle noted, they had no trouble keeping busy, "balls, parties, and receptions having been continuous for a week or more."[3]

As was evident by such society news, Bryan had changed considerably
in the last few decades. While more than a dozen saloons still lined Main
Street and adjacent alleys, and the city marshal routinely filled the jail with
various miscreants and drunken troublemakers, Bryan had settled down
into a somewhat more mature life as an established town with some 3,000
residents. Sarah Dodson, who had complained in an 1866 letter to friends
back in Alabama about the raucous street life of Bryan and the deplorable

lack of "a particle of culture of any kind," would no doubt have been grat-
ified to see the changes that had taken place. Whereas in Dodson's day
not a single church could be found within a mile of the town, now no less
than eleven congregations gathered regularly: seven white churches, two of
which were Catholic, at least three churches attended by black residents,
and even a Jewish community that met privately in homes. Moreover, civic
organizations and social clubs had sprung up, such as the Mutual Improvement Circle, the forerunner of the Bryan Woman's Club, which would
soon spearhead the construction of the Carnegie Library on Main Street. A
chapter of the Daughters of the Confederacy was in the process of forming,
assorted fraternal lodges met frequently, and a municipal brass band was
about to add its collective voice to the town's cultural offerings. Two "opera
houses" also offered various traveling shows and theater performances, and
three newspapers kept area residents informed about Brazos County doings
and the wider world beyond.[4]

Major technological change was also taking place. By 1896 Bryan was
entering the modern age, though only by fits and starts. Cows, stray horses,
and chickens could still be found roaming Main Street, much of which was
still lined by ramshackle wooden structures that housed a variety of dry
goods merchants, groceries, hardware stores, livery stables, and of course,
the ever-present saloons. But increasingly, substantial brick buildings were
replacing wooden ones, and one of them even soared three stories high.
Although sandstorms frequently raged down Main Street—when rains had
not turned it into a muddy quagmire—the town aldermen were investing
in new road improvement equipment such as ox- or mule-driven bulldozers
and water sprinklers.

Most important, electricity, running water, and telephone service—
three hallmarks of modern life—had more or less arrived by 1896. Only a
few years earlier, Main Street had been suddenly illuminated when the new
light company turned on the electrically operated bulbs that hung across
the street by wires, though widespread residential service appeared to be
some years away. About the same time, the city had contracted with a private water company to supply residents with running water, but the service
initially was too expensive for the overwhelming majority of the city dwellers to afford. The few who could pony up the $50 connection fee found the
actual availability of water fitful at best, and the company frequently irri-
tated city officials by shutting down at inconvenient times, such as during
fire insurance inspections. The city seemed to have better luck with the telephone company, which was up and operating by the spring of 1895, at first

on a strictly local basis, and then with long-distance service as telephone lines reached other counties and nearby towns. The *Eagle* obligingly published detailed instructions for those who had never used the device before: "When you wish a connection, give one ring and immediately talk down the receiver, pressing it firmly to the ear, and when Central answers speak in an ordinary tone of voice . . ."[5]

Despite such initial kinks and quirks, city leaders seemed to be enormously pleased with the progress the city had recently made. The *Eagle* joined the chorus of approval by frequently boasting about the city's accomplishments: "Bryan [is] the chief little city of central Texas" and "Bryan is now enjoying an era of prosperity which few if any town in Texas can boast." Every so often the newspaper, in its role as Bryan's chief booster, would catalogue the city's attractions, listing the number of cotton warehouses, brickyards, and small factories, and lauding the enterprising spirit of its merchants and businessmen.[6]

But a closer look reveals that all was not well. Despite such optimism and cheery forecasts of a rosy future, the *Eagle* also bore witness that Brazos County, and Bryan itself, had not been spared various economic and political shock waves that were rocking rural communities across Texas and the South at the time. The mid-1890s was not a good time to be a farmer, especially a cotton farmer, and many in Brazos County were suffering. The *Eagle* published lists of landowners throughout the county and city whose property was about to be auctioned at a sheriff's sale for failure to pay taxes, and more than a hundred names were listed. Cotton prices had been steadily sliding downward for some years, and a national economic recession that hit in 1893 had hung on in areas like Brazos County like a severe chest cold. More and more farmers, unable to pay debts, were either losing their land and joining the ranks of sharecroppers and tenant farmers, or finding themselves unable to buy the land they had dreamed of one day owning. By the 1890s more than two-thirds of farms in the county were rented, a considerable increase from the decade before.[7]

Most of those listed in the newspaper's announcement of the sheriff's sale were owners of small plots of land, ranging around 100 acres or less. Indeed, the average farm in the county was only 97 acres, compared to a statewide average size of 357 acres. Brazos County was a county of small farmers, notwithstanding the wealthy plantation owners of the Brazos Bottom, and such small landowners were hit hardest as they had little or no cushion to soften any blows. Many others were affected as well, including the businessmen and merchants in Bryan who ginned, baled, and shipped the cotton to other dealers, and who depended on farmers' purchases to survive. By the 1890s Bryan was a cotton town through and through, and its fortunes were intimately tied to an international commodity whose trading value was largely beyond the control of any of the county's residents.[8]

That summer of 1896 would prove to be a particularly difficult season for Brazos County's farmers and cotton-dependent merchants. In the coming fall, owners of cotton gins and warehouses would report lower numbers of processed bales than the year before, which also had been a bad year for cotton production. The weather would be uncooperative; county residents were in for another long, hot, and dry summer. That year Bryan was hit both by lower crop yields and by a catastrophic incident that took place at the beginning of the summer. Not long after noon on Sunday, June 7, just as Bryan's churchgoers were leaving services and starting for home, a fire of mysterious origin broke out in the town's cotton compress. The building was completely destroyed and the machinery severely damaged. "The loss to Bryan is more than can be estimated, for in addition to paying out several thousand dollars each season for labor, it also added much to Bryan's prestige as a business and enterprising city," the *Eagle* lamented. "We truly regret its loss." The compress—which reduced the size of cotton bales, and therefore shipping costs—was one of the city's star attractions, luring farmers into town who might otherwise have hauled their bales to railroad shipping points farther north or south. Without the compress, Bryan's merchants stood to lose even more business in the coming fall harvest. It was a serious blow, indeed, and an ominous beginning of the summer season.[9]

Three days later, violence erupted. Though seemingly the violence had nothing to do with the cotton compress fire or any aspect of the cotton economy, the economic blow that the fire signified could only have raised the tension that the area's farmers already were suffering. Emotional release was ready at hand, and it came quickly. On Sunday night, only hours after the compress fire, a white girl in Kurten, a farming community east of Bryan, woke screaming that someone had tried to drag her through the open window near where she lay sleeping. The girl was the twelve-year-old daughter of Dr. R. H. Wilson, a respected physician and farmer in the eastern part of the county. The next morning suspicion fell on two of the doctor's African American farm workers, Louis Whitehead and George Johnson, who immediately fled the community.[10]

On Tuesday, several neighbors of the doctor's family tracked the two men to a saloon in Bryan, where they were arrested. They were thrown in jail, joining another black man, Jim Reddick, who had been sitting in the county jail for about a year and a half waiting to be tried on rape charges. In December 1894 an Italian woman had accused him of attacking her, and a Bryan jury had convicted him and sentenced him to hang. But the state appeals court had questioned the evidence used against him and ordered a new trial, which had not yet been set. Apparently the presence of three accused rapists in the city jail was more than some residents of Brazos County could bear. Learning that the sheriff conveniently was out of town, a lynch mob formed that Tuesday night, but dispersed when word spread that the prisoners had been sent away somewhere else for safekeeping.

The next night another, larger mob formed. They reached the jail door at 9:45 P.M. on Wednesday, surprising the deputy sheriff on guard, who immediately got out of the way but apparently did not hand over any keys. Undeterred by the imposing, castle-like walls and obviously well prepared, members of the mob beat on the door locks with axes and blacksmith's cleavers until they were smashed open. While the deputy sheriff watched, "powerless to resist," the mob rushed into the jail, beat open the cell door locks, and hauled out the three black prisoners. They loaded them onto a wagon and carried them out to Boonville Road, one of the highways leading into the city from the east. Stopping when they got to the edge of Carter's Creek, the mob kindled a bonfire for light. There they hanged Jim Reddick, Louis Whitehead, and George Johnson from separate limbs of the same large oak tree.

By the time Sheriff Tom Nunn returned to Bryan a few days later from Galveston, rumors were already circulating that he had left town on purpose because of the lynching. Not so, the sheriff responded forcefully. Nunn seemed outraged both by the lynching and by the rumors about his absence. In a long letter to the community that he published a week later in the *Eagle*, he vehemently denied any prior knowledge that a lynching had been planned. Furthermore, he wrote, the merits of the case did not require this sort of justice. "Under all the circumstances," Nunn wrote, "this lynching was certainly uncalled for." He emphasized that point even further in a letter he felt obligated to write to the state governor: "I think that it was the most uncalled-for lynching that has ever been committed in Texas."[11]

Nunn did not clearly explain just why the lynching was so "uncalled-for." What seemed to trouble Nunn most of all was the type of people who had led the mob. The "unknown parties" were of course known, and apparently quite well known to the sheriff. These were not the "good people of Brazos county," Nunn wrote in his newspaper letter. Rather, "there was

The lynching of Jim Reddick, Louis Whitehead, and George Johnson on Boonville Road, just east of Bryan, on June 10, 1896. Photo courtesy Prints and Photographs Collection, Center for American History, University of Texas at Austin

certainly some people in the crowd who were far from being good citizens. Certainly it is a dangerous precedent for men of this character to take the law in their hands; when such men lead mobs who is safe." Insisting that "such men" be restrained, Nunn took the highly unusual step on the day his letter was published of arresting four men on charges of murder in connection with the lynching, and their names also were published in the *Eagle*. Nunn hinted strongly in his letter to the town's newspaper readers that there was considerably more to this lynching than met the eye. "If the curtain could be raised and the good people could see the very bottom of this move, they would see some other motive at the bottom of the lynching," Nunn wrote.

Moreover, while he was all in favor of defending "the fair women of this county" against the "rape fiend," such defense should be done only by the right sort of people, Nunn argued. "I further believe that when the people undertake to take the law in their own hands, it should be a general uprising by the best citizens of the county, and what they do should be done after great caution and due deliberation in broad open day." In Nunn's view, that had not happened in this case. It was the violent presence of an uncontrollable mob "with their shot guns in one hand and dynamite in the other and

murder in their hearts"—more than the alleged actions of Reddick, Johnson, and Whitehead—that seemed to bother the sheriff deeply.

Whatever was "at the bottom of the lynching," the arrests of the mob
leaders caused consternation in Bryan. The next day 500 citizens gathered
in the courthouse to discuss this latest development. Nunn gave a speech,
"expressing the hope that the good people of the county would put their
heads together calmly and dispassionately and uphold the law with justice
to all parties." An ad-hoc committee of eight citizens met to decide what
action should be taken, and Nunn's arguments prevailed. The committee
was chaired by Milton Parker, one of the wealthiest and most respected
white residents of Bryan. Parker and his committee resolved "to stand by
our sheriff in the discharge of his duty" and wait for the "fair and impartial
trial" of the prisoners.[12]

The arrested men were allowed out on bond the following Monday, and
neither their charges nor their court case was mentioned again in the pages
of the *Eagle*. Brazos County District Court records do not list their names,
likely indicating they were never indicted by a grand jury and thus were
never tried. If so, it was a win-win solution for all of the whites involved—
though not, of course, for African Americans in Brazos County or for those
who were lynched. Sheriff Nunn and business elites who had chaired the
committee retained their sense of authority and preeminence by seeing that
the men who were arrested remained in jail at least over the weekend and
were released through proper court procedure rather than through the work
of a mob. Meanwhile, those who supported the lynching saw that its leaders
were not put on trial for murder and eventually were allowed to go free.[13]

As it turned out, many of the "men of this character" who had so offended the sheriff were from the Kurten area, where Dr. Wilson and his
family lived, and from other nearby communities in the eastern half of Brazos County. And so at this point we need to stop and explore the Kurten
community, especially its political landscape, because the political situation
there had a great deal to do with how its residents regarded the county
sheriff, and vice versa. The political features of Kurten formed the backdrop
against which the Bryan lynching took place and helps in no small way to
reveal why it happened. Understanding Kurten also requires some exami-
nation of the political landscape of the rest of the county, which for decades
had remained uncertain and at times even volatile.

Dr. Wilson, whose twelve-year-old daughter's screams helped to ignite
the lynching, lived in a contentious area of Brazos County that often sim-
mered with political discord. Such contentiousness had helped to fracture

the county's Democratic party after the Civil War, and it had spawned other political movements that had attracted a host of restless and discontented voters. Quite a number of such disgruntled voters seemed to live in or near Kurten, but they were also scattered elsewhere across the county. The result was that the white vote in Brazos County was thoroughly splintered, and the black Republican vote was strengthened to such a high degree that the local Democratic party could not control the county's electoral outcomes until the end of the nineteenth century. Indeed, the party was virtually shut out of power on the county level for several decades after the war. This was particularly annoying to local Democratic leaders, because although their party had been able to dominate the state government since the early 1870s, they seemed to have made little headway in Brazos County. The tried-and-true solution was to inflate racial fear among whites. As they did in other counties throughout the state and across the South, Democratic leaders were able to heat up anxiety about black political power and then eventually use such fear to cement the white vote into a more or less cohesive whole. Brazos County's neighbors to the north, east, and south—Robertson, Grimes, and Washington Counties—also experienced political discord during this time, and Democrats in those counties used similar solutions. Indeed, racial fears and violent outbursts on the part of anxious whites played no small part throughout the Brazos region and across the South in settling the question of how most whites would vote, particularly at the local level.

The small rural community of Kurten, near where Dr. Wilson lived, had been formed after the Civil War by German settlers, many of whom had been recruited to the area by the prominent, German-born landowner Henry Kurten. But it had also attracted settlers from other southern states, Georgia in particular. The area where Wilson lived was known as "Little Georgia," because about a dozen or so families from a single county in that state had moved there in the 1880s. Also known as Reliance, after the name of a local Baptist church, Little Georgia was one of a string of small settlements in northeastern Brazos County with names such as Tabor, Edge, Steep Hollow, and Bethel. Such communities took their names from the first white settlers to arrive, or from nearby streams or churches, and most of them at least had a schoolhouse to give the community some cohesion, if not also a church, general store, cotton gin, and grist mill.[14]

In the years before the Civil War, relatively few of the county's slaves had lived here, as the larger plantations were mostly on the western side of the county, in the Millican and Mudville areas near the Brazos River. On this eastern side of the county, which drained toward the Navasota River, farmers tended to have smaller, less productive farms than their Brazos Bottom counterparts. They remained that way after the war as well. The soil here was sandier, underlain by a hard clay, and crop yields of cotton and corn were more uncertain and often meager compared to what the Brazos bottomlands could produce. Until the 1890s, when population growth spurred more attempts at crop farming, especially cotton, most of the farmers here raised cattle instead of cotton. And because the Houston & Texas Central Railroad ran though the western side of the county, there was no nearby train service here on the eastern side to provide quick connections to the rest of the county and state. So by and large, most of the area's residents spent most of their days within the sphere of these small communities, following relentless agricultural cycles of clearing and breaking land, planting and cultivating gardens and fields, harvesting and preserving crops and foods, and tending to their livestock. On Saturdays some of the farmers might ride into Bryan to visit saloons, do business with cotton merchants and bankers, or stop by the town's blacksmith shops or dry goods stores, but their families tended to stay nearer home. Occasionally the routine would be broken by a community picnic, church singing convention, or wedding, and families from neighboring settlements often visited one another for Sunday dinners.[15]

Beneath the seemingly peaceful and unvarying nature of rural life, however, lay a hotbed of political insurgency. On the whole, the northeastern upland of Brazos County was home to a large group of feisty and independent farmers, whose votes could never be counted on by the local Democratic party leadership in the decades following the Civil War. Despite the presence of large numbers of Germans—or perhaps in reaction to them—this area was home to the county's strongest supporters of prohibition during the late 1880s. This is also where much of the county's support lay for the Farmer's Alliance, and for Populism, the third-party political movement of the 1890s. The Farmer's Alliance, a sort of combination self-help and agrarian protest movement, had spread into Brazos County from its origin in north-central Texas in the 1880s. Focusing at first on a new concept of cooperative buying and selling as a means of empowering farmers, the organization soon gave birth to a rapidly growing political protest movement that in 1891 called itself the People's party, and its followers became known as Populists. At the top of the list of the new party's platform were calls for a more flexible money supply, a government-sponsored credit and crop-marketing system, and government regulation of railroads—most of which were eventually adopted by Democrats years later, but at the time seemed outrageously radical to many in the party, including those in Brazos County.[16]

Falling crop prices, tight credit, and the lingering economic depression of the 1890s spurred much of the unrest in Brazos County, as it did in similar areas across central and north-central Texas. Much of the wrath of these unhappy farmers was directed at Democrats, whom Populists accused of ignoring the increasing economic woes of farmers and laborers. Brazos County farmers in the Kurten, Edge, and Steep Hollow communities were angry not only with their state and national leadership; they also directed a considerable amount of vitriol at county leadership as well. After Populist candidates were defeated in state and national elections in 1896, sending the movement into a nosedive toward oblivion, the farmers in eastern Brazos County continued to stir up trouble for county Democrats. In 1898 this area produced a brief, strictly local political insurgency that provided a means for some of the discontented farmers in the area to vent their frustrations with the county's Democratic leadership. Leaders of the "non-partisan citizens' movement," as they called it, had become incensed at the autocratic way in which Democratic elites had picked the candidates for local elections coming up in the fall. "We heartily condemn the action of certain gentlemen in trying to take the whole matter of naming a county ticket in their own hands," griped a committee of Kurten farmers who were about to attend their upcoming "citizens' convention." The movement failed to capture any of the offices it sought—namely, sheriff, county judge, and tax collector. Nonetheless, the political brouhaha signified that farmers in the eastern part of the county would not be ready to return wholeheartedly to the Democratic party following the collapse of Populism.[17]

Adding to the political stew in these eastern uplands were German-born and German American farmers, many of whom tended to vote Republican but were not necessarily active in party activities and county politics. Such loose affiliation was typical of other Germans in nearby counties to the south, such as Washington County, where large concentrations of German settlers had exhibited ambiguous voting patterns that frustrated Democrats and Republicans alike. "We are not quite able to locate their political status," reported a somewhat anxious Democratic newspaper editor in Washington County during the 1870s. "God forbid that they should ever affiliate with that rank leprosy the Radical [Republican] Party, that has so long rankled like a festering sore in the heart of our body politic."[18]

Germans had been part of the county population since the 1850s, and many of them were well-respected farmers. One of the first Germans to arrive in Brazos County proved to be something of a boon to the Confederacy. Henry Kurten walked away from his German military assignment while on furlough in Galveston in 1851 and kept on going until he got to Brazos County. He spent the Civil War years running cotton down to Mexico, an activity that was both patriotic and profitable. With the money he earned—and the respect he must have generated as a loyal southerner—he was able to buy a sizable quantity of land in the eastern area of the county. Kurten subsequently enticed some of his fellow countrymen back in Germany to join him in Texas. Thanks in part to his efforts, Germans were by far the largest European immigrant group in Brazos County in 1880 and 1890, just as they were in the rest of the state.[19]

Arguably the most prominent German in Brazos County was Henry Kurten. He clearly had Republican sympathies, as was evident when he agreed to be one of the underwriters for the $10,000 personal bond that J. Allen Myers needed to secure his new appointment as Bryan's postmaster in 1882. Myers, the son of a controversial Republican leader in Millican, had been exonerated in court in 1876 on charges of murdering his father's assassin in a revenge shooting. By 1882 he had become the leading white Republican in the county, but apparently had drawn enmity from some of the city's Democrats, who he thought were determined to keep him from obtaining the post office job. As he wrote years later, "my enemies began to work to prevent me making the bond" immediately after his return from Washington, D.C., where he had gone to obtain the post office appointment. To the rescue came an assortment of European immigrants. They included Henry Kurten; Hugh Reed, an Irish-born farmer, former justice of the peace, and county census taker; and Adam Royder, another wealthy and prominent German-born landowner who lived southeast of Bryan in the Rock Prairie community and who had fought for the Confederacy during the Civil War. Thanks to such help, Myers made his bond and was duly installed as the city's postmaster.[20]

The incident suggests that some of Myers's Republican support included the county's wealthier Germans, most of whom lived in the eastern uplands in and around the Kurten community. These Germans did not appear to be actively involved with the Republican party, however, as very few if any of their names were listed among Republican leaders in news accounts of party doings. Instead, Henry Kurten's name appeared on a list of Democratic precinct delegates for a countywide "white man's primary" in 1890, and later on he even served as the precinct chairman for the Kurten Democrats. Thus his political status may have been as uncertain to Brazos

County Democrats as his fellow Germans in Washington County were to local party leaders there.[21]

Kurten may have been playing both sides of the fence in order to maintain his socially prominent position in the county, and there is some evidence to suggest that at least a few of his German neighbors had the same tendencies. Two of Henry Kurten's German neighbors, a couple of prominent farmers and general store merchants named August and Henry Prinzel, were arrested in 1895 for violating the local-option ordinance in Kurten. This was an area of the county—probably the only one—where prohibition-minded voters had been able to pass a local option law forbidding the sale of alcohol. A similar option had come up for a vote in Millican in the late 1890s, but it had been heartily defeated in a more than three-to-one rout. While such active support for alcohol prohibition in the Kurten area surely would have alienated many local German residents, who enjoyed drinking beer, the Prinzels apparently had voted in favor of the option, according to the *Eagle*. But somewhere along the line, the Prinzels nonetheless had run afoul of their prohibitionist neighbors by turning around and selling the very alcohol they had voted to forbid, possibly to their fellow Germans. The Kurten area was also home to a large number of active white Baptists, and some of the offensive alcohol sold by the Prinzels no doubt was being consumed on Sundays, favorite beer-drinking days for German settlers. Such habits could only have further outraged their prohibitionist neighbors.

In any case, the jury in Bryan, where a dozen or more saloons lined the main street and where nearly every grocery stocked liquor, was ambivalent about the case. First it acquitted August Prinzel on one charge of selling alcohol, deadlocked in a second trial involving another charge, and then sent Henry Prinzel to the county jail for a twenty-day visit. However, Henry Prinzel was quickly pardoned by the state governor, Charles A. Culberson, and released, much to the approval of the Bryan newspaper editor, whose writings through the 1890s never showed any sympathy for prohibition.[22]

It is possible that the Prinzels alienated their neighbors because of Democratic, rather than Republican, sympathies. While they may have leaned toward "that festering sore in the heart of our body politic," as the Democratic Brenham newspaper editor referred to the Republican party, the Prinzels, like Henry Kurten, had publicly aligned themselves with the Democrats during the 1890 election cycle and continued to do so in later elections. August Prinzel served as Kurten's postmaster beginning around 1893, a job usually given to the faithful of the party then in power. He was likely appointed to the job by the higher ranking Bryan postmaster, who at that point happened to be a Democrat because the current occupant of the White House, President Grover Cleveland, who approved all city postmaster appointments, was a Democrat. And then in 1900 Henry Prinzel's name was listed among the Kurten delegates to a Democratic county convention that met to choose delegates to various other state conventions.[23]

The Prinzels' political affiliation with the Democratic party could have caused serious problems with neighborly relations because by 1895, when the arrests took place, many of the Prinzels' neighbors had bolted the Democratic party and joined the Populist movement, and were no longer among the party faithful. Election returns suggest that in the 1890s most residents of the Kurten community also had no admiration for Republicans. Unlike the situation in neighboring Grimes County, Populists and Republicans in Brazos County did not seem to find much in the way of common cause despite their common hostility to Democrats. As we shall see, this political gulf among voters was particularly evident in the local sheriff's races.

Along with the heavy concentrations of black Republicans in the Brazos Bottom area on the western side, these independent farmers in the eastern county were one of the reasons why the county's Democrats had such a hard time gaining any kind of control over the county's electorate. Like these farmers in the eastern uplands, county voters as a whole threw their support behind a series of Greenback, Independent, Populist, and Republican gubernatorial and presidential candidates in the 1870s, 1880s, and 1890s. The result was a political imbroglio of shifting loyalties and fragmentary coalitions, in which no single group or individual dominated the county for any length of time until after the turn of the century, some years after Democrats in neighboring Washington, Robertson, and Grimes Counties had already settled their political affairs by thoroughly and violently squashing their opposition.[24]

Statewide races seemed particularly volatile in Brazos County. The Democrats carried the county in only seven out of thirteen gubernatorial elections between 1876 and 1900, and many of those wins were very close. Though Democrat governor Lawrence Sullivan Ross carried Brazos County in the 1886 gubernatorial election, for example, by 1888 his support in the county was usurped by the prohibitionist candidate Marion Martin, even though prohibition had failed in Brazos County the year before. Next, the Republican candidate for governor, William K. Makemson, carried the county in 1892, and the Populist gubernatorial candidate, Jerome C.

Kearby, won the county's majority vote in 1894, although both candidates were soundly defeated statewide.

As for presidential politics, things were hardly more stable. Support for Democrat Grover Cleveland waxed and waned, though this was typical of ambivalence toward him throughout the South. Cleveland narrowly carried the county by 125 votes in the 1884 election, in a vote of 1,474 to 1,349. Apparently he won in the county by a mere eleven votes in the 1888 presidential election, according to published election returns, although the Galveston newspaper reported that Republican Benjamin Harrison carried Brazos County. The county's Democratic leaders also seemed to have been under the strong impression that Harrison carried the county, judging from the teeth-gnashing and deep chagrin that was expressed in the county's Democratic-controlled newspaper two years later. And in the politically explosive presidential election of 1896, Republican William McKinley carried the county, surmounting the combined vote for William Jennings Bryan by both Democrats and Populists.[25]

The Republican vote in Brazos County remained strong and in many cases decisive through the end of the nineteenth century. If the politically uncontrollable farmers on the eastern side gave the county's Democratic leaders headaches, it was the continued strength of the county's Republicans, and especially of black voters, that caused no end of serious annoyance. For most of the last half of the nineteenth century, while Brazos County Democrats had their hands full trying to consolidate power and take control of the county's political life, which had never been particularly stable, their chief bugbear was the African American vote. County Democrat leaders, many of whom lived in Bryan, were hardly alone in their frustrations. All through the Brazos Bottom—the long, riverine corridor stretching from Waco down to the Gulf—large percentages of black voters had been able to keep the Republican party alive, if only at the local level. Even though Reconstruction was over and the Democrats were back in power at the state level by 1874, in the dozen or so counties along the Brazos River and in a few other clusters of counties, the Republicans remained politically viable for at least two more decades. African Americans in the Brazos Bottom continued to exercise political muscle, and their voices had been consistently and loudly heard at local polls. So it is useful at this point to take a passing glance at the political terrain and racial violence that occurred in some of these neighboring counties to better understand the context of what happened in Brazos County.

For example, in Washington County, Brazos County's southern neighbor, a powerful Republican party emerged after the Civil War, generated by a formidable combination of African American and German residents. Until the turn of the twentieth century, more than half of the county's population was black and another quarter was of German extraction. Possibly half of the German vote had been brought into the Republican camp, thus enabling the party to dominate county government until the mid-1880s, including the county's representation in the state legislature. Meanwhile, in Robertson County, the northern neighbor of Brazos County, a large African American vote also had put several blacks in county offices, and kept Democratic gubernatorial candidates from carrying the county in a number of elections. Black voters had also put the county in the Republican column for every presidential election from 1876 onward. By 1896, Robertson County's Republicans were poised to maintain their domination through a fusion ticket with Populists, and white Democrats there were fit to be tied. And in Grimes County to the southeast, also bordered in part by the Brazos River, black voters had been able to send black legislators to Austin well after the end of Reconstrucgtion. Various groups of Grimes County whites, in opposition to the county's Democrats, had combined forces with African American Republican voters to elect a number of non-Democratic men, some of whom were black, to county offices during the 1880s and 1890s. Such Democratic opposition in Grimes County culminated in 1898, when a white Populist was reelected county sheriff through a strong Populist-Republican coalition, causing a high level of anxiety among white Democrats.[26]

Racial fear provided the perfect solution for Democrats in these counties. It offered a unifying rallying cry the Democrats could use to gather white voters from all parts of the county into the same camp, and it was a highly effective tool, especially when used violently, to intimidate black voters from using their political strength. Of the three counties just mentioned, Washington experienced the first waves of furious retaliation. In 1884 and 1886 a series of violent incidents enabled Democrats to take control of Washington County by stealing ballot boxes, shooting black election judges, lynching at least three black Republicans, and ordering white Republican leaders out of the county. "The Republican Party in Washington County is done for once and for all; the mobsters have complete control," reported one of the exiles, a German named Carl Shutze, in a gloomy letter from his California refuge to a friend back in Texas.[27]

Ten years later, in 1896, violence erupted in Robertson County when a murderous county judge, O. D. Cannon, and other armed whites stood outside polling places with their guns in view to keep African Americans from voting. No one who witnessed such scenes would have doubted that the legendary Cannon would use his weapons if given half a chance. At that point the judge had already killed three men while in office, escaping conviction each time. The most notorious incident had occurred in his own court, when black lawyer and former state legislator Harold Geiger offended him by failing to show enough respect during a trial. Cannon pulled out his gun and shot Geiger five times. In this election in November 1896 Cannon indeed got the chance to shoot again—this time at the black candidate for state representative, Alexander Asberry, who had the temerity to publicly protest the blatant fraud that had robbed him of victory. Cannon only managed to wound Asberry in the arm, but the incident convinced another black candidate, who won his race for county commissioner by too great a margin to lose it by fraud, to decline the office, thus allowing his white Democrat opponent to take the job instead. Cannon, incidentally, was finally sent to the state penitentiary for shooting the white former county school superintendent in 1899. But he was eventually pardoned and sent back home, where he went to work on writing a book about the Bible.[28]

Finally, over in Grimes County to the east, white Democrats spent the last half of the 1890s simmering with resentment at the power that Republicans were able to wield, especially when allied with a rising number of Populists. Most offensive of all, it seemed, was that such a coalition had put a white Populist, Garrett Scott, in the sheriff's office in 1898, and this sheriff had gone so far as to hire black deputies. It was not to be borne, and in the spring of 1899 a group of defeated Democratic candidates created the White Man's Union, whose stated goals were to prevent blacks from voting. Violent intimidation over the next eighteen months convinced thousands of the county's African American residents not only to abstain from voting, but also to leave the county altogether. The terrorism culminated in the November 1900 election. Less than half the usual number of voters made it to the polls, and the White Man's Union candidates won by a landslide. To ensure Scott would not challenge the election, Union members, bristling with guns, converged in Anderson, the county seat. There they occupied the courthouse. A shootout ensued, leaving three men dead, including Scott's brother, and the defeated sheriff with a bullet wound in his leg. Scott holed up in the county jail, where he remained during the five-day siege, leaving only when the state militia from Houston arrived to escort him safely out of town.[29]

Brazos County's newspaper readers probably followed the events unfolding in Anderson with great interest, as the *Eagle* reported the story in
detail. The newspaper's coverage was aided by a somewhat comic eyewit-
ness account of an Anderson lawyer, G. B. Abercrombie, who told the
newspaper he had been in the jail with Scott, but had escaped the siege by
dressing in women's clothing. He made his way across the countryside to
Millican, where he caught a northbound train to Bryan, presumably after
shedding his skirts. The lawyer remained in town for a few days to recuperate and wait for the violence at home to die down, and in the meantime he
regaled Bryanites with his version of the Anderson events. More than a few
white residents of the town would have taken a particular interest in Grimes
County affairs, as they reflected to some degree what had been happening
in Brazos County during the same decade. Such convulsive political storms
eventually resulted in the silencing of African American voices throughout the Brazos Valley for many decades, including those in Brazos County.
Although Brazos County apparently did not experience the kind of widespread terrorism that characterized political activity in neighbor counties,
black voters were nonetheless effectively silenced here as well. But Brazos
County was perhaps the last county in the Brazos valley region where that
silence fell.[30]

Brazos County's African Americans were largely concentrated in the
Millican area and in the other fertile bottomland area in the northwest corner of the county known as Mudville, or Steele's Store.[31] African American
voters from these communities were able to send at least one, and sometimes
two, blacks to the county commissioners court in the 1880s, 1890s, and early
1900s. Mudville maintained a black elected presence in the form of county
commissioner, justice of the peace, or constable from 1880 until 1914. As the
Eagle reported, blacks in Millican, Mudville, and throughout the county
voted solidly Republican, though election returns and newspaper coverage
showed considerable support for other non-Democratic candidates. It was
a strategy that kept the party alive and kicking until nearly the end of the
nineteenth century. As the editor of the *Bryan Eagle* wryly admitted in 1894,
"The Republican party, if dead, is a pretty lively corpse."[32]

In the early 1870s, despite the erosion of power at the state level, Republicans had dominated the county government and also held important offices in Bryan and Millican. Through the late 1870s and 1880s, Republicans
had formed various coalitions with first Greenback and then Independent
candidates, a strategy that successfully kept Democrats out of major county
offices, such as county judge, sheriff, clerk, and tax assessor. The Greenback

party mainly focused on the issue of increasing the nation's paper money supply, and because of its opposition to the Democratic party, state leaders of the Republican party, such as former governor E. J. Davis, had agreed to support Greenback candidates in 1878. Although the strategy failed at the state level, it had stunning success in Brazos County. Among other victors in the county, Elias Mays, an African American farmer and Methodist pastor, won a trip to Austin in 1878 as a victorious candidate for the state legislature on the Greenback ticket.[33]

His victory was galling to the county's white Democrats, who had fielded a respected white physician and "straightout Democrat" in Bryan, Dr. A. R. Canfield, who later became the party chairman. The *Galveston Daily News* summed up the assessment that had been published in a Bryan newspaper: "The Pilot expresses its mortification and indignation of the result of the election for a member of the legislature from Brazos County." Mays was the second African American to be sent to the statehouse as the county's representative; the first was John Mitchell, elected in the early 1870s. Clearly, by the end of that decade, the Democrats had made no progress in gaining control of the county. The sheriff, a New York native named William Forman, was a Republican who had been serving as the county's chief law enforcer since at least 1870, and the Democrats could only sit and watch a majority of the county's voters return him to office every two years. The same was true for the county judgeship: through the entire decade, Republicans had a lock on that office as well.[34]

Things were no better for the Democrats during the 1880s. As a newspaper in neighboring Washington County noted glumly, "In Brazos County the white vote is divided and split up, leaving the county virtually in the hands of Africa. In the county election the contest is for the African vote." The only consolation could have been that the victors were largely white; no blacks actually held any of the county-level offices, though a black farmer had been elected to the county commissioners court from the Mudville precinct.[35]

By the 1880s the Greenback party had faded away, and now Brazos County Republicans were allying themselves with white Independent candidates. Just as in the 1870s, the strategy failed in contests for state offices, but it continued to work splendidly in Brazos County. In 1882, 1884, and 1886, Independent/Republican candidates swept the local elections, losing only the contest for state representative. But not for long: in 1888 Elias Mays won again. Republican/Independent incumbents in all other county posts also hung on to their jobs, except for the district court clerk. Mudville's voters had been particularly victorious in the 1888 election. Precinct 5 had elected a black commissioner, justice of the peace, and constable. Blacks in Millican also had managed to elect a black county commissioner.[36]

After the 1888 election the county's Democrats were fed up with trying to gain control over such an unruly political environment, and in 1890 they pulled out what was about to become an old southern standby for winning elections. Fear of "negro domination"—a rallying cry that echoed across the South with particular resonance in the 1890s when whites sought various means to disfranchise black voters—became the slogan of a "white man's campaign" launched in Brazos County in the spring and summer of 1890. In a similar, though apparently less violent plan than what Grimes County would follow ten years later, the goal of Brazos County's Democrats was to rid the county of Republican officeholders, especially African American ones, and draw together the fractious and contentious elements of the white vote into the fold of the Democratic party. Party leaders appealed to memories of "Old Brazos," a nostalgic term that was meant to evoke what in their view had been the good old days of antebellum Texas, when slavery held blacks in firm control, and whites were completely in charge of the county's affairs.[37]

The 1890 campaign in Brazos County was more than mere political manipulation to round up errant white voters. Racial anxiety had some basis in reality for many of the county's whites; that is to say, fear of "negro supremacy," as the *Bryan Eagle* phrased it, was not entirely unfounded. The 1888 elections had put no fewer than five black men in elected office, including Elias Mays, who enjoyed a second trip to the statehouse. The county thus earned what to Brazos County's whites was the highly dubious distinction of having one of the state's two black state representatives as their man in Austin for that legislative session.

J. Allen Myers, the leader of the county Republicans, was reelected as the county clerk, a post he had first won two years earlier to replace the postmaster's job that he had just lost because a shift in federal patronage following Democrat Grover Cleveland's presidential victory. What was worse, from the Democrats' point of view, was that Myers stood a good chance of being reinstated as postmaster because Benjamin Harrison had won the presidency back for the Republicans in that same 1888 election. Two years later, in 1890, Myers was indeed back at his old job in the post office, and the move caused no small measure of unease among Democrats, who feared Myers's prominence would only hurt their party further. As county clerk, Myers had been somewhat dependent on non-Republican white voters to keep him in office. Now, however, as a Republican federal appointee, he could give his full attention to keeping his party going full throttle. As the *Eagle* editor commented regretfully, "We candidly believe that the reinstatement of Mr. Myers in the Bryan post office will strengthen and solidify the republican forces in this county . . . and it is to be expected that he will hold his party well in hand, as in days of yore, when the rank and file of Brazos county Republicans 'hearkened to his voice' all along the line." [38]

Many whites fully recognized that such success on the part of the black electorate was due not only to the splintered white vote, or to the leadership of white Republicans such as Myers, but also to the growing black population itself. The 1890 census showed a black majority for the first time, though it was slim: 8,433 blacks to 8,213 whites. Ten years earlier, the census had shown a startling trend. The county had grown by more than 2,000 percent since 1850, but the growth rate had not been racially even. Blacks were outpacing whites. While the white population had increased by about 30 percent since 1870, the black population had nearly doubled during the same time period, and continued to increase through the 1880s. [39]

Part of the growth stemmed from efforts by planters to recruit laborers for their burgeoning cotton plantations. Probably because foreign immigrants showed little inclination to work as day laborers for landowners outside their families, some planters turned to older southern states to recruit more labor in the form of black workers, whom they brought into the county by the train carload. Despite rising fears among whites over the increasing black population, the local newspaper noted the arrival of black laborers with approval in 1889:

> Capt. C. B. Black returned from South Carolina a few days ago, bringing with him about 40 families of negroes, who have since been located on one of Mr. Wm. Koppe's plantations in Burleson county. If there is any one thing this section needs more than anything else, it is good farm labor and plenty of it. Therefore, Mr. Koppe has set an example that other Brazos bottom planters ought to follow. Some may object on political grounds, to an increase of the colored population, while others will contend that more negro voters will mitigate the evils that have heretofore resulted from their presence in our political affairs. There is a plausibility about the latter theory, for it is a fact that wherever the negroes are largely in the majority in a community, the whites are fully alive to the perils of the situation and never fail to do their full duty as white citizens of a white man's government. [40]

Meanwhile, in the Millican area, blacks were by far the majority already by 1880, making up more than two-thirds of the population. With such a black majority, white fear and hostility in Millican remained high, and whites there did indeed seem to be "fully alive to the perils of the situation," as the *Eagle* had phrased it. The Millican community remained racially oppressive through the end of the century, with reports of lynchings and mysterious deaths surfacing every few years. "Many Negroes have met their death at the hands of overseers and landlords; in fact, the number of Negroes who have been murdered and thrown into the Brazos River will never be known," wrote Elmer Marshall in a 1937 study of the county's history. "No one seems to know the number that have been hanged by mobs." Though Marshall's study covered the entire county and was largely based on anecdotal recollections ranging back to fifty years earlier, a survey of press reports from the 1870s, 1880s, and 1890s corroborates Marshall's assessment, particularly for the Millican area.[41]

Convict labor camps provided another aspect of brutality and punishment in Millican. Most, if not all, of the county's convict camps were in or near Millican. Several others were nearby in Robertson County, in a community named Mumford. Convict labor arrived in the county after 1878, when the state began leasing its prisoners to a private company that in turn subleased them to various privately owned sugar and cotton plantations along the Brazos River, among other places in the state. By 1880 there were dozens of such convict camps scattered across east Texas, and they were known for their appalling living conditions. Landowners had no incentive to keep their leased laborers alive. If one died, as a planter notoriously said, all he needed to do was "get another."[42]

"The reports of nearly all the penitentiaries where convicts are worked outside the walls show fearful death rates," wrote Thomas Goree, the state penitentiary superintendent, in an 1880 report to the state. The 1880 census showed a total convict camp population in Brazos County of ninety-six, all black, with a guard work force that was all white. By the 1890s, more than 400 convicts worked in six Brazos County camps.[43]

Nonetheless, despite the oppression and violence, the African American population had continued to grow. Brazos County was one of the few counties along the Brazos River corridor that continued to experience steady increases in the percentage of its black population during this period. Robertson County also saw blacks reach the majority by 1890, but elsewhere percentages were slipping, although the absolute numbers of African Americans were climbing slightly. Washington and Grimes counties already had black majorities by 1880, but those majorities were beginning to ebb. Even Brazoria County on the Gulf coast, which was close to 80 percent black during the 1870s and 1880s, had decreased to about 74 percent black by 1890, a trend that would continue until by 1910 blacks would be in the minority there. Uneven population growth explains the change. Throughout the state a large and continuing influx of white newcomers, including foreign-born, was outpacing the growth of the black population. Statewide, African Americans slipped from nearly a quarter of the population in 1880 to just over a fifth in 1890.[44]

But the African American population in Brazos County had seen a whopping 35 percent increase during that decade, causing deep unease among the county's white voters, whose political divisions had been partially responsible for black success at the polls. The county's rapid growth since the Civil War had accelerated during the 1880s, and many black families had been attracted—or in some cases, recruited by large plantation owners—by the offers of work and the possibility of owning their own land. A soaring increase in the number of black residents, many of whom were new and unknown to whites in the area, was a threat to every aspect of white supremacy in Brazos County—socially, economically, and politically. Such racial unease, simmering in 1890, was heated further by the political turmoil of the early years in that decade, and finally boiled over when a series of lynchings erupted in 1896 and 1897. Other studies of lynch-prone areas of the South have shown that lynchings tended to occur when whites felt threatened by their black neighbors, especially when those black neighbors were dominating the census returns.[45]

In the summer of 1890 the political threat of the county's black majority seemed paramount to white leaders. Among those who were outraged that blacks were exercising such political muscle was W. D. Ward, editor of the *Millican News,* whose article complaining about the distressing state of affairs in county politics was reprinted in the *Bryan Eagle:*

> The democratic majority in the county, from what we can learn, is remarkably small, and should there be many discontents in the party ranks after nominations were made it might result in the defeat of the entire ticket. We would hail with pleasure the organization of the democracy of Brazos county, and rejoice to see every office from the constable to congressman filled with simon-pure white democrats. But the question is: can this be done? The negro element will vote solidly against a democratic nominee, no matter who he may be, and will naturally prefer one of their own color to a white republican even. This element is large in the county, and one which it would be policy to be chary of. A glimpse at the result of the last election reveals to view a negro representative to first warm the seat Brazos county holds in the new and grand capitol at the seat of government. Also from this, precinct 1, a negro

county commissioner, who had not sufficient friends in the precinct to make his bond, but had to call on parties in Bryan to make it for him. There are still other positions in this county filled by this off-color race. And of what benefit are they to the county as officers? What has Elias May done for any portion of this state while a member of the last legislature except to bring water and draw his salary? What has our (God save the mark) commissioner done for this end of the county since he has been in office? Simply nothing. Neither of them have influence nor weight with their fellow-members, nor even the respect of the tax-paying white element of this county. And still they must be preferred to worthy men who are capable of furthering our interests in matters pertaining to necessary and requisite legislation. It is about time something were done.[46]

That "something" was the creation of "white men's clubs" throughout the county and Brazos County's first "white man's primary" that would field a single, cohesive Democratic slate intended to lay waste to any Republican or otherwise upstart opposition. Get-out-the-vote barbecues and festive gatherings were held the night before the July 25 primary, culminating in a torchlight parade through downtown Bryan replete with fireworks, flags, a brass band, and speeches.[47] The slate was duly elected by a large turnout, but party leaders were still nervous about what would happen in November. Malcolm Carnes, editor of the *Bryan Eagle* and an active member of the Democratic party, warned his readers in September about the possibility of political perfidy:

> About seventeen hundred whites voted in the primary—a handsome majority of the entire vote of the county. Therefore, the fate of opposition would simply turn on the integrity of the white voters of the county. No man of personal honor or political integrity who took part in the primary election, will countenance or encourage an opposition ticket, and the man who figures on defeating a nominee of that election certainly bases his calculation on a supposed lack of honor and integrity on the part of a large number of white voters of the county. If there are in Brazos county a sufficient number of white men so degraded, so completely lost to every manly virtue and patriotic instinct as to bolt the primary, go with the negroes and elect an opposition ticket, our cause is hopeless, and the sooner we know it the better it will be for all hands. Decent people can then go elsewhere, and leave this county to its negro-ridden destiny.[48]

The 1890 campaign turned out to be only partially successful. In the fall election Elias Mays was defeated, thus ending white embarrassment over having a black representative in Austin. Despite repeated attempts in coming years, Mays would never again be reelected; he was the last black state representative Brazos County would ever send to the statehouse. Other black local officials were knocked down at the polls, including a county commissioner, justice of the peace, and constable. One official, however, remained standing: Dennis Ballard, a stubborn and indefatigable political combatant from the Brazos Bottom, near Mudville, who would end up serving no fewer than nine two-year terms on the county commissioners court.

Ballard's story will figure more prominently in chapter 5, but suffice it to say here that his political survival must have given heart to Mudville's black voters. By the next election, they regrouped for another try at putting at least one of their own in office, and this time they were successful—and stayed so for some years following. In 1892 the Mudville precinct elected another black justice of the peace, Matt Eaton, who held onto the job for twelve more years. And in the election after that a black man, Powell Harvey, regained his old constable position, a job he would keep until 1914. Election returns for the county as a whole suggest that African Americans—who by the *Eagle's* estimation made up the overwhelming majority of Republican voters—were hardly cowed by the machinations of those who had organized the 1890 "white man's movement." Whatever success the movement had had in uniting white voters for that single summer primary—which was probably only a fleeting unity—it had done nothing to quell the black vote for the next several November elections.

Because of the state political connections of postmaster J. Allen Myers, Brazos County Republicans closely followed the urgings of state Republican leaders, such as former governor E. J. Davis, and the African American leader, Norris Wright Cuney, who led the party after Davis's death in 1883. Cuney, a remarkable politician, was the son of a slave mother and a white planter in neighboring Washington County. In the decades after the war Cuney held a variety of elected and appointed positions, including collector of customs in Galveston, and he also enjoyed strong connections with the national Republican party. With such local, state, and national stature, he garnered strong respect among Brazos County's black Republicans. In 1892, 1894, and 1896, the county's Republican voters successfully kept the county out of the Democratic column of gubernatorial victories. For most of the 1890s, it appeared the only permanent victory the "white man's movement" had won was the battle over which racial category would provide the county's representation in the state's House of Representatives.[49]

But there were other casualties of the 1890 white man's primary besides state representative Elias Mays. These casualties were two white men, and it can be argued that their defeat lit slow-burning resentments and frustrations that eventually exploded in the 1896 lynching. Seemingly hidden beneath the racial animosity and desperate appeal to Democratic unity that the 1890 "white man's campaign" signified was a contest for the county judge's office, and a bitter race for the sheriff's seat. Both incumbents lost to active members of the Democratic party. The losers were J. A. Buckholts, the county judge, and D. D. Dawson, the sheriff. Their defeat in the primary could only have worsened a significant political and social rift between whites in the eastern uplands and those in the western bottomlands of the county. The irony, of course, is that the rift widened during a political campaign that was meant to increase white solidarity but instead may have only served to deepen resentment by demonstrating the eroding political power in the eastern uplands.[50]

Buckholts's and Dawson's defeat and the rift it amplified had great significance in later years, particularly in the 1896 triple lynching. It signified that the Democrats finally were beginning to gain what would become an iron grip on county leadership and to shut out other independent political movements that had kept the white vote fractured. It would take the rest of the decade for the Democrats to achieve a complete victory, but the defeat of Buckholts and Dawson signaled the end of white opposition to Brazos County's Democrats. And that in turn heralded the end of black Republican voting power, though it would not be fully realized until the early twentieth century. So while the "white man's campaign" initially had little impact other than the defeat of an African American state legislator, it set in motion a slow but inexorable political realignment that would eventually strangle any Democratic opposition for a good part of the twentieth century.

In a newspaper notice that ran as the "white man's campaign" got under way in the summer of 1890, County Judge J. A. Buckholts described himself as a Democrat, but his affiliation seemed somewhat tenuous at best. Born in Mississippi, he had fought in the war against Mexico and then settled in Texas sometime before the Civil War, where he served in the state legislature from another county. He arrived in Bryan in 1870, and served at one point as a district judge. The 1880 census listed his occupation as a lawyer, and news accounts in the 1890s reported him as an active member of the Bryan bar and one of the oldest lawyers in the area. It is possible that his political sympathies, if not outright ties, were to either the Greenback or Independent movements, both of which had strong support in Brazos County during the 1870s and 1880s. It is not clear just what his political affiliation was in 1888 when he was elected county judge, and it is doubtful that his loyalties were wholeheartedly Democratic, because news accounts a few years later made much of the fact that the Democrats had fielded no ticket during that election. By the mid-1890s, a few years after the "white man's primary," Buckholts's loyalties became clear when he publicly bolted the Democrats to become an active leader of the county Populists. He and Dawson apparently were fellow travelers, politically speaking, as they both ended up rotating the county chairmanship of the local Populist party during the 1890s. Such a move seemed to represent a permanent fall from grace in the eyes of Bryan's Democrats, because when Buckholts died in 1898, the staunchly Democratic *Eagle* noticed his passing with a mere three paragraphs and never mentioned that he had held the county's highest local office ten years earlier. It was a stark contrast to the long and effusive stories the paper normally ran when prominent men in the county died.[51]

Buckholts lost the 1890 primary in a four-way race in which all the candidates were Bryan lawyers. While the contest for county judge would certainly have stirred some interest, particularly among Bryan's courthouse crowd, the real attention-grabber throughout the county was the sheriff's race. Here the candidates were not the well-educated, elite town dwellers who were vying for the county judgeship, but a couple of scrappy political opportunists who represented very different segments of Brazos County's population and who were contending for the most prominent law enforcement job the county had to offer.

The incumbent, D. D. Dawson, was a native of Georgia. After a stay in Alabama he, like nearly everyone else in Brazos County, it seemed, had moved to Texas following the Civil War. He settled first in Burleson County across the river from Brazos County, where he worked as a farm hand, and possibly as a sharecropper or tenant farmer. Sometime in the 1870s he moved to Brazos County and quickly got himself elected county commissioner from the eastern side of the county. By 1879 he was the owner of a 120-acre farm in the Reliance community, near where Dr. R. H. Wilson lived. Apparently he soon made friends with the county's Republican/Greenback/Independent power brokers, because in 1880 he was appointed to the sheriff's post to fill an unexpired term of the previous sheriff, the Republican William Forman, who had resigned after serving ten years. Dawson held the job for less than five months before being ousted in the November election, but he made a comeback bid in 1882, and this time was successful. He stayed through two more election cycles. During that time he also substantially increased his land and livestock holdings in the

Thomas C. Nunn was elected sheriff of Brazos County in a hotly con-
tested race in 1890. He served as sheriff for close to twenty years during a racially turbulent time in the county, and was unable to prevent
at least two lynchings. Photo courtesy George Hamilton

Reliance area, bought a parcel of land in Bryan where he erected a new
home, and probably to most observers appeared set to keep his prominent
place in county affairs for some time to come.[52]

But in 1888 a serious political challenge surfaced in the form of Tom C.
Nunn, a local saloonkeeper and former cattle trail driver. Nunn, thirty-five
years old, was a native Texan. One newspaper account in the 1890s had it
that he had been born in neighboring Burleson County, but census data
suggest he actually may have spent his early childhood before the Civil War
in Washington County in a slaveholding family. His obituary in 1927 listed
his birthplace as Washington County. In any case, at around age twelve or
fifteen, just after the end of the war, he had moved with his father to Brazos
County, where he raised cattle. Eventually drifting west, he spent some time

as a trail driver in New Mexico and Wyoming, among other states, before returning to Bryan in 1878 to work in a saloon, which he owned by the late 1880s. Then, in 1888, he apparently needed a fresh challenge and decided to take on Sheriff Dawson, who was a prohibitionist and an active Baptist. Although prohibition had failed in Brazos County in the statewide 1887 vote, the saloon keeping Nunn was not able to wrest the sheriff's job from Dawson, though it was a close call. Nunn lost by 183 votes. Looking back two years later, the *Eagle* called the 1888 sheriff's race "the hottest one" in the county that year. Precinct returns show that the election pitted the eastern prohibitionist farmers, allied with similarly minded Bryanites, against an odd coalition of whiskey-drinkers in Bryan, African Americans of the Brazos Bottom, and Czech and German settlers in the Wellborn and College Station areas in the central area of the county. It was clear from these precinct returns that Nunn's support was largely from the western side of the county, near the Brazos River, while Dawson's base of support was in the eastern uplands, near the Navasota River. Bryan voters leaned heavily toward Dawson. Veiled references in the *Eagle* to divisions in support along racial lines also seemed to indicate a further separation between the two contenders: by 1890, as the newspaper reported, Dawson "is now stronger than ever among the white people," while Nunn "is popular with all classes."[53]

When the 1890 election season rolled around, Nunn was ready to do whatever it took to win the election this time. Realizing that his saloon was a major liability, especially among Bryan teetotalers, he published an open letter to the community in the *Eagle* in the middle of the campaign that year, during the height of the "white man's movement." To reassure potential voters that his saloon would not stand in the way of doing his duty as sheriff, Nunn announced he "would abandon the liquor business in the event of any election to the sheriff's office." But a few days later, he decided not to wait until the election to divest himself of his saloon, and instead publicly announced that he was selling his saloon immediately to John N. Nunn, probably his brother. As a campaign tactic, it worked. It may also have helped that the *Eagle* seemed to favor Nunn—who after all had supported the newspaper by advertising heavily while still a saloon keeper. According to the newspaper, Nunn was "physically a splendid specimen of Southern manhood and is first-class material for the office to which he aspires." Nunn beat Dawson by a 100-vote margin in the primary, edging out Dawson even in Bryan, where the incumbent sheriff had previously enjoyed strong support. As the sole candidate on the Democratic ticket, Nunn won the general election in November, and would continue to win for six more terms.[54]

The curious coalition that supported Nunn unsuccessfully in the 1888 election had now prevailed. It was probably the statewide vote on the proposed constitutional prohibition amendment in 1887 that helped to coalesce these two otherwise disparate groups of voters—white, business-minded, anti-prohibitionist Democrats, and black Republicans—into a solid and enduring base of support for a former saloon keeper turned sheriff. As several historians have noted, the bitter 1887 prohibition campaign loosened party ties, particularly for prohibitionists such as D. D. Dawson and his supporters, many of whom left the Democratic party soon after the election to become active Populists in the 1890s. The prohibition campaign caused a great deal of factional turmoil within communities, and created long-lasting resentments in Brazos County, particularly on the eastern side where support for prohibition was strongest. How individuals voted on prohibition was so divisive that years later voters remembered the 1887 election as a time "when friendships were severed and family ties subject to the keenest trial," as Randolph B. Campbell noted in his history of Texas. Indeed, nearly five decades after the vote, elderly Brazos County residents could still remember just how much dust had been kicked up by the election: "Throughout the campaign people remained in a state of mind bordering on frenzy."[55]

Election returns for the 1890s show an interesting change: whereas Greenback and Independent voters seemed to be ready and willing to form coalitions with Republicans, the Populists—though many were former Greenbackers and Independents—made few such liaisons. Other than possible agreements in the 1896 gubernatorial and presidential elections, local races did not show a great deal of cooperation between the two groups. Many of the Populists in Brazos County also seemed to be prohibitionists and active Baptists, and they likely blamed the Republicans—specifically, the county's African American voters—for the defeat of the state prohibition amendment in 1887.[56]

Many of these Populists were owners of small, less fertile farms, in a county where the average farm was 98 acres, and where two of every three farmers worked as tenants or sharecroppers. They were hurting. In the long, hot summer of 1896, many of their political hopes and economic dreams were focused on the upcoming fall elections, which would determine not only who would hold the nation's highest political office, but also who would be Brazos County's most visible lawman. Several white farmers from the eastern side of the county no doubt decided to take advantage of a volatile situation created by the accusations of Dr. Wilson's daughter. The sheriff's comments about the mob and the identities of the mob leaders suggest that the incident at Dr. Wilson's farm offered a chance for those who formed the mob to express their resentment of Nunn by staging a lynching. At the same time, killing the three African American men also demonstrated the mob's ability to assert control over the county's growing black population. These farmers surely recognized that a healthy chunk of Nunn's support came from African American voters in the western side of the county, who, in this case at least, were allied with a number of white Democrats, some of whom lived in Bryan and were wealthy landowners of Brazos Bottom cotton plantations. Murder must have been irresistible. It enabled disgruntled eastern upland farmers to demonstrate what they considered to be their superior ability to maintain law and order in the county, tweak the wealthier Democratic elite in Bryan, and discredit the sheriff, who was not even in town during the entire episode.

Nunn and his wife, along with the county judge and his wife, had all left town Monday afternoon, the day after the Sunday night alleged attack on Wilson's daughter, to attend a "good roads" convention in Galveston. Nunn said he was unaware that problems were brewing in the Reliance area. "When I left home, I never heard a word of the attack," he wrote in his letter to the community, published in the *Eagle* a week after the lynching. On the Tuesday after the attack, his deputy notified him in Galveston, probably by telegraph, of the arrests of the two black men. Nunn telephoned the deputy to discuss the situation and then assumed the deputy would be able to keep things under control—which of course turned out to be a serious error in judgment.[57]

As noted earlier, Nunn was outraged more than anything by the type of men who had led the lynch mob, "who were far from being good citizens," as he wrote in a letter to the community. He also suggested that the rumors alleging he had deliberately left town to avoid responsibility for the lynching were being circulated for "political purposes" by "some who are not my friends." In another letter written to the state governor at about the same time, Nunn was more explicit about the possible political motives of the mob by pointing to their political affiliation, which by his inference was Populist: "There may have been some democrats among them, but I doubt it."

It is highly significant that W. N. Smith, one of the mob leaders whom Nunn had arrested, was former sheriff Dawson's brother-in-law and lived in the Reliance and Kurten area. Smith was also one of Dr. Wilson's neighbors who had helped the deputy sheriff to track down the fleeing black farm laborers, Louis Whitehead and George Johnson, to a Bryan saloon, where they were arrested and jailed—and then promptly lynched. Smith's arrest suggests an underlying connection between Nunn's longstanding political opposition in the eastern uplands and the lynching. Nunn's mysterious allusion to hidden motives for the lynching no doubt was a reference to this political opposition.[58]

The sheriff was facing another reelection campaign in the fall, and he clearly ran a huge political risk by arresting Smith and the other mob leaders. Nunn was acutely aware that most people in the county seemed to believe that the lynching had been done "under the guise," as he put it to the governor, of defending the virtue of white women. "It is hard to enforce the law against men for lynching Negro rapists, no matter what their motive is," Nunn commented with evident frustration. Indeed, the decision to arrest the leaders had prompted some 500 people to converge at the courthouse in a state of high consternation. Nonetheless the sheriff was vindicated when the ad hoc committee voted to leave the men in jail, if only temporarily. Significantly, wealthy Brazos Bottom plantation owner Milton Parker, who lived in a large mansion in Bryan and was arguably the most socially prominent man in town, chaired the committee. It seems likely that Parker and a majority of the committee also recognized the underlying political motivations for the lynching. In any case, Nunn's move to arrest the men paid off politically, because in the election that fall Nunn was returned to office, defeating his Reliance opposition once again. In November 1896, six months after Bryan's triple lynching, another farmer from the same eastern county area, W. A. Stewart, joined Dawson as one of Nunn's vanquished contenders. Stewart had been one of the eight men chosen to serve on the ad hoc committee that met to decide what to do about Nunn's decision to jail the four lynch mob leaders. Significantly, Stewart lived in Reliance near Dawson's cattle farm, and thus was also a neighbor of Dr. Wilson and a prominent member of the community. Although he evidently had been unable to prevail against the power of committee chairman and wealthy Bryanite Milton Parker, Stewart continued to keep alive the opposition to Nunn. In the following years, Nunn's political opposition remained centered, as it had from the beginning, in the same eastern uplands where Dawson had enjoyed his greatest support.[59]

Such underlying associations and motives behind the 1896 lynching reflect the intimate connections between race and politics in late nineteenth-century Texas. Lynchings often resulted from complicated relationships among neighbors and within communities, where all sorts of hostilities and bitter resentments might simmer for years until an incident—such as the night screams of Wilson's daughter—offered a sudden, explosive release.

The 1890s were particularly volatile in that respect throughout the South and in Texas, where economic troubles, combined with political upheaval and social dislocations, produced furious eruptions that often targeted African Americans as scapegoats. Such was the case in Brazos County, as in other counties along the Brazos River. A long history of slavery, family feuds, murderous outbursts by whites against other whites, and lawless behavior of every sort had created an environment where one more brutal episode, such as a lynching, could not have been unexpected. Those who felt most beleaguered by economic troubles and political powerlessness may have welcomed it, and found some measure of vindication for their woes in the deaths of three black men.

But the frustrated farmers of the Kurten area were not the only ones to feel vindicated that June night in 1896. In addition to Dr. Wilson's two black farm workers, the mob murdered another African American, a man who had been accused of raping an Italian woman some eighteen months earlier. In that highly racialized environment of the late nineteenth century, the Italian community had much to gain through the lynching of this particular man. Though they likely were not part of the mob that night, the Italians of Brazos County nonetheless benefited from his death.

Chapter 3

THE ITALIANS

Trouble between the negroes and the Italians is becoming often [sic] and the bitterness engendered has already reached a point of almost continuous hostility which bodes no good for the future.

BRYAN EAGLE, 6 December 1894

On the night Jim Reddick, Louis Whitehead, and George Johnson were lynched on a dark road on the outskirts of Bryan, the young, wealthy white daughters of Milton Parker were holding an elegant reception in honor of their visiting out-of-town friends. At least on a symbolic level, the two events were not unrelated. Perhaps it was by chance that both occurred within blocks of each other, but it was no coincidence that both ended up on the same page of the newspaper the next morning as news items of equal interest. Pure white women and lynched black men were equally important as racial symbols, and their meanings were inextricably linked in the minds of many southerners, including the white people of Bryan. The purity of one inspired the killing of the other, and never more so than in the waning years of the nineteenth century.[1]

Just why that was so has kept scores of historians, sociologists, and literary critics busy in recent years, but no one has come up with a definitive explanation. Lynching has been examined with many different analytical lenses, political, economic, psychosexual, social, religious, and cultural. As we saw in chapter 2, political conflict played a significant role in this particular lynching, but the event also was deeply suffused with notions of gender, and especially what it meant to be a white woman. Chapter 2 examined the political conflict that underlay this lynching; this chapter will tell the story as it affected a number of women in Bryan and in outlying rural areas. The events leading up to the 1896 Bryan lynching clearly demonstrate the role that southern white women often played in creating and sustaining a lynching culture. And in this episode, one of the starring roles was played by an immigrant woman, an Italian, who desperately needed—but did not quite receive—the status that whiteness conferred.[2]

The 1890 "white man's primary" election that put Sheriff Nunn in office created seething resentment in the Kurten area and other eastern county communities, which eventually erupted in the 1896 lynching. But elsewhere in the county, especially in Bryan, political agitation and electoral anxieties over "negro domination" seemed to die down after the 1890 elections, or at least such fears were not expressed so clearly in the local newspaper. Brazos County's white Democratic leaders seemed willing to concede Precinct 5—the Mudville, or Steele Store, area—to its black residents, at least for the time being. There was no more grumbling in local news accounts after 1890 about "negro supremacy" or any repeat of the "white man's campaign." Perhaps removing Elias Mays from the highly visible post of state representative and reducing the black representation on the county commissioners court from two commissioners to one was enough to make Democrats feel that they had drawn the teeth from the threat of black political strength. Perhaps they recognized the value of allowing a black justice of the peace and a black constable to exercise control in what was largely a black population; Bryan aldermen, after all, had hired a black policeman for years to deal with black lawbreakers.

That is not to say that Democratic leaders completely ignored the potential of a black electorate to upset the county power structure. A few incidents suggest that at least some anxiety over black political power remained. In 1899 the county commissioners voted to remove the voting boxes from Mudville and from another area near Millican where high concentrations of blacks voted. Such a move did not eliminate the black vote from this part of the county, as events would later show. But it would have increased the voting difficulties for these residents, especially in Mudville, by requiring them to travel farther to find a polling place. And in 1900 white Bryanites kept black voters away from a city election by openly threatening violence. A Grimes County newspaper, the *Navasota Daily Examiner,* reported that friends of two Bryan mayoral candidates "made a display of force and permitted no Negroes to vote. All white citizens went to the polls, quietly deposited their ballots for whom they pleased and went on about their business." Nonetheless, the county as a whole did not seem to experience the high level of violent convulsions that swept over Grimes, Robertson, and Washington Counties. This may have been because Sheriff Nunn, one of the most visible political officeholders in the county and the man with whom most citizens would have first contact in judicial and legal matters, was a white man firmly endorsed by the Democratic elite. That he also seemed to enjoy the support of the thousands of black residents near the Brazos Bottom could only have helped to reduce panic among Democratic leaders.[3]

Perhaps white county leaders also recognized there were other, less troublesome but equally effective ways to control black aspiration. In the fall of 1890 Jim Crow segregation formally arrived when the city rebuilt its train depot with separate waiting rooms for African Americans and whites. Officials were proud they had found a way to separate the races further. "The enforcement of this rule will be hailed with delight by the citizens of Bryan," predicted the *Eagle*. In the late 1890s and early 1900s the population of the county's black convict labor camps nearly doubled, providing a brutal object lesson about white racial domination in the very areas where the county's black population was most concentrated. Arrests and convictions of African Americans accused of assault and theft substantially increased from earlier in the decade. At the same time, the county began using its own black convicts on road projects and enforcing spurious vagrancy laws with the acknowledged intention of boosting a badly needed labor source. Perhaps most effective of all were the series of lynchings and a legal execution that proclaimed white dominance with a vengeance.[4]

In Mudville one other factor may have helped account for whites essentially shrugging their shoulders at the continuing black political success in Precinct 5. While various waves of political turbulence were breaking over the county, eastern and southern European immigrants were settling into their farmsteads and businesses and slowly becoming naturalized Americans, as well as racialized southerners. In Precinct 5, not far from the Brazos River, hundreds of Italians and Bohemians were renting and buying land. Because they tended to be newly arrived immigrants, not many were naturalized. They were in no position to challenge or even complain about black political power, or to assert any claims of white dominance. Judging from the few comments in the *Bryan Eagle* about their presence, they represented little challenge to white Democrats.

The racial unrest that surrounded them provided a way for Brazos County's European immigrants to settle the question of their own racial ambiguity. Democratic party leaders may have been initially puzzled by the racial status and anxious about the political loyalties of these newcomers, but as time went on there were indications that many of the new, naturalized citizens would vote Democratic and thus would continue to pose no threat. White county leaders could afford to tolerate the existence of a black constable and justice of the peace—and even a black county commissioner— in an area inhabited chiefly by African Americans and strange-speaking foreigners. The political invisibility of Precinct 5 would change, but not until the twentieth century was well under way and these eastern and southern Europeans began to vote in larger numbers. By that time, thanks in part to the racial violence of the 1890s and new, restrictive electoral laws, the Democratic party had gained full control over Brazos County politics. The way would be open for naturalized immigrants to prove their whiteness in political terms and to reap the benefits that political power could bring.

Most certainly the Italians of Brazos County who witnessed the events surrounding the lynchings of 1896 learned important lessons about racial hierarchy. What they may not have understood quite so clearly at first was the political backdrop against which these lynchings took place and the ways in which race and southern politics were so intimately connected. But there is no doubt that they and other immigrants eventually learned these racial and political lessons from native-born white southerners quite well. They, and especially their children, would be among the chief beneficiaries of the Democrats' consolidation of political power at the end of the nineteenth century and of the seeming social equality among whites that racial violence wrought.

At the time these new European immigrants were beginning their new lives as Brazos County farmers, many of their native-born neighbors were suffering a variety of economic problems. But not everyone in the county was hurting. The wealthiest members of Bryan's white elite were able to ride out that summer of 1896, as well as the entire turbulent decade, with little apparent trouble, as evidenced by the building boom in which they took part with gusto. Some were renovating older homes, while others replaced them with new and elegant abodes, and still others bought empty lots and erected brand-new monuments to their high social standing. Palatial Greek Revival mansions, complete with fluted columns and massive porches, were beginning to rise on the east side of town, along with turreted Queen Anne-style houses with wide verandas and a dozen or more rooms. Many of these homes were owned by prosperous landowners of large, fertile Brazos Bottom cotton plantations, whose crops were harvested by a mixture of sharecroppers and day laborers, many of whom were black and some of whom increasingly were Italian immigrants.[5]

One of these landowners was Milton Parker, perhaps the city's most eminent citizen at the time. As a twelve-year-old boy, Parker had moved to Texas in 1852 with his family, settling across the river in Burleson County. Parker served in the Confederate Army, then after the war moved to Galveston to work briefly as a cotton merchant before deciding to move back to the Brazos Bottom, this time to Millican. In Millican he launched various businesses, including a bank, which later became the First National Bank when it was sold to Guy Bryan, son of the town's namesake, William Joel Bryan. With profits from the sale, Parker added to his substantial cotton acreage in neighboring Burleson County, on the other side of the Brazos River from Brazos County. Like Brazos County, Burleson has substantial river bottomlands that by the end of the nineteenth century were largely planted in cotton and were mostly owned by wealthy planters such as Parker. By the 1880s Milton Parker had moved to Bryan. There he went on to develop a prosperous lumber company, which he sold to his son, G. S. Parker, in 1890.

Another son, John Parker, ran a dry goods store in town. All three Parkers also owned cotton gins in the Brazos Bottom, and they were involved in various other banking, business, and development projects in the county. Just about anything family members did made news, whether it was visiting friends in Dallas or launching a new company to build a bridge across the Brazos River that would help to link their farmlands in Burleson County with railroad connections in Bryan. The Parker family also had impeccable social connections to other prominent families in the area. Milton Parker's stepmother was the sister of Harvey Mitchell, one of the county's earliest settlers and the "father of Brazos County," as the *Eagle* had designated him, and the Parkers were also closely related to other wealthy families in town.[6]

Especially interesting to Bryan's newspaper readers, it seemed, was the Parkers' social life, especially that of their three daughters still at home, who were in their late teens and early twenties. Nearly every summer during the 1890s, the Parkers could be counted on to entertain Bryan's elite with an assortment of receptions, card parties, dinners, and eventually, fashionable weddings at St. Andrew Episcopal Church. They lived on the prestigious west side of town, where in 1885 Parker had built a spacious, $6,000 multistory home with the aid of German carpenters from Dallas. Though it lacked the Corinthian columns, turrets, and monumental porticoes of other homes that had been or were soon to be erected across town, the Parker house nonetheless was a model of elegance for the up and coming of Bryan.[7]

That summer of 1896, Milton Parker seemed to have spared no expense for his three daughters, Winnie, Kate, and Fanny. Their lavish party on Wednesday evening, June 10, had attracted great interest. According to the next morning's edition of the *Bryan Eagle,* theirs was a scene of "unusual brilliance and gaiety." Parker had imported a dance ensemble, Herb's Light

The Parker Lumber Company was one of the Parker family's many successful businesses in Bryan. Parker family members also owned productive cotton plantations in Brazos and Burleson Counties. Photo courtesy Carnegie Center of Brazos Valley History

Guard Band, from Houston, and the music drifted out across the verandas and wide lawn on the warm summer evening. "Ices and salads were temptingly served," the newspaper noted, and the large number of guests entertained themselves with conversation and dancing.[8]

Meanwhile, about twelve blocks away from Parker's mansion, a "party" of a different sort altogether was taking place. Several hundred angry white men, who were "armed to the teeth," were surging toward the county jail with axes and sledgehammers, intent on murder. The jail was a stout-looking, two-story brick affair with ornate masonry that lined the edge of the upper story and roof line with rows of miniature battlements and turrets. Built "on the style of the old English castles," as a newspaper in a nearby town described it, the seemingly impregnable jail stood next to the county courthouse, also an elaborate Victorian structure.

Unlike the layout of most southern towns, Brazos County's courthouse did not dominate the town square by standing in its center with the town's major streets radiating outward, although that had been the original plan. Instead, Bryan had been skewered, as it were, by the very railroad that gave it birth. Before the town had been built, Bryan's first businessmen had quickly realized that the lots next to where the train tracks were to be laid were cheaper than the lots surrounding the courthouse. So they set up their

Parker-Bernath House, the home of the Milton Parker family, built in 1885. It was the scene of many social gatherings in Bryan, including a lavish party held on the same night in June 1896 that a triple lynching took place several blocks away. Photo courtesy Carnegie Center of Brazos Valley History

shops a few blocks westward instead of clustering around the more expensive property near the courthouse. Bryan's Main Street therefore developed as a long, straight corridor paralleling the train tracks, and the courthouse and jail were left standing virtually alone on the other side of the tracks. Thus, when the Houston & Texas Central trains rolled through every day, they cut the town in half, separating the business district, which stretched out on the west side, from the courthouse and developing neighborhoods on the east side. For generations to come, the town layout would cause endless annoyance to county and city residents, who often found themselves trying to cross from one side to the other just as a train was coming through.[9]

Parker's mansion, situated on the west side of town, was therefore separated from the courthouse by both Main Street and the train tracks. The distance was not far, however, and there would have been nothing to mask the sounds of an impending riot other than the rumble of passing trains and possibly a handful of industrial-type machines near the downtown. So it is hard to imagine that at least some of the partygoers at the Parkers'— especially those who were lingering outside on the verandas and lawn—did not hear some of the raging tumult that was erupting on the other side of town. Some of them may even have made sudden excuses and left to see what could be taking place at the courthouse. The newspaper reported the

Brazos County Jail, built in 1878 and demolished in the 1920s to make way for a new jail, which was torn down in the 1950s. The 1878 jail stood next to the Brazos County Courthouse on the corner of 25th and Washington Streets. It saw the beginning of several lynchings, including the triple lynching in 1896 and another lynching in 1897. Photo courtesy George Hamilton

next day that the large crowd trailing behind the lynch mob included "parties who went out from the town from curiosity."[10]

Until that point, Jim Reddick had been sitting in jail for about eighteen months on charges of raping an Italian woman named Fannie Palazzo in early December 1894. But apparently Reddick's attack had not stirred a great deal of interest in the larger Bryan community, because no lynch mob had appeared to carry out its version of justice, as would ordinarily have happened in rape cases such as this. Other than acts of murder, nothing could incite southern whites to frenzy in these years quite like the accusations of sexual offenses by black men against white women. "The unspeakable crime," the rape of a white woman, was an abhorrent and feared crime that loomed large in the imagination of whites at that time, including the newspaper readers of Bryan, who were regularly treated to accounts of rape-inspired lynchings then occurring across the South. The absence of a lynch mob strongly suggests that for whatever reason, Brazos County's whites

View of the east side of Bryan, looking along 26th Street from Main Street, with the county courthouse in the upper left corner. The photograph is undated, but was probably taken around the turn of the twentieth century. Photo courtesy Carnegie Center of Brazos Valley History

were not particularly disturbed by Reddick's crime, and were content to leave him in jail.[11]

However, many of the Italians, who were in the process of settling the Mudville area, west of town near the Brazos River, and another area just east of Bryan, had become riled immediately after the incident occurred. The newspaper's account suggests they possibly considered forming a lynch mob of their own. But the Italians had since quieted down, apparently believing the assurances of the sheriff that he had things well in hand. "The Italians are very much incensed by the outrage and would have made things lively for the negro had not Sheriff Nunn told them firmly that the law must be allowed to take its course," the newspaper reported the day after the rape.[12]

In April 1895 the law took its course, and a Bryan jury convicted Reddick of rape and sentenced him to hang. But his lawyers successfully appealed the case to a higher court. In February 1896 the Texas Court of Criminal Appeals overturned the verdict on grounds of shaky evidence and remanded the case to Bryan. Local court officials set a new trial date for March, then postponed it when a key defense witness for Reddick could not be found. Months passed, and still Reddick sat in jail. Then on Tuesday, June 9, two African American men, Louis Whitehead and George Johnson, were arrested for attempting to rape the twelve-year-old daughter of

Dr. Wilson in Kurten two nights earlier. The next night, the mob stormed the jail, and apparently for good measure, they hung Reddick along with Whitehead and Johnson, though he had had nothing to do with the alleged assault on Dr. Wilson's daughter.[13]

The lynching was one of about six in the state that year, contributing to what would be at least 400 violent deaths of men, women, and youths at the hands of Texas lynch mobs between 1880 and 1930. Across the South the total was at least 5,000. Exact numbers are difficult to come by, and historians widely agree that recorded totals were most likely seriously underreported. Official compilations, such as those kept by the *Chicago Tribune* and the Tuskegee Institute, mostly relied on reports published in a limited number of newspapers. The numbers are also inexact because these sources employed varying definitions of lynching, a problem that continues to bedevil modern scholars who struggle to give an exact meaning to the word *lynching,* as historian Christopher Waldrep has noted. Part of the problem is the difficulty of trying to pinpoint the type of victim, circumstances, and number of perpetrators that would constitute a lynching. But historians generally agree that the most basic element of any lynching is the broad support that the surrounding community gave to such extralegal violence. As Waldrep wrote, "Lynching means many things, but one meaning is murder endorsed by community . . . nineteenth-century folk understood lynching to mean an act of violence sanctioned, endorsed, or carried out by the neighborhood or community outside the law."[14]

In any case, the peak year for lynchings in the South appears to have been 1892. In Texas, lynching apparently peaked in several different years, including just before and after the Bryan triple lynching. In 1895 and 1897, Texas mobs killed at least twenty-six victims each year; in 1915 the body count soared to at least twenty-nine. From the 1890s onward, brutal torture and sexual mutilations characterized an increasing number of these mob killings. Lynchings sometimes became festive, ritualized, daytime public spectacles that drew thousands of white men, women, and even children to watch. But perhaps one-third or less of these lynchings were perpetrated by mass mobs, and even fewer were mass spectacles involving burning and torturing victims before thousands of onlookers. The majority were less public, conducted on back roads and at night, erupting beyond the purview of photographers and seething, bloodthirsty crowds.[15]

The 1896 Bryan lynching was not a gruesome public spectacle, and no torture or prolonged death ritual was mentioned in news accounts. Thus in some sense it was more typical. But there are curious aspects of it that raise questions, especially about the role that women played in the unfolding of the violence. With few exceptions, most lynching studies focus on white men, probing why they engaged in and supported such extralegal and brutal racial violence. But when one looks closely at the Bryan lynching, the meaning of this particular story, as well as its impact on the community, becomes clearer when the women—especially the Italian woman, Fannie Palazzo—are brought into focus as well.

While they were not reported to be among the Bryan lynch mob, white women nonetheless filled major roles in this lynching episode. They included Palazzo, who accused Reddick of raping her; the twelve-year-old daughter of Dr. Wilson, who claimed to have been attacked by her father's employees, and her mother, Mrs. Wilson, who was the first to call publicly for the death of Whitehead and Johnson. Black women also figure in the story as well, as alibi witnesses for Reddick, whose testimony the Bryan jury ignored but the appeals court considered. And last but not least were the three Parker sisters, who were numbered among the community's most elite white women, in whose name—and those like them—lynchings across the South were conducted. Questions abound about these women. Why did Reddick sit in jail unmolested for so long? Why did a mob form so quickly on behalf of Wilson's daughter, but not for Palazzo? What role might the Parker reception have played in the events going on twelve blocks away? And what did the lynching of three black men mean to the white women of Bryan, and specifically to Fannie Palazzo, an Italian woman who did not yet speak English?

A review of some important developments in southern women's history and lynching can provide a framework for understanding what happened in Bryan in 1896. New studies have raised the question of agency on the part of white women, of their complicity in creating and sustaining an environment in which lynching became an acceptable form of social control and a means through which to assert white identity and privilege. By the late nineteenth century the overwhelming majority of lynch victims in the South were African Americans. The justification often given for these lynchings was the notion that black men were turning into black beast rapists, imperiling the virtue and purity of white women. Less than 30 percent of these lynchings throughout the South had anything to do with assaults on white women, but the rape-lynching rationale was so widely circulated that most Americans, whether in the North or South, believed it. Ida B. Wells, a turn-of-the-twentieth-century black journalist and activist, has been widely acknowledged as the first to publicly call attention to the fact that lynching was about far more than avenging the rape of white women and instead often involved economic and political oppression.[16]

Wells recognized that while the lynching rationale manipulated white women and increased their subordination and sense of dependency on white men for protection, white women themselves were also guilty of complicity in sustaining the lynching myth. Wells suggested that many so-called assaults were in fact consensual relationships covered up by cries of rape. In a much-quoted newspaper editorial in 1892, Wells wrote: "Nobody in this section of the country believes the old thread-bare lie that Negro men rape white women. If Southern white men are not careful, they will over-reach themselves and public sentiment will have a reaction; a conclusion will then be reached which will be very damaging to the moral reputation of their women."[17]

But Wells's gendered analysis of racial violence stayed dormant for nearly a century. It largely remained to historians in the late 1980s and 1990s, when gender became a compelling category of historical analysis, to explore more fully the complex interplay between race and gender in the turbulent decades in the South following the Civil War. It was this unstable time that caught the attention of historian Martha Hodes, who analyzed gender and race as they pertained to violence, particularly the violence of lynching. Hodes argued that before the Civil War, white southerners strongly disapproved of sexual relations between black men and white women, but that they did not usually react violently against such liaisons by lynching black men until after slavery—and a secure racial hierarchy—had ended. Hodes probed the political implications of lynching, and like Ida B. Wells, she also recognized that lynching involved not only the subordination of white women, but their active complicity as well. Discussing the agency of white women, Hodes pointed to cases where white women—most of them from nonelite social classes—attempted to cover up the racial transgression of an interracial affair by pretending to be the victim of a rape. In many cases, outraged family members coerced them into making rape charges.[18]

Crystal Nicole Feimster provided still another analysis showing white women as active agents in creating racial oppression. She closely examined the degree to which southern women participated in lynching in the late nineteenth and early twentieth centuries, and discovered the presence of women at every stage of lynching rituals, from start to finish. "By alleging rape, identifying alleged assailants, inciting the crowd with calls for lynching, cheering, providing fuel for the execution pyre, lighting the pyre, shooting at the lynched victim, scavenging for souvenirs, praising men for the violent actions, and engaging in a variety of other actions, women participated in multiple ways and for many reasons."[19]

Feimster's main argument focused on the public power that white women sought through the lynching of black men. She argued that through their actions white women asserted power over African Americans, especially African American men. Through their publicized rhetoric at rallies and in newspaper articles, they also laid claim to power in the public sphere, particularly in relation to white men. They called for women to take up arms themselves for their own protection, clearly implying that men were doing a less than adequate job of protecting their women. One could argue, however, that for both white men and women, lynching was not only about power, but also—perhaps even primarily—about identity. The two concepts, power and identity, are inextricably linked. Historians from Winthrop Jordan onward have rooted American racial thinking and white supremacist behavior in the quest for white identity. In his landmark study of the origins of American racism, *White over Black: American Attitudes toward the Negro, 1550–1812* (1968), Jordan skillfully used a variety of colonial records to show how white Americans formed their own identity by contrasting themselves with the black image they created.

It was an identity that was constantly in process, and constantly needed to be remade as the American nation continued to grow and change. Historian Lisa Lindquist Dorr analyzed the ways in which the character and behavior of southern white women of the New South were scrutinized through court trials of black men who were charged with rape. Dorr noted cases in early twentieth-century Virginia where judges overturned convictions or substantially reduced sentences of black men when clemency hearings revealed that their accusers turned out to have less than virtuous reputations as white women. In one case, a defense attorney discovered that his client's accuser had opened a bawdyhouse three years after the trial. In another, the supposed rape victim had not shown herself to be sufficiently frail and victim-like in the aftermath of the alleged attack. Dorr argued that the original rape accusations in many cases revealed the strategies women used to reassert their white womanhood and to lay claim to the privileges such status might bestow. Such claims, however, did not go unchallenged. If the women's character and behavior could be shown to be beyond the pale of ideal southern white womanhood, the accused black men often were exonerated.[20]

Fannie Palazzo, the Italian woman who accused Jim Reddick, an African American, of raping her, may well have found herself in just such a situation of having her character and behavior weighed and ultimately found wanting. But before her story can be told, a few words first need to be said about the Italian community in which she lived. Italians first began appearing on the county census rolls in 1870, along with a host of other Europeans who were making their way to Texas to begin new lives. As a new railroad town, Bryan was attracting every sort of newcomer imaginable. Adding to Bryan's bustling atmosphere was a growing variety of foreign-speaking arrivals, whose different languages contributed to the general cacophony of the town. Throughout the county, Irish and Germans dominated, but about a dozen other countries were now represented. Most of them lived in or near Bryan, where one could find Brazilian shoemakers; Italian bakers and fruit sellers; a Danish blacksmith; French, Russian, West Indian, and Polish dry goods merchants; a Spanish restaurateur; a Swiss watchmaker; Norwegian house servants; and Mexican laborers. Most of the Irish were single men who worked as laborers, principally on the railroad, though a few Irish families—especially those who had arrived before the war—prospered as farmers. Most of the Germans, who arrived in family units, were farmers.[21]

Over the next decade, still more newcomers arrived, buying up or renting farmland from older residents and opening up new businesses in Bryan. Like many other communities throughout the South in the 1870s, Brazos County had tried to attract foreign immigrants to replace laborers lost through the demise of slavery, by sending out advertisements in foreign languages that listed the attractions of the county. One scheme involved running an immigrant home in Bryan where newly arrived foreign settlers could stay until settled on farms, and various gala fundraisers were held to raise money for the house. It is difficult to say how successful the house was as a recruiting tool; elsewhere in the South similar efforts came to naught when few foreign immigrants arrived or remained long enough to meet planters' expectations. Nevertheless, a relatively large number of immigrants eventually made their way to Brazos County, though they tended to rent or buy their own land rather than work as day laborers for established planters.[22]

Czech-speaking Bohemians made their first appearance in the county during the 1870s. Numbering only about forty, they were only a trickle of those who would arrive in the next two decades, and with the exception of a cabinetmaker and a store clerk, they were all farmers. More than a score of Moravian families, another Czech-speaking group, moved into a central area of the county, taking up residence in another new railroad community between Millican and Bryan, called Wellborn. Smaller communities of Czechs appeared east of Bryan, where they lived side by side with German farmers. Other new nationalities appeared as well, though usually only in ones or twos—Swedes, Hungarians, Dutch, and Belgians. One group that increased slightly during this time was Mexican farmers, through the addition of about a dozen farm families in the Millican area. However, their numbers remained very small: Mexicans remained a tiny percentage of the foreign-born population until about 1920. Curious cross-cultural marriages showed up in the 1880 census: a Mexican farmer was married to an English-woman; a Scotsman married a Prussian woman; other Prussians married Hungarians, Austrians, and Belgian nationals. Perhaps the most unusual case was a fifty-year-old Italian-born barber living in Bryan whose parents had been born in Prussia, and who had married a twenty-year-old Bohemian woman. Significantly, with one exception—a Mexican man—none was married to an African American. Only the year before, after all, a white man named T. L. D. Brandon had been charged with "unlawful marriage" after wedding a black woman, Arabella Perkins.[23]

By the 1880s increasing numbers of Italians were moving into Brazos County. The 1890 census shows they were now beginning to dominate the official tallies of foreign-born county residents, pulling up even with the Germans, whose numbers they would surpass in the coming decades. Fannie Palazzo and her husband were part of this first large influx of Italians into the county, most of whom originally hailed from two villages in Sicily, Poggioreale and Corleone. The Palazzos were from Corleone. Like most of the Italians in Brazos County who originally hailed from Corleone, they had settled east of Bryan, not far from an area known as Dilly Shaw. Another, probably larger group, from Poggioreale, was steadily moving onto land west of Bryan, near the Brazos River in the area called Mudville, though natives of both Italian towns could be found in either area.[24]

Many of these Italians came to work as sharecroppers and day laborers on cotton farms owned by white elites, with the intention of eventually becoming landowners themselves. One of those white landowners was Milton Parker, who employed Italian farm workers to grow cotton on his holdings in the bottomlands of Brazos and Burleson Counties. Several accounts of Italians in Texas hold that a large number of Sicilians first discovered Brazos County as a likely spot in which to settle through their work for the Houston & Central Texas railroad as section hands. When the railroad company no longer needed their labor, they settled in Brazos County and began working on land near the Brazos River. Although the 1880 and 1900 census data for Brazos County list very few railroad section hands with

Italian origins, it is possible that these Sicilians had worked in other counties and had noticed the fertile land while traveling through by train. It is also very likely they would have sent word back home to Italy about the prospective farmland they had found in Texas, thus initiating a large flow from Sicily to Brazos County. When they first appeared on the county tax rolls in the mid-1880s, few if any of the new Italians owned any land and were taxed instead for the farm equipment and livestock they owned. Later many were able to scrape together enough ready cash and loans to acquire their own land. Milton Parker's son, G. S. "Sam" Parker, also had close connections with these new Italian farmers and even loaned money to some of them to help make their first land purchases.[25]

The 1890 census showed an Italian-born population in Brazos County of 216, a substantial increase from a community that numbered less than two dozen in 1880. Nearly all of them were listed as farmers or farm laborers, a significant shift from previous decades. Few if any of the Italians listed on the 1870 and 1880 manuscript census returns were listed as farmers. Most of them worked in Bryan at a variety of jobs, including fruit vendors, shoemakers, barbers, and restaurateurs. At the time, foreign-born and American newcomers alike were seeking a fresh start in an up-an-coming railroad town that was also the county seat. Land was bought and sold, new buildings erected, businesses launched, new homes built. It was an ideal time for any person with at least a little money and a willingness to risk it in a new business venture, and some of these early risk-takers were Italian. For some of these men, the risks paid off when they did quite well financially and became established members of Bryan's white society.[26]

An Italian saloon keeper-turned-gunsmith and confectioner, F. C. Zanetti, for example, arrived sometime in the mid-1870s. By the 1890s he had acquired enough Bryan real estate to have his name attached to a city block known simply as "the Zanetti block." Zanetti's investment paid off. His town lots that were valued at $500 in 1876 ballooned up to a value of $6,300 ten years later. In a town whose citizens rarely referred to streets by name until the 1920s, having one's name constantly used in reference to location—plus the prestige of owning valuable, high-traffic property on the town's main street, not far from the county courthouse—evidently conferred respectability. The comings and goings of Zanetti and his various family members, especially his wife, were frequently noted in the newspaper's social news. No doubt it helped that his wife, Mollie, had been born in Mississippi of parents born in Georgia, and thus perhaps had impeccable white Southern credentials.[27]

Bryan Fire Department with members of the city fire department showing off their equipment, probably around the turn of the century. The son of an Italian family, Louis Zanetti,
was hired to be the engine driver in 1898. Photo courtesy Carnegie Center of Brazos Valley
History

His son, Louis Zanetti, was also of interest to the newspaper. The
younger Zanetti made news for his zealous patriotism during the Spanish-
American war in 1898 when he hung a 9-foot American flag that he had
painted himself over the family property on Main Street. A few months
later—after an apparently unsuccessful attempt to help form a military
company to head for Cuba—he was elected driver of the city fire department's engine.

In 1902 F. C. Zanetti's daughter married a locally respected man with
the very Anglo name of William F. Thompson, in a ceremony performed
at the Zanetti home by a local Baptist pastor. The *Bryan Eagle* bestowed its
blessing: "Miss Zanetti is well known in Bryan, having been reared here,
and is a most excellent young lady; while the groom is a popular conductor
on the I&GN railroad. Both have a number of friends who wish them every
success in life." [28]

Clearly, the Zanetti family and several others like them had achieved insider status in Bryan society, and their ranking as white citizens was without
question. But such status was not so clear for the hundreds of other Italian-
born newcomers, who were by and large Sicilians, and who were arriving in

Brazos County after Zanetti had already established himself in Bryan. The Bryan cemetery registers, as well as the inquest reports from the turn of the century, in which various justices of the peace occasionally would determine how an individual came by his or her death, can provide glimpses of these new immigrants' ambivalent racial status. Zanetti died in 1891, and his name was listed in the cemetery register without any additional racial designation, as was the case for all whites. African Americans, on the other hand, were always listed with the additional designation after their name, "colored," and the few Mexicans listed were given the additional designation, "Mexican." But beginning in 1895—the same time as Jim Reddick's rape trial—a change took place. Italians were given an additional designation, "Italian," after their name, while whites continued to be listed without designation. Even children who had been born in Brazos County and thus were American citizens, but who had Italian-born parents, were listed as "Italian." In the inquest reports, the racial ambivalence was more pronounced. The deceased persons were described as "white," "white of German birth," "Italian," "Bohemian," or "Negro." Italians and Bohemians were never listed as, say, "white of Italian birth" or "white of Bohemian birth." Only Germans received the clear status of "white"; other immigrants, such as the Italians, evidently were somewhere in between white and black.[29]

Brief glimpses of these newcomers also can be caught in the pages of the *Eagle,* and they reveal an ambiguous attitude on the part of the newspaper's editors. The *Eagle*'s first editor, R. M. Smith, left Bryan in 1894 to serve a term in Austin as state representative, whereupon his pen was taken up by Malcolm Carnes, an active member of the city's Democratic party elite. Smith and Carnes offered little editorial comment on the growing presence of Italian farmers and laborers in Brazos County. Instead, their viewpoint—which likely reflected that of Bryan's conservative Democratic business class—must be teased out of the type of news coverage they gave the Italians in the 1890s and early 1900s. It was by no means consistent. Occasionally the paper lauded an enterprising and innovative farmer, such as Joe Saladina, whose attempts in 1898 to grow tobacco in the Brazos Bottom were featured and praised, especially when he won a prize in a Houston agricultural show. "Joe Saladina is a model for other citizens," proclaimed the newspaper, which for several years had been urging county farmers to plant something—anything—other than cotton to reduce dependency on an unpredictable market, advice that went largely unheeded.[30]

The Italians were also objects of curiosity to native-born county residents, who seemed to find their foreign language and customs mildly amusing. The *Eagle* took note once of the "jovial jabberings" of one land-owner's Italian tenants during an outdoor barbecue, and reported that a local factory was manufacturing a large number of pasta machines for its Italian clientele. "The average person is apt to think there is a lot of mystery connected with the manufacture of macaroni, spaghetti, and vermicelli," the paper observed.[31]

More frequently highlighted were various shootings, stabbings, poison-ings, and other assassination attempts among Italians in the Mudville area near the Brazos River, where most of these new immigrants were settling. In this sense the newspaper coverage of Italians reflected the sort of report-ing the *Eagle* used for African Americans, who usually made news only after either committing a crime or becoming a victim of one. Such coverage also reflected stereotypes of the era that portrayed Italians, especially Sicil-ians, as violent and crime-prone, and seemed to echo the out-of-state news about Italian crime that the *Eagle* reprinted from time to time. But even here one can see the ambivalence that Brazos County's whites seem to have felt toward these Italians, and the uncertainty of their racial status. The out-comes of court cases involving Italians were by no means as predictable as they were for African Americans, who almost always were found guilty of whatever they were charged with.

A young Italian woman named Rosa Schittino, for example, made headlines when she shot a Bryan shoemaker, Tony Todaro, twice in the back on Main Street around daybreak one Sunday in March 1901, just as Todaro was entering his shoe shop. He died on his doorstep in the presence of several witnesses. As the newspaper explained, "It is asserted that Todaro was soon to be married to another woman and that jealousy was the cause of the killing." Schittino's father, a prosperous fruit vendor, owned property on Main Street in or near the Zanetti block, where Todaro, who was also Italian, operated his shoe shop two doors down from the Schittino fam-ily. Rosa Schittino was jailed, charged with murder, and then released on a $3,000 bond. The following September a jury found her guilty only of man-slaughter and sentenced her to four years in the state penitentiary. Schittino obtained a new trial, and in the next session of the district court in March 1902 she was acquitted.[32]

The newspaper offered no explanation as to why the jury judged her to be innocent. One possible explanation, though highly speculative, is that Schittino defended herself by arguing that Todaro had jilted her and was guilty himself of "breach of promise," a crime of seduction that could send a man to jail in the late nineteenth century. Such accusations from women had particular resonance in the South, where the image of a respectable woman was pure, chaste, and vulnerable. Schittino may have been able to present herself as a vulnerable white woman whose virtue had been compromised by Todaro's perfidy. If so, her whiteness became visible only by degrees, as she was first charged with murder, then convicted of manslaughter, and finally acquitted. The recognition of her father as a successful Bryan businessman and property owner, who like F. C. Zanetti, had contributed to the growth and development of the town, may also have enhanced her status.[33]

But if the *Eagle* seemed eager to report local Italian crime, it passed over a far more significant source of activity in which the Italian community was then engaged. Missing from the coverage was any sense of the substantial contribution that Italians as a whole were on the verge of making to the county's agricultural economy. By the early 1900s these former sharecroppers were buying and clearing large sections of land along the Brazos River in the Mudville area, land that southern-born white farmers were willing to sell because of the high risks of flooding. By the time investigative agents for the U.S. Commission on Immigration showed up in Brazos County sometime between 1907 and 1910 to take a look at what was by then "the largest Italian agricultural community in the United States," Mudville's newest farmers were doing very well indeed. More than half of them owned their land, and were reported to "make a better cotton crop than many of the Americans or Bohemians." Moreover, their success had more than doubled the price of land, to the point where other Italians were forced to migrate northward toward Hearne in Robertson County and westward into Burleson County to find cheaper land. Cotton and the fertile Brazos bottomlands eventually would make some of these farmers quite wealthy, including an immigrant named Brazos Antonio Varisco, whose holdings one day would include an airfield in Mudville, substantial high-rise property in downtown Bryan, and the most respected hardware store in town.[34]

But in the mid-1890s, at the time of Palazzo's rape incident, few southern-born whites in Brazos County appeared to recognize the rising economic power of the Italian community. Although they were valued as agricultural laborers, their status as white citizens of Brazos County was ambiguous. Elsewhere at that time, Italians were not considered fully white, and Brazos County residents, many of whom traveled out of state frequently and subscribed to Houston, Galveston, and San Antonio newspapers, would have been aware of the uncertain racial image that Italian immigrants carried in other areas of the nation, especially in the South. A veiled reference to the racial differences of Italians can be seen in a letter to the editor of the

Washington Post that an unhappy white resident of Brazos County wrote in 1899 to protest published reports that a recent and severe flooding of the Brazos River "was divine punishment for recent Negro lynchings." The letter writer, Dr. J. N. Johnson, argued that far from abusing their workers by lynching them, white residents of Brazos County instead enjoyed close personal relationships with African Americans, especially those living and working on the rich cotton-producing bottomlands near the Brazos River. "No people in the South get along better than the people in the bottoms. The white people and colored have learned to depend upon each other so that the latter will never quit the river bottoms and rented lands till death takes them out, nor will the white landlords supplant them with other races," Johnson wrote.[35]

Besides revealing a breathtaking misperception of the poverty, lack of opportunity, and constant threat of violence suffered by the overwhelming majority of African Americans in Brazos County at the time, Johnson also gave an interesting view of the alternate labor supply that was becoming available to white landowners. The "other races" to which Johnson referred could only have been the growing numbers of Italian laborers and tenant farmers, and to a lesser extent, Czech-speaking workers, who were then moving onto lands near the river. Johnson did not call these newcomers "strangers" or "foreigners" or even "immigrants." He called them "other races," indicating a curious inability to pinpoint just what sort of laborers these new people actually were. And his blithe assurance that these "other races" would never usurp the place of the seemingly loyal and faithful black workers also indicates an uneasy sense of the indefinably alien quality that white landowners such as Johnson saw in the new Italian and Czech-speaking immigrants.

White Democrats living in Brazos County's western neighbor, Burleson County, finally resolved the issue by declaring that Italians definitely were not white. In April 1904 Democrats restricted their primary to white men, ruling that the word *white* should be interpreted to "exclude Mexicans and Italians as well as negroes." White Democrats of Burleson County may have felt that they had settled the issue, but elsewhere Italians remained something of a racial puzzle to many white southerners, as historian Matthew Frye Jacobson discovered. In his study of European immigrants and white identity, Jacobson noted that Italians lived in a racial middle ground in certain places in the Jim Crow South: "Politically Italians were indeed white enough for naturalization and for the ballot, but socially they represented a problem population at best."[36]

Louisiana had attracted more of this "problem population" than any other southern state. Most of the state's Italians remained in New Orleans where they had disembarked from steamships arriving directly from Italian ports, but many others fanned out across sugar parishes and cotton-growing regions, where they encountered a variety of reactions. While state officials and wealthy planters encouraged the arrival of Italians as an able substitute for black labor, whites in local communities frequently showed resentment and hostility to these foreign newcomers by equating them with African Americans because of their landless status and stereotype as murderous and violence-prone. Deadly racial discrimination against Italians broke out in the form of three lynching incidents in Louisiana in 1891, 1896, and 1899, the most famous of which was the 1891 lynching by a white mob of eleven Italians who were accused of shooting the New Orleans police chief. [37]

Elsewhere in the South, Italians—who were at this point nearly all Sicilians—also encountered severe prejudice and violence. Historian Clive Webb found that twenty-nine Sicilians died at the hands of lynch mobs between 1886 and 1910 across the South. Most of these lynch victims had been accused of or implicated in the murder of a white person, or they had posed a threat to local white businesses through economic success. Webb noted that Sicilians were viewed as "alien outsiders" who seriously complicated the color line because of their ambiguous racial status, to the point where they were widely regarded as "white Negroes." [38]

Part of the Italians' image problem stemmed from their initial willingness to live and work alongside or near blacks. Italians quickly learned the social handicaps of such associations, however, and soon placed wider distances between themselves and blacks as they were able to leave day labor and tenant farming and buy land or open businesses. Historian Jean Scarpaci studied Sicilian accommodation to white southern racial mores in Louisiana during this time period. She noted, "A change in Sicilian patterns of behavior developed both out of the native Whites' initial hostility towards the immigrant and out of the immigrant's desire to improve his economic situation. . . . When they faced social discrimination, they realized that they had to identify with the group in power, the Whites." [39]

This was exactly the lesson Fannie Palazzo learned in Brazos County. Many of the Brazos County Sicilians had worked on sugar and cotton plantations in Louisiana before moving to Texas, and thus would have been acquainted with southern racial culture to some degree before arriving in Brazos County. Palazzo and her husband and a son entered the United States through the port at New Orleans in 1885, and soon after they journeyed on to Texas. It is not clear how long Palazzo and her family were in Louisiana, or what they experienced there before coming to Texas. Palazzo's husband, Charles, and brother-in-law, Joe, first appeared on the county tax rolls in 1887. At that point, Charles Palazzo owned 100 acres just west of Bryan, and Joe Palazzo, Charles's brother, owned only a wagon and horse. Joe Palazzo was the older of the two brothers. He had arrived in the United States earlier in 1880, and would prove to be the more prosperous. By 1890 Joe Palazzo had moved into the ranks of landowners through the acquisition of 100 acres near the parcel owned by Charles Palazzo. In the following years, Joe continued to buy up land, and by 1904 he was paying taxes on seven parcels of land that added up to 642 acres. Charles Palazzo, meanwhile, never expanded his 100-acre farm, probably because mental disorders kept him away from home in a state asylum. According to family history, Charles was thrown by a tornado against a tree or building, probably within a few years after arriving in Brazos County. The injuries apparently affected his mind, and he was subsequently sent to the state "Lunatic Asylum," as it was then known, in Austin.[40]

Fannie Palazzo was thus left to farm alone, with several children to care for. By 1894 they included a fourteen-year-old son, also named Charles, who had been born in Italy, and two other sons, about five and seven years old, who had been born in Texas, probably in Brazos County. Most of her neighbors were Italian, but census reports show that several black families, probably sharecroppers, farmed nearby. And judging from information later revealed in court, Fannie Palazzo apparently had not yet learned to give these African Americans a wide enough berth. Her fellow Italians, however, were indeed distancing themselves from the African Americans to the point where hostilities between the two groups were becoming noticeable. As the *Eagle* reported, "Trouble between the negroes and the Italians is becoming [sic] often and the bitterness engendered has already reached a point of almost continuous hostility which bodes no good for the future." Fannie Palazzo may not have felt quite as much hostility, but she quickly learned how to distance herself from at least one African American, and how to identify herself as white.[41]

The attack occurred around 3:00 A.M. on Sunday, December 4. As Palazzo later testified in court—with the help of an Italian shoemaker in Bryan who translated for her—she had been awakened by a pounding at her door. She said she noticed the time because she had glanced at a clock when she lit a lamp. Her eldest son went to answer the door, and when her son lifted the latch to see who was there, a man shoved his way into the home, brandishing a pistol and demanding money. When he learned they had no money, the man began to attack Fannie Palazzo on her bed, but was in turn attacked by Palazzo's son Charles. The man then grabbed her and dragged her outside, where he raped her on the ground. He finally left, she later testified, after about two hours. At daylight, Palazzo went to the home of her brother-in-law, Joe Palazzo, who sent for the sheriff.[42]

As it turned out, the man charged as her assailant, Jim Reddick, farmed a piece of land next to hers, and thus was a neighbor. He had been over to her home before the attack to borrow an ax, and so she obviously knew him. Other Brazos County residents may have wondered just how well she knew him. Her husband had been gone for some time, possibly six years, at the state mental hospital in Austin. Did other white residents suspect any intimacy between Palazzo and Reddick, which she felt necessary to hide by charging rape? Did they view her as one of the nonelite or poorer white women that historian Martha Hodes examined, who attempted to cover up an interracial affair by pretending to be the victim of a rape? Or was it possible that family members, such as her brother-in-law Joe Palazzo, coerced her and her son, who said he witnessed the attack, into making the accusation in order to salvage the family honor? Given the utter lack of any form of mob justice, and the later verdict of the appeals court, local whites may well have speculated in such directions—simply because she was Italian and of ambiguous racial status, and because Reddick lived nearby and had already visited her home at least once.

Palazzo's subsequent actions indicate that she seemed to feel the need to establish some degree of respectability and to enhance her credibility, which she may have realized was compromised by her Sicilian origins. One way to do that was to claim the character of a frail white southern woman in need of protection, as historian Lisa Lindquist Dorr has shown was so necessary in cases of rape. Despite Reddick's status as a known neighbor, the Brazos County sheriff, Tom C. Nunn, arranged to have a lineup of eight men and brought both Palazzo and her son in to town to identify her attacker. Census data suggest that two of the men in the lineup also may have been neighbors, part of another African American family named Eaverhart who rented a farm a few homes away from Fannie Palazzo. Nunn had arrested both of the Eaverhart men along with Reddick, and we can only speculate that Nunn suspected one of these Eaverhart neighbors was actually the attacker. But Palazzo herself pointed to Reddick instead. As Nunn later described the scene, "She at once pointed out the defendant as the man who committed the rape on her. As soon as she saw him she bit her thumb and seemed to faint and would have fallen had someone close by not caught her."[43]

The fainting spell was classic, well-recognized behavior at the time for truly vulnerable white women of the nineteenth century. Unlike the more robust African American women or even lower-class white women, a "true woman" was supposed to be physically weak, among other attributes, and fainting was considered a particularly appropriate way to demonstrate such weakness. There is no evidence that Palazzo's near faint was intentional or contrived to demonstrate her status as a "true" white woman, and we can only speculate about her emotions at the time of the lineup. Nonetheless, it is worth asking why she behaved as if she were about to faint in the sheriff's presence, especially in light of other research that has shown that such behavior clearly helped to win rape convictions. And in this case her close faint was subsequently introduced as key evidence during Reddick's trial, which helped the jury to convict him and sentence him to hang. But the larger Bryan community did not seem as convinced—either of Reddick's guilt or of Palazzo's status as a vulnerable white woman whose rape threatened the white supremacist social order. Indeed, the *Eagle* used a curious phrase in reference to the rape: "This is the woman's version of the affair as told to Sheriff Nunn." To introduce the word *version* was to suggest that there was more than one account of what had happened, a suggestion that was never implied in later news accounts of the attack on Wilson's daughter, or in other local stories of rape and assault.[44]

Reddick, after all, had been able to provide no fewer than nine alibi witnesses who testified he had been at a party with them some miles away all that night. They testified to the grand jury that he had danced with them and lingered at the party until early the next morning, and thus could not have been anywhere near the home of Fannie Palazzo in time for the 3:00 A.M. assault. According to these witnesses, Reddick had escorted some of them home from the party with a rented buggy and horse, remained at the stable in Bryan after returning the rentals, and was spotted on Main Street at dawn making a vain effort to buy a bottle of whiskey at a closed saloon. The problem for Reddick, however, was that most, if not all, of these witnesses were black, and the key witnesses, who testified he had been dancing and riding with them, were women. Texana Asberry remembered holding his coat while he was dancing; Jennie Harrison said he had left her home around 3:00 A.M. after dropping her and her husband off after the dance; Jane McMillan recalled she had last seen him at 4:00 A.M. But what all-white jury would believe the testimony of these black women, when their

word was held up against such contrasting evidence as the dramatic fainting episode of the victim herself? Faced with such a compelling choice, the
grand jury indicted Reddick on charges of murder, and the District Court
jury convicted him.[45]

Nonetheless, Reddick was allowed to sit in the jail unmolested while
his case wound its way through the Texas appeals system. No lynch mob
appeared, and the *Eagle* ignored him, except to list his name occasionally
with other inmates of the city jail. Finally, his case was heard on appeal,
and the Court of Criminal Appeals clearly was unconvinced by the evidence against him. The court cited the use of the fainting spell as evidence,
among other problems, as an "error in this matter of a very material character." The court also noted the large number of witnesses who could put
Reddick far from the Palazzo home at the time of the assault. Without giving details, the court raised the possibility that Palazzo's testimony "was
recently fabricated" and had been given "under the influence of improper
motives." The court reversed the original judgment and remanded the case
back to Bryan.[46]

All the while Reddick remained in the Bryan jail. Then on June 9, 1896,
George Johnson and Louis Whitehead were arrested for allegedly attempting to rape the twelve-year-old daughter of Dr. R. H. Wilson, who lived
near Kurten. Johnson, nineteen, and Whitehead, an ex-convict in his early
thirties, worked for Wilson and lived on his land. Wilson owned a 100-acre
farm and raised cattle, evidently supplementing his income as a physician.
Sometime during the night of June 7, Wilson's daughter woke and ran into
her parents' bedroom, screaming that "some scoundrel" had tried to attack
her through an open window near where she lay sleeping. Newspaper accounts had it that the assailant had stolen what he thought was chloroform
from the doctor's office and poured it on her, and had then tried unsuccessfully to seize her and pull her through the window.[47]

Waiting until morning, Wilson accosted his two black workers, who
had shown up for work as usual, apparently thinking nothing was amiss.
Suspecting they were the culprits, Wilson had them whipped until they
confessed. At that point Wilson's thirst for personal vengeance seems to
have been satiated, and he sent a message to a law official for papers to arrest
the workers. But his wife intervened, insisting that the two be shot on the
spot. As the sheriff reported later in an open letter to the community that
was printed in the newspaper, "his wife begged him to avenge the wrong
that had been done their daughter, and this he refused, and failed to avenge
this great wrong, and either turned the negroes loose or let them get away

and come to town." A day later, the pair was arrested in a saloon in Bryan, and a day after that, they and Reddick were lynched by a "mob of 300 unknown parties."[48]

As we have already seen, the story did not end there, as it would have in many other southern towns where lynchings occurred. Despite his apparent contempt for the way Wilson had bungled his job as family protector, Sheriff Nunn was outraged by the lynching and by rumors that he had purposely left town so as to allow the lynching to take place. About a week after the killings he arrested four leaders of the mob. In a letter to the governor, Nunn strongly hinted at hostile political motivations behind the lynching. The four men he arrested included W. N. Smith, who had helped to track down Whitehead and Johnson in the Bryan saloon, and a man named Tom Wilson. W. N. Smith was the brother-in-law of the sheriff's chief political rival. But what about Tom Wilson? Could he have been related to Dr. Wilson? Census reports do not make clear any family relationship between the two, but one could speculate that as a possible member of the family, he may have attempted to make up for Dr. Wilson's patriarchal failure to carry out the summary justice for which Mrs. Wilson had pleaded. He lived in the eastern part of the county, and thus may also have been among those Kurten residents who bitterly resented Nunn's continuing political success and who saw the attack on Wilson's daughter as a way to cause trouble for the sheriff.

What is curious about this story is that even though it involved accusations of rape, clearly none of the white men who took leading roles was predominantly concerned about the defense of white womanhood or the threat to white supremacy that the rape and threatened rape posed. Sheriff Nunn worried more about the threat to law and order that the mob presented and about the political problems the lynching signified. Dr. Wilson ignored his wife and allowed his black employees to escape with only a whipping. The mob leaders, Smith and Wilson, had other motives for storming the jail than avenging the insult to Dr. Wilson's daughter. And Milton Parker—the city's leading citizen, who had the most to lose should the social hierarchy be overturned by unruly residents of a rural part of the county—was all for leaving the mob leaders that Nunn had arrested in jail, at least temporarily. Parker, it may be recalled, served as the chairman of the ad hoc committee that hurriedly met to decide whether to abide by the sheriff's decision to make arrests and then voted in favor of the sheriff.

And what of the women? If the lynching revealed political and economic fissures among the men who participated in the events surrounding the killing, the episode also held deep meaning for the women of the story, though on a different level—the nebulous and shifting terrain of racial identity. Fannie Palazzo provided the opening act with her accusation of Reddick. Several black women appeared on the scene to provide an alibi for Reddick, which though ignored at first, might eventually have saved him if two other black men had not ended up in jail with him. Dr. Wilson's daughter appeared in the second act, a more dramatic scene because her accusation involved not one, but two black men. As a twelve-year-old whose whiteness was unquestioned, she clearly presented a more vulnerable and credible victim than did Palazzo. Then there was Mrs. Wilson, whose cries for summary execution eventually galvanized a lynch mob.

And silent—but nonetheless present—through the entire show were Milton Parker's three daughters, who represented just the sort of white virginal purity that lynching throughout the South was supposed to uphold. There is no evidence to suggest that the Parker sisters or their family had anything to do with the lynching. But it must be remembered that their lavish party occurred at exactly the same time. It is possible that some of their male guests were dancing with the Parker sisters or their friends when the sounds of the angry mob storming the jail mingled with the music flowing out from the open doors and windows of the Parker home. Their minds would have been filled with idealized images of white southern womanhood, and some of these guests may have slipped away from the festivities to join an established ritual of southern white racial hierarchy occurring only a few blocks away. At least on a symbolic level, the Parkers' party provided a vivid backdrop to the violent celebration of white dominance over black life, of white power to punish and kill.

If the Parkers' party provided the backdrop, the women who were on center stage of the drama were in a very different racial and social position relative to the Parkers. It is worth taking a closer look at how they compared, socially speaking, with the Parker sisters. The Misses Parker were wealthy and privileged, and the white womanhood they represented was well established and unassailable, as their father's willingness to jail the lynchers demonstrated. Clearly their identity as pure white women was rock solid. Not so for Fannie Palazzo, an Italian immigrant who spoke English so poorly that she needed an interpreter during Reddick's trial. As a Sicilian, and with a husband in the lunatic asylum, Palazzo had two strikes against her, racial and social. Thus she had only a tentative claim to the rights and privileges of southern white womanhood, to the credibility of a southern lady, or to the protection offered by southern white patriarchy. Regardless of whether

her accusation was just—that is, if Reddick actually had raped her—she may well have realized her own testimony was not sufficient to convict him. Whatever she intended by it, the near faint and dramatic fall into someone's arms could only have helped her case. As proof positive of violated white womanhood, it worked for the jury—but only for a while. The Bryan community and the Texas Court of Appeals concluded otherwise, and for the time being, Reddick's life was spared. He might have been sent instead to a convict labor camp, or might even have walked out of jail as a free man, had it not been for Dr. Wilson's daughter.

Wilson's daughter and wife represent a sort of social middle ground between the elite Parker sisters at one end of the social scale and Fannie Palazzo at the other. The Wilsons were white, well known, and highly respectable. But they were also rural, and without the wealth and power of a family such as the Parkers. Why was Mrs. Wilson so intent on having her husband's two black employees shot on the spot, when her daughter clearly had not been harmed and might have imagined the entire episode? By calling for the summary execution of Johnson and Whitehead, was she trying to claim the sort of protection—and thus the identity of vulnerable white womanhood—for herself and her daughter that the Parker girls automatically received by virtue of their social status? Was this, in effect, an attempt on the part of Mrs. Wilson or her daughter, possibly like that of Fannie Palazzo, to raise the family's social status?

Curious also are the changes that took place in the status of the black women who testified that they were with Reddick at the time of Palazzo's alleged rape, changes that seemed to be directly related to the changes in Palazzo's status as an endangered white southern woman. In the minds of the Bryan jury, women such as Texana Asberry, Jennie Harrison, and Jane McMillan were not legitimate witnesses in light of the convincing story of Palazzo's near faint. For that brief moment, Palazzo had achieved legitimacy as a frail white woman, and the testimony of the black women was virtually erased from consideration. Later, however, when the Texas Court of Appeals raised the possibility that Palazzo might have concocted the rape story and might thus have been a less than virtuous woman, the alibi these women provided suddenly became visible. In the eyes of the appeals justices, their testimony "tended very cogently to show that the defendant was not present at the time the rape was charged to have been committed." So compelling was this alibi that the court concluded "that there was error in this matter of a very material character." The rising credibility of these black women underscored the degree to which Fannie Palazzo's identity as a pure southern white woman was quickly disappearing. Class mattered, and so did race, and the perception of virtue meant everything. The protection and maintenance of southern white womanhood was not as much of an overwhelming concern for white men as it was for the white women of the story, and most particularly for Fannie Palazzo.[49]

But in the end, one might argue that they were all of them vindicated. The man whom Palazzo pointed out in a lineup was lynched after all, even if it was a year and a half after the attack. And Mrs. Wilson finally got the justice she sought for her daughter. The morning after the hanging, hundreds of residents traveled up and down the Boonville road to view the bodies dangling from the oak tree at Carter's Creek. Someone eventually cut down the dead men, hauled them back to town and back to the courthouse, and laid them out on a patch of lawn near the jail. Anyone who had missed the hanging or the sight of three black corpses looming over Boonville Road that morning could still view what southern justice had achieved. A more explicit lesson about white power and privilege could not have been given to the county's African Americans, as well as to its European immigrants. As the *Eagle* noted with dramatic relish, it was a scene "which gave a fearful lesson of the swift and terrible retribution which overtakes the fiend in human form who places himself outside the pale of human sympathy and must take the consequences of his own acts when the indignant and outraged people cry out for vengeance." And in that brutal moment, as the bodies of the three men lay side by side, their anonymous and contorted faces turned upward to the passing crowds, the status of Fannie Palazzo and Mrs. Wilson and her daughter, together with the Parker sisters, surely became fused in the minds of onlookers. The purity of Brazos County's white women—all of them—had been redeemed.[50]

The story of the 1896 Bryan lynching was thus a complicated affair indeed. It began with an immigrant Italian woman whose accusations of rape landed one of her neighbors in jail but whose credibility was too low—and racial ambiguity too high—to hang him. The story ended a year and a half later with the arrest and release of four white mob leaders whose motives for killing had nothing to do with defending feminine virtue. Instead, they were far more interested in trying to discredit a sheriff whose continued victory in the polls had eroded the social standing and political power of their community and its leaders. Both groups of instigators—Italian immigrants and Populist farmers—had much to gain through the lynching, though the Italians were by far the greater beneficiaries in the long run by the enhanced whiteness that the lynching conferred on them. And literally caught in the racial and political maelstrom were three African American men, who may or may not have committed the offenses of which they were accused. Guilty or not, they became convenient vessels into which a deadly mix of jealousy, alienation, fear, ambition, and rage—concocted by widely dissimilar groups of Brazos County residents—was poured.

The Italians were not the only European immigrants in Brazos County whose racial ambiguity took some time to settle, and who eventually benefited through the violence and political upheaval of that era. Like the Italians, the Irish of Brazos County had their own battles to fight to establish their social equality with native-born whites. Like other such battles, this one would be won in part through racial violence.

Chapter 4

THE IRISH

Our neighboring county, Brazos, seems to be afflicted with an unprecendent [sic] era of lawlessness.

BRENHAM DAILY BANNER, 23 January 1897

About seven months after Jim Reddick, Louis Whitehead, and George Johnson were lynched on Boonville Road, another lynching took place in Brazos County. This time the mob stayed closer to home, choosing to kill its victim in the open, in daylight, and in the presence of anyone who happened to be in town and cared to watch. The lynching took place on Main Street, in front of the First National Bank, at around supper time, and it attracted a crowd perhaps two to three times the size of the earlier lynching. It began with a similar scenario: a teenage girl in the Benchley area north of Bryan claimed a black man had raped her. He was a stranger who had entered her home in the middle of the afternoon, assaulted her, and then fled by jumping out the window.[1]

But unlike the earlier case, this time the crucial testimony that led to the lynching was not provided by the teenage victim, or by any white woman. Instead, an anonymous Irishman would take center stage. The Irish of Brazos County, like the Italians, followed an uneven if somewhat different path to assimilation. Unlike the Italians, Irish farmers had been among the county's first settlers in the 1820s, and in the following decades they had blended seamlessly in with other, American-born, newcomers in many ways. But they had not yet blended in completely. At times their differences were noticeable to the white southerners of Brazos County. Even as late as the 1890s their racial status in this part of Texas remained ambiguous to white southerners. In racial terms, the Irish were not quite as problematic as the newly arriving Italians, but some uncertainty still clung to them, especially those who were poorer. And for the Irish as well as the Italians, progress toward becoming part of southern white society was enhanced by the racial violence unfolding around them. This would be particularly true in the political sphere. Just after the turn of the twentieth century, as white Democrats were finally successful in shoving African American Republican voters away from the polls, the door would be wide open for a small Irish community to gain entrance to the county's political arena. For the Irish of Brazos County, racial violence helped to make their whiteness more visible than ever.

This next lynching story began in late January 1897. The seventeen- or eighteen-year-old rape victim, identified in the *San Antonio News* as Miss DeHart, was living at the time in Benchley with her sister and her sister's husband, a tenant farmer named Brooks Wright. Miss DeHart had been home alone that Thursday afternoon, January 21, because Wright had gone to Bryan on business, and his wife was visiting at another home to help a friend with a sick child. Immediately after the attack, Miss DeHart "gave the alarm" and word was sent to Bryan to her brother-in-law and to Sheriff Tom Nunn. The news flooded the county, and soon Nunn, the city marshal, and a posse of outraged county residents swarmed to Benchley looking for clues. Thanks to newly installed telephone lines that were beginning to lace across the county, Nunn was able to call a convict farm in the Mudville area before he left Bryan to request that a pack of dogs be sent over to Benchley to help with the tracking.

But the dogs were long in coming, so Sheriff Nunn, using his own tracking skills, picked up the traces of the attacker as far as the railroad tracks about 400 yards away. But he could trace him no farther, despite the assistance of an assortment of citizens who had joined in to help. It was now nightfall, and Nunn went back to Bryan to send word to other counties, also by telephone. He made sure area newspapers were informed, and offered a $50 reward for information leading to the arrest and conviction of the mysterious black man.

Nunn, however, probably already knew where to start looking. The next day, apparently unaided, he located a "Bryan negro of bad repute, about 21 years old, 5 feet 7 or 8 inches high" who seemed to answer to the description the girl had given him. The unlucky African American, Eugene Washington, was duly arrested and lodged in the Bryan jail. The newspapers did not mention where Washington lived, but likely his home, or his family's home, was in a small neighborhood bordering the city cemetery called "Freedman town." Like many southern towns and cities of the era, Bryan had a designated residential area for its black populatiion, and as its name signified, Freedman town was home to the area's freed slaves and their descendants. The neighborhood was on the east side of the railroad tracks, and it bordered the north side of white neighborhoods that were then spreading eastward. Wealthy or middle-class white Bryanites, many of them merchants and craftsmen, were busy building new homes here, and it was no coincidence that their neighborhoods bordered Freedman town. In the compact, crowded community of Freedman town dwelled a small army of washerwomen, cooks, nannies, and laborers of every sort, who provided needed services within easy walking distance of the homes of Bryan's whites.[2]

Another African American neighborhood was spreading westward, on the opposite side of the railroad tracks, just to the north of where the wealthy planters Milton Parker, James Chance, and others had built their homes. Like Freedman town, this area was also home to many washerwomen, cooks, and day laborers who worked for white homeowners just to the south. But the two neighborhoods—Freedman town and the west side community, which apparently had no particular name—also were home to somewhat more prosperous African Americans, the teachers, ministers, physicians, craftsmen, and business owners who also made up much of the political leadership of the local Republican party. Wealthier black homeowners lived side by side with less fortunate renters in a hodgepodge of dwellings and crowded alleys.

In between the two black neighborhoods lay a black business district of sorts near the north end of Main Street, known derogatorily to whites as Rat Row. Here were saloons, barbershops, and other businesses that were black-owned or catered to blacks. In later decades African Americans spread farther into west Bryan, and on the east, into a neighborhood known as Candy Hill, but by and large they did not spread south until much later in the twentieth century. To the south of Freedman town and the west side black neighborhood stretched the white neighborhoods, and they remained white for a very long time. Bryan's African Americans, who made up perhaps one-third to one-half of the city's population, thus were largely confined to the north end. So when Sheriff Nunn wanted to find a particular African American man in town who apparently already had a reputation for misbehavior, he would have been able to limit his search to one general area—the north end of Bryan.

After locating his quarry—possibly in Freedman town—Nunn's next move was a staple feature of most lynching dramas in the South at this time. The sheriff brought Washington out to Benchley that same day so that Miss DeHart could identify him—a scene that Fannie Palazzo had performed with great drama when she bit her thumb and fainted. In most cases the accused attacker was brought to the victim for identification, but in Palazzo's case Nunn had made her come to the jail instead to view a lineup of suspects, perhaps because he doubted her credibility or because she did not seem as vulnerable a victim. As young, single, and Anglo, however, Miss DeHart obviously fit the part of a frail white woman, and so Washington was brought to her.

But here is where the problems started. Face to face with her alleged attacker, Miss DeHart could not be sure Washington was the right man. Admitting her confusion to Nunn, "she told him the negro looked like her assailant and she believed he was the right man, but her identification was not positive," the *Bryan Eagle* reported. Despite his protests that he could provide an alibi, back went Washington to the city jail "to await further developments."

Further developments were not long in coming. That same afternoon—now Friday—word reached Nunn that an Irishman had been walking northward along the Houston & Central Texas railroad tracks near Benchley the day before in the company of a black man who matched the description of Miss DeHart's attacker. The Irishman was now in Hearne, a town about 20 miles north of Bryan. Having heard reports of the rape, he had notified authorities in Benchley of what he had seen. According to the Irishman, when they passed near the Wright home, the African American had told the Irishman he was going to a house nearby "to get some water or something to eat." The African American had then left in the direction of the Wright home. The time of the conversation corresponded with the time of the attack. The Irishman left his name with the Benchley authorities in case anyone wanted to speak to him further. The next day, Saturday, Nunn took a train to Hearne to locate the surprise witness and bring him back to Bryan. Meanwhile, reports of the rape began appearing in Galveston and San Antonio newspapers, and interest in the case in Bryan seemed to be increasing by the hour. When Nunn and his witness stepped off the 3:40 P.M. train from Hearne, a large crowd had gathered at the depot to greet them. Surrounding them like an enormous cloud of bees, the crowd followed the two back to the jail to await the Irishman's verdict.

Unlike Miss DeHart, the Irishman had no trouble identifying his walking companion. Nunn rounded up about a dozen black men for a lineup, and the Irishman picked out Washington "at a glance." To add a touch of credibility, the Irishman told Nunn that Washington had a torn pocket on the inside of his jacket. Deputies checked the coat, and sure enough, there was the torn pocket. Meanwhile, the crowd waiting outside the jail had swelled to about 500. Despite the uncertainty of the victim's testimony, when it was announced that the Irishman had made a positive identification of Washington, the crowd—now a mob—began to demand the prisoner.

Already some curious aspects of this story have emerged. Assuming the Irishman was telling the truth, it is worth asking first of all why Washington suddenly veered off the tracks he was walking along to visit the Wright home. Given that he lived in Bryan, either near or with his mother, would he suddenly stop by an unfamiliar home to beg for food? But he might veer off to go to a home where he knew he would be welcome. In other words, had he been to the Wright home before and did he know Miss DeHart already? Of course it is possible he was genuinely hungry and thought he could get food there, and ended up startling the teenager, who then over-reacted and leveled a rape charge. However, in light of anti-lynching activist Ida B. Wells's charges that many so-called rape accusations were cover-ups for consensual relationships between white women and black men, and in view of historian Martha Hode's investigations of women who cried rape for the same reason, it is worth asking whether Washington was on intimate terms with Miss DeHart and had stopped by to see if she might be alone. There is no evidence that the two knew each other, much less that they were intimately involved. But at the same time, evidence in other, similar cases elsewhere in the South shows that a consensual relationship that ended in accusation of rape was not a rare thing.[3]

It is also entirely possible that when Washington veered off the tracks, he was actually aiming for another home in the area. Census data show black families living in the Benchley area, including some whose last name was Washington, and Eugene Washington may well have had family or friends in the area whom he knew would provide him with food and drink. Perhaps Washington passed near the Wright home—too near for the comfort of Miss DeHart, who may have misread his intentions as she saw him approach the house.

In any case, what is curious is Miss DeHart's inability—or unwillingness—to positively identify Washington as her attacker, in view of the precise description she had given Nunn only the day before, on the very day of the alleged attack. She said her attacker's face was "bumpy, sore and bleeding, hands also sore." Washington was later "said to be suffering from a loathsome disease," although it is impossible to know whether he actually had a skin disorder or whether the newspaper bestowed the description on him to make a better match. The phrase "said to be" suggests a level of hearsay and uncertainty, rather than verifiable fact. Although the attack had happened in afternoon daylight less than twenty-four hours earlier, Miss DeHart could not point her finger at Washington with certainty. But neither would she exonerate him.[4]

Most curious of all is the way the confusion was resolved. Although the Irishman had left his name with Benchley authorities—probably with the postmaster—none of the newspapers in Bryan, Brenham, Galveston, San Antonio, Austin, or Dallas that carried the story ever mentioned him by name. Apparently he was not from Brazos County and no one in the Bryan area seemed to know him. He was simply "the Irishman," without history, family, or antecedents, without any tie to the county except as a surprise witness who could give the damning testimony a lynch mob craved. And this raises several more questions. First, why would the Irishman go out of his way to offer testimony that he surely knew would result in the tortured death of a black man? And second, why would the mob willingly embrace such testimony from an alien, a nameless stranger, a foreign immigrant un-tethered to any social connections in the county?

To answer the second question first, by the time the Irishman was brought to Bryan to identify Washington, more than forty-eight hours had passed since the alleged rape. There had been no other drama or high excitement to relieve the growing tension of an unresolved case. Nunn had simply arrested Washington and brought him to jail in what must have been fairly mundane circumstances, as there were no reports of desperate escape attempts or spectacular chases—usually another staple feature of southern lynching narratives and one that surely would have been reported if it had happened in Brazos County. So there had been plenty of time for restless and hostile white citizens of Brazos County—who had been given little involvement in the drama to this point—to get even more restless and hostile.

It was now late afternoon on a Saturday. While on a weekday many of them would have been out working on their farms, on this day crowds of farmers, ranchmen, sharecroppers, and laborers, white as well as black, were in town. Main Street and adjacent alleys would have been jammed with wagons and carts, horses and mule teams, and lined with groups of lounging men. They were there to do business with Bryan's merchants and craftsmen, indulge in some horse trading and bartering with each other, visit the town's many saloons, and catch up on local news. And here was news in the making. For whites, it was a chance to make news themselves. Here also was ready-made entertainment, violence at its best, and it offered far more drama than, say, the cockfights occasionally sponsored by a popular drinking establishment on Main Street, the Taylor & Cox Saloon.[5]

Unlike the case six months earlier, this time news accounts carried no suggestion or hint that this lynching had local political undertones, but many Brazos County farmers were still suffering economic distress, perhaps even more so than the previous summer. The harvest that fall had been meager again compared to previous years, cotton prices were still falling, and the Bryan cotton compress, which had burned in June, had not yet been rebuilt. Even without a looming political campaign to add fuel to simmering tensions, white farmers of Brazos County would still have been a largely unhappy lot, fearful of the future and uncertain how they were going to pay off current debt. Washington, represented as a black fiend who had robbed a pure white woman of her most prized possession, her virtue, likely was seen as leveling a serious blow at white honor—and honor was something these farmers no doubt felt was in increasingly short supply. Washington, in short, made a most excellent scapegoat.

Likely the crowd would have tried to lynch Washington had the Irishman never appeared. Jim Reddick, after all, had been lynched despite the questionable credibility of Fannie Palazzo, and Louis Whitehead and George Johnson had also been killed despite the lack of injury or positive identification on the part of Dr. R. H. Wilson's daughter. Nonetheless, the testimony of the Irishman was like a lit match thrown on the highly combustible and growing rage of the crowd, who eagerly embraced his word as if it had been a divinely given judgment. Doubtless it was the mob's raving hunger for any justification to lynch Washington, rather than the testimony of the Irishman himself, that caused the crowd to believe Washington was Miss DeHart's attacker.

The Irishman's credibility surely was not enhanced by his nationality, which likely would have weakened his testimony under other circumstances. In Brazos County, as elsewhere in the nineteenth-century South, Irish residents varied greatly in occupation, economic standing, and social class. Some had been slaveholders of considerable wealth; others were lowly ditch diggers and railroad laborers. Assimilation in the South had been an uneven process, as most of the region's Irish immigrants had settled in cities where they retained their culture by living in ethnic communities. They had been prominent in antebellum port cities such as New Orleans, where they tended to work at menial, unskilled jobs, leading to the stereotype that the Irish would do work that was too dangerous for slaves. Such low occupational status also led to racial stereotypes about their tendency toward violence, crime, and alcohol abuse. Such images reflected racial stereotypes that had been in circulation in northern cities such as New York and Boston since the 1830s, where nativists described and pictured Irish immigrants in terms not unlike those used for African Americans. The Irish, it was widely recognized, were not of Anglo-Saxon descent. Instead, they were Celtic, and thus had much lower standing in the racial hierarchy of the nineteenth century. They were described as apelike, as lazy and unreliable, and very prone to disorderly conduct.[6]

In Texas, Irish immigrants had been recruited early on by Irish impresarios to settle in the San Patricio and Refugio colonies near the Gulf, and others had been part of Stephen F. Austin's "Old Three Hundred" colonists. Irish nationals had been among Brazos County's pioneers. One of the state's early Irish communities was in northern Brazos County, in Staggers Point, a settlement of Irish immigrants who began arriving in the 1830s, about ten years after Robert Millican. Staggers Point was at the opposite end of the county from the Millican community, at the northern border with Robertson County. Now called Benchley, the community straddled the county line and was known to other residents in the area as Irish Town. Still more Irish settled in a southeastern part of the county near the Navasota River, forming a community led by Joseph Ferguson, in whose home was held the county's first court in 1841.[7]

By 1850 there were some 1,400 Irish in Texas, a number that would nearly triple in the next decade. As part of the nation's first massive wave of foreign immigration, the Irish who settled in Brazos County were distinct in several ways from their compatriots arriving by the thousands elsewhere in the nation, particularly in the northern states. Less than 10 percent of the Irish who came to America settled south of the Mason-Dixon line, and few of these settled in rural areas, either too poor to buy land or too disillusioned with farming to consider an agrarian life. Historian David T. Gleeson noted that most of the Irish in the South who did manage to acquire farms were not refugees from the Great Famine of the late 1840s, but were earlier migrants. Robert Henry, who arrived in Charleston, South Carolina, in the 1820s before moving on to Staggers Point in Brazos County in 1829, was part of this earlier wave. Henry, his brothers, and other family members eventually acquired large tracts of land in both Robertson and Brazos Counties. Unlike later arrivals of Irish Catholics, these first Irish in Brazos County were Protestants—Scots Irish who were staunch Presbyterians. The Dunns were another prominent Irish family that settled in the same area. The wealth of these early families was also enhanced by the possession of slaves, which was not uncommon among well-off Irish farmers in the South, who had quickly realized that one of the best ways to ensure one's white standing—and to refute the low racial stereotypes—was to join the ranks of slaveholders.[8]

When the H&TC railroad reached Bryan in 1867, the town began to grow immediately, attracting a wide variety of other European immigrants, including more Irish. Their numbers were never very large, peaking in 1870 at about eighty, which represented about 28 percent of Brazos County's foreign-born population at that time. The 1880 census showed that none of Brazos County's neighboring counties had attracted significant numbers of Irish either, with counts ranging from as low as five in Madison County, to ninety-nine in Robertson County and eighty-eight in Washington County.[9]

One of those Irish who arrived in Bryan in the 1870s was Thomas Dunn, who emigrated from Ireland in 1849 as a twenty-four-year-old, settling in New Orleans where he eventually acquired the wherewithal to open saloons on seven steamboats plying the Mississippi River. Unlike the Irish families who earlier had settled in Benchley, this Dunn was Catholic, and the time of his arrival in the United States suggests he may have been among the "famine Irish" of the late 1840s. His wife's health deteriorated in the early 1870s, and after a visit to relatives and friends in Bryan, Dunn decided to start over as a Texan so his wife could benefit from a drier climate. He also brought with him a partner named John Daly, a native New Yorker born to Irish immigrants, who was related to him by marriage. The subsequent Dunn & Daly Saloon on Main Street became a highly successful local watering hole. Despite the competition of at least a half-dozen other drinking establishments, the saloon was arguably "the largest retail liquor business of any one house in any of the smaller Texas cities, and has a wholesale trade that covers the entire surrounding country," boasted the *Eagle* in a special edition published in 1895 to highlight the county's most successful businesses. In the *Eagle*'s eyes, the Irish background of the saloon's proprietors seemed to add a slightly exotic flavor, as the newspaper noted with a hint of pride that they could trace "their lineage back many, many years in the land of St. Patrick and the shamrock." About six months after the notice appeared, Thomas Dunn died "from the effects of rheumatism," and was lauded again in an obituary, where again the connection with St. Patrick was noted in approving tones. His pallbearers included some of the city's most notable citizens: a former city clerk, the city tax collector, a prominent merchant, and the postmaster, J. Allen Myers.[10]

St. Patrick and shamrocks, however, did not seem to enhance the image of other Irish in Brazos County, most notably Mrs. Kelly, the wife of an "aged Irishman" who was a tenant farmer living in the Brazos Bottom, in the Millican area. E. D. Kelly worked on land owned by a lawyer and wealthy planter named Lon Holiday, and their relations were not amicable. In early May 1889 Kelly and his wife were jailed on charges of "murderous assault" on Holiday. No details were given as to what had motivated the Kellys to attack their landlord, but a clue emerged about a week later. The newspaper reported, "Complaint has been filed against Lon Holiday, a prominent farmer near Millican, charging him with raping Mrs. Kelly, the wife of one of his tenants. The rape is alleged to have been committed March 1st."[11]

Like the Millican family, members of the Holiday family also had been linked to various violent episodes in the county history, though usually not as directly as the Millican clan. It was Andrew Holiday, Lon Holiday's brother, then twenty-one years old, who helped to launch the Millican "race riot" in 1868. Holiday was rumored to have lynched a black member of the pro-Union Loyal League. The rumor may have been unfounded, but when added to Holiday's subsequent public warning that he and other whites were about to be massacred by angry blacks, it sparked a series of armed confrontations between whites and blacks that eventually left six blacks dead.[12]

It was not the last time the Holiday name would be linked to racial conflict. In 1880 one of Lon Holiday's white tenants or laborers, Frind Peoples, got into a drunken argument on Holiday's farm with a black man named Wash Taliaferro. Peoples accused Taliaferro of stealing money and forcibly had him searched; in retaliation later that evening, Taliaferro grabbed an ax and whacked Peoples hard enough in the neck and head to kill him. Knowing the penalty for killing a white man, Taliaferro took to his heels but was caught by a white posse in neighboring Washington County. He was brought back to Millican where he was lodged in a convict camp. Later that night, another mob of about forty masked men took him from the camp and hanged him from a tree near Holiday's farm. Whether Holiday was among the mob is not known, as no one was identified. But given that the white victim, Peoples, was one of his tenants who was murdered on his land, it is not improbable that Holiday might have been among the avengers.[13]

By the late 1880s, when he began contracting with Irish tenants, Holiday was well known throughout the county, enjoying wide social and political connections. The Brenham newspaper that ran the small article about Mrs. Kelly's rape charge in May 1889 added a seemingly disconnected fact about

Holiday that spoke volumes about his social standing relative to Mrs. Kelly: "Holiday ran for the legislature at the last session." Against so well known and relatively wealthy a personage as Lon Holiday, Mrs. Kelly did not stand a chance. About a week after she leveled her rape accusation against Holiday, Brazos County attorney V. B. Hudson—who would later be elected county judge—came down to Millican to investigate. He concluded that Mrs. Kelly was not a credible victim and that her charges were without merit: "From the fact of complainant waiting several months before making the charge and other circumstances connected with the affair, he threw the case out of court."[14]

Mrs. Kelly and her husband presumably remained in jail until the assault charges against them could be examined in court, and it is not known how that case turned out. But in a sense Mrs. Kelly had already been tried in a court of sorts, where she had been judged not to be a vulnerable white woman in need of protection. Mrs. Kelly's in-between racial status can be clearly seen here. On the one hand, Hudson took the charges seriously enough to investigate—something he would have been very unlikely to do had Mrs. Kelly been black. On the other hand, after meeting her he refused to take the accusation seriously, which he—and other members of the community—would have been bound to do had she been viewed as a white woman, her tenant status notwithstanding. Miss DeHart of Benchley, after all, was the sister-in-law of another tenant farmer, at about the same economic level as Mrs. Kelly. And Miss DeHart's accusations had been taken very seriously, to the point where it seemed that half the county had gone looking for her attacker.

From the scanty evidence it is impossible to say whether Hudson dismissed Mrs. Kelly's rape accusation because of a genuine lack of credibility, or because of her low social and economic class relative to Holiday, or because of her Irish connection. Likely it was a tangled combination of all three factors, in which class significantly affected Mrs. Kelly's racial status. Another case a few years later clearly shows that when victimized, the Irish in Brazos County, especially if they were poor, were not treated with the same respect as southern-born whites. What happened that time was a bloody massacre of Irish and other immigrant railroad workers by a mentally unstable local white man living in the Millican area.

From the late 1850s at least through the turn of the twentieth century, the Houston & Central Texas Railroad, as well as other railways, had brought immigrant laborers to Brazos County to build and maintain the railroads. Many of them lived together in boardinghouses known as "section houses" that were located at intervals along the railroad tracks, with a large concentration in the Benchley area. Writing his memoirs in the 1920s, Bryan businessman and postmaster J. Allen Myers remembered seeing large groups of Irish railroad workers during his youth in the early 1870s, when he worked for the H&TC Railroad as a brakeman on a construction train.

> The men employed on this work were all Irishmen. There were sixty-five of them. . . . This crowd would build three big bonfires every night all set around and talk, tell yarns, etc. . . . They were the wittiest bunch I ever saw and they always had a witty answer for everything you talked about. But all at once the Irish disappeared, out of the employ of the RR and section houses. I asked an old friend of mine one day what on earth had become of all the Irish that once worked on our railroads. In amazement he said don't you know what became of them. I said no. He said they all had gone to New York, Philadelphia and Chicago and were all holding political office. Well I said that is true. I think that the short time I spent on that construction train at Benchley, Tex, was one of the bright spots in my boyhood life. I enjoyed every minute of the time and I was always glad when the time came at the end of the day for all of us to go to camps and assemble around the bog heaps and listen to the bright witty sayings of this jolly Irish crowd.[15]

In addition to the Irish, workers living in the section houses included a scattering of French, English, Italian, German, Mexican, Canadian, Danish, Swedish, and Polish nationals. But most were Irish. They were single men, ranging from the twenties to the sixties in age, though by the 1890s many were in their fifties and beyond. Such was the case in 1895 at Section House No. 12, located about 3 miles south of Millican. In late January thirty-three-year-old Will Ward joined the railroad work crew as one of the very few American-born white workers. He moved into the section house, a three-bedroom home occupied by six other workers, an elderly landlady named Mrs. Yeager, and her daughter, Miss Rica Yeager.[16]

By all accounts, Ward was something of a misfit and had been unable to hold down a job for any length of time. Despite family connections in Washington County that included an uncle who worked as the county jailer there, Ward had been unemployed for a while before joining the section crew. Within days of starting work, he began to have problems with his fellow laborers. As he said later with considerable bitterness, "They wouldn't let me get along with them." It is not clear from news reports just what the problem was, but the *Eagle* referred to Ward's "consuming enemy within"—possibly some personality disorder—that "made him the subject of ridicule and aversion" from the largely Irish work crew. Apparently, what to J. Allen Myers was "a jolly Irish crowd" was to Will Ward an unbearable source of annoyance.

Nine days into his new occupation, Ward walked off the job in the afternoon, complaining about the weather. He stopped by the home of a friend, found a Winchester rifle there and left with it, then visited another friend's house and went with that friend to the town of Millican where he bought some morphine. Later that evening he returned by himself with the Winchester to the section house, where the other men were relaxing after supper with pipes and newspapers. Once he was in the house, Ward opened fire. Clearly the men had no warning of what was about to happen when Ward walked through the door. One died in his bed, newspaper in hand; three others fell haphazardly to the floor, where their bodies were later found scattered over the rugs. Ward also tried to murder Mrs. Yeager and her daughter, but they had locked themselves in their bedroom and retreated to the closet when the shooting started. At one point Ward heard groans coming from the bedroom where he had begun the massacre, and returned there to continue shooting at the men to make sure they were all dead. At that point, Miss Rica Yeager escaped from the house to run for help. But by the time aid arrived, Ward had set fire to the house and returned to one of the homes he had visited earlier in the evening, where he tried unsuccessfully to commit suicide by drinking the morphine.

The dead included Martin Murray, a sixty-five-year-old Irishman who had been working for the H&TC "for a long time"; another sixty-five-year-old Irishman named John Cosgrove who had been an Ohio river boatman before coming to Texas; John Costello, a sixty-year-old Irishman who had been working for the railroad about six months; and a fifty-two-year-old Swedish ex-sailor named Charles Carlamber. Wounded were the foreman, a German named William Rohl, who had been with the railroad for eleven years; and Martin Oelshlager, a farmer who was working for the railroad while he had no other work, and judging from his name, was probably German as well.

A few days after Ward was safely lodged in the Bryan jail, a reporter from the *Eagle* stopped by to look in on him and hear his story. The unrepentant Ward continued to pour out anger and vitriol against his now dead and wounded coworkers. His only regret was that he had not killed every last one. "All I hate is that I didn't get the whole layout," he was quoted as saying. "All I hate is that I didn't get them two old women." Here he added a curious statement that may hold the meaning of the slaughter, at least from Ward's perspective: "Well, the next American boy who goes to work there they will treat him right." While Ward's murderous nativism was not typical of other Brazos County residents, his contempt for these immigrants may have been widely shared, judging from what happened—or rather, what did not happen—next.[17]

One of Ward's jailmates, as it turned out, was Jim Reddick, the African American accused of raping the Italian woman, Fannie Palazzo. Reddick had been in jail for about two months, and the trials for both Reddick and Ward were set for April. But Reddick ended up going on trial first, and at the end of March he was convicted, largely on the basis of Fannie Palazzo's faint. But he appealed the verdict, had his case remanded back to Bryan, and so remained in jail. Meantime, with both a convicted black rapist and a self-confessed mass murderer sitting in jail, no lynch mob formed. The lack of mob violence could not have been due to any lack of coverage of the Millican massacre in the *Eagle*. The newspaper eagerly reported the gory details of the crime scene, and described Ward in terms similar to what southern newspapers usually reserved for "black beast rape fiends."

> One of the most awful and appalling crimes ever committed within the confines of the state now stares the authorities of this county in the face and the public awaits their action with impatient interest. A red handed self-confessed murderer who has almost bathed himself in a sea of blood lies incarcerated behind steel bars to await judgment. His life was snatched from the slippery brink of a yawning grave that he might stand up and answer for his diabolical work. . . . Revenge, insatiate revenge impelled the dead, if we are to believe the meager and disconnected statements of the prisoner. . . . He shot to kill and gloried in the killing. The gurgling of blood was the laughter of fiends. Insane? No. The devil in him was uppermost.

The lack of mob action was not lost on the *Eagle*, which commented on possible reasons why a "necktie party" had not occurred: "We are glad the spirit of mob violence has not manifested itself, which, had the victims been men of prominence, doubtless would have been the case." For those regretting the absence of a lynch mob, the *Eagle* seemed to offer consolation by predicting that Ward would certainly get the death penalty.

The jury, however, sentenced Ward to life in prison because—according to the *Eagle*—he had made a full confession of his crime in what must have been an early version of a plea bargain.[18] While Reddick waited for the Court of Criminal Appeals to hear his case, Ward continued to sit in jail for several more weeks awaiting transport to prison. Meanwhile, the *Eagle* reprinted grumblings about the life sentence from other newspapers, such as the *Navasota Review*'s comment: "Ward, the murderer in cold blood of four section men, was given a life term in the penitentiary at Bryan last week. And still it is said there is justice in the land." Brazos County residents, however, seemed to offer a collective shrug, as still no lynch mob appeared at the jail door.[19]

Finally, the day came for Ward and several other prisoners to be shipped away, and the *Eagle* reporter went to see "Ward, the quadruple murderer" off at the train depot, noting with some disgust that he was in high spirits.

> He wore a full red beard and a broad smile indicating he was very well pleased with his fate, which is indeed mild when compared with the enormity of his crime. All outside criticisms we have observed indicate the general desire of the public was that his life should pay the penalty, and indeed he only saved it by a plea of guilty which disarmed the prosecution.[20]

More likely his life was spared because of the identity of his victims and their in-between racial status. As the *Eagle* had recognized, old Irish rail-road laborers were not "men of prominence." But neither were they as low on the scale as African Americans, whose murder would not have resulted in a life sentence for a white man such as Ward. For example, in April that year—about the same time Ward went on trial—a white boy named Martie Hearn shot an unnamed black man in the Brazos Bottom area, but was acquitted of "negligent homicide." In October of that year a white man named John Rains barged into the home of a black man named Si Jones and shot him dead. In court, Rains claimed he had killed Jones in self-defense and was acquitted. As historian Leon Litwack has pointed out, courts through-out the South at this time granted virtual immunity to whites accused of crimes against black men and women. In those few cases in Brazos County where whites were convicted of killing blacks, the killer was given a short sentence, as in the case of John Greer, who was found guilty of second-degree murder in the shooting deaths of two black men at Allenfarm in October 1901. The jury sent Greer to the penitentiary for five years.[21]

In Brazos County, whites who killed other whites were themselves often shot dead by avenging relatives before their case could be heard in court, especially in the feud-prone Millican area. After several shootings in a complicated family feud, J. Allen Myers was acquitted in 1875 of murder-ing John Millican, but that case was so fraught with political overtones that it is difficult to use as an example. Perhaps more typical was a rape case in 1902, in which Joshua "Tobe" Price, a white man, was sentenced to death for sexually assaulting his fourteen-year-old daughter. He appealed, but the Texas Court of Criminal Appeals affirmed the death penalty. Finally, about a week before he was scheduled to hang, the governor commuted his sentence to life in prison, and Price was turned over to a penitentiary agent instead of the hangman.[22]

Ward's sensationalized killing of the railroad workers was too deliberate and involved too many victims for an acquittal, especially as he had freely and with obvious relish admitted to the deed. But at the same time the jury would not give Ward the death penalty, as it likely would have done had his victims been unassailably white. Part of the reluctance of the jury to sentence Ward to death may also have been the low status of his victims: they were poor, they were old, and they were not well known to most people in Brazos County. Indeed, by any measure they were "not men of prominence." But there was one part of their identity that seemed to hold significance, at least in the eyes of the *Eagle* editor, who made a point of listing it in the news stories: most of the victims were Irish. They were alien outsiders in every respect, and the jury's decision shows a high level of ambiguity, a confounded sense of how to avenge four victims who seemed neither black nor fully white. In the end the murders, willful and brutal and numerous as they were, were not enough to send a white killer to the scaffold. Like Mrs. Kelly, the Irish tenant farmer's wife whose accusations of rape were both considered and ignored, these immigrant railroad workers were fixed in a racial twilight that was likely the murkier because of their poverty. Seeming to be neither fully white on one hand, nor black on the other, the murdered immigrants remained somewhere "in between."

Let us return to the winter of 1897, and to the doorway of the Bryan city jail. An angry mob of 500 Brazos County residents were clamoring for the black prisoner, Eugene Washington, because an Irishman had fingered him as a rapist. City officials tried to calm the raging crowd. Brazos County attorney A. G. Board, who was the county's chief prosecutor, and Sheriff Tom Nunn appeared in the doorway. Board spoke first with "an eloquent appeal" to the mob "to let the law take its course." Nunn came next with an emotional appeal, pleading "with tears in his eyes," and telling them "that he loved every man in the crowd, but that they had elected him sheriff and it was his sworn duty to protect his prisoner even with his life, and that he would do it, so help him God." Nunn had already been through a lynching six months earlier and had felt obligated afterward to write to the governor explaining his failure to stop it. He had written a similar letter to the Brazos County community at large through the newspaper about the hazards of mob rule. Apparently unwilling this time to clean up the mess following another lynching, Nunn now refused to budge from the jail door. Given the ease with which many law officers gave way before threatening crowds in lynching episodes elsewhere in Texas and the South, Nunn's resistance was perhaps genuine.[23]

Nunn, now forty-two years old, had been sheriff of Brazos County for about six years. He had just survived an electoral challenge by defeating yet another Kurten-area farmer, and now seemed to be confident of his standing among Brazos County voters. If he had been ready to do whatever it took to win his first victorious election in 1890, when he sold his saloon in the middle of the summer campaign, he now seemed to be considerably less sensitive to the mood of his constituents. This time Nunn was not as disposed to accommodate himself to the mood of the town. He continued to resist the cries of the crowd to hand over Washington, and his obstinacy inspired other county officials to do likewise. Joining him at the jailhouse door were county judge W. H. Harmon, county treasurer R. W. Carr, district judge Taliaferro, another judge, A. C. Brietz, and several other prominent men. As if at an election rally, the men proceeded to give a series of speeches, "all making pleas to maintain the majesty of the law." Taliaferro reminded the crowd that the court would convene within six weeks, and that Washington would be sure to get his just deserts. "The mob listened respectfully, but was determined, and when Judge Taliaferro, the last speaker, had finished, made a rush on the door."[24]

Nunn stalled the crowd by firing pistols from inside the jail, giving time for Taliaferro to send a telegram to the governor in Austin asking for military aid. During the standoff, the crowd grew still larger, swelled by the presence of "law-abiding and substantial persons of Bryan." A large committee of this elite group who were "not identified with the mob" made their way into the jail and tried to convince Nunn to stand aside, telling him that members of the crowd had now acquired some dynamite, which they were in the process of planting beneath the jail in order to blow it up. But still Nunn refused to give way. Finally, the "best citizens of Bryan," in order to save the jail and their favorite sheriff, overpowered him, as the newspapers phrased it, allowing the mob to rush in and take Washington away.[25]

A debate ensued over whether to burn Washington alive, or merely hang him. After first voting to burn, the mob decided to hang him instead, possibly swayed by the "best citizens" who realized a burning might not enhance the reputation of the growing and progressive business community that they were working so hard to create. Washington, meanwhile, continued to assert his innocence. A *San Antonio Daily Express* reporter who worked his way to the front of the crowd found the doomed man on his knees, "praying to God to forgive a poor sinner." Finally, at about 6:30 P.M., the crowd moved off toward Main Street, with Washington in tow, while some continued to cry, "Burn him!" A cottonwood tree stood in front of the First National Bank, offering a convenient gallows. News accounts presented a rather serpentine image of one of the men helping to prepare the execution: "The form of a man bearing a rope was seen gliding up the leafless tree." Within minutes, Washington was dead. Someone pinned a note to his body to warn other would-be rapists, while others kindled a bonfire in the street to warm the crowd, which lingered for some time afterward.[26]

Unaccountably, after the hanging the crowd decided to salute the sheriff with a three-cheer hurrah, which might cause one to doubt whether Nunn's resistance to the lynching was truly as determined as news reports made it out to be. But mob members might also have cheered Nunn simply for arresting Washington in the first place, and then for speedily tracking down the Irishman, whose testimony had been crucial in providing justification for the lynching. The Irishman himself had not been forgotten. He was still on hand, evidently having joined the throng as it hauled Washington down to Main Street to kill him. The last thing the crowd did before dispersing was to take up a collection and give it to its star witness. Two days earlier, Nunn had offered a $50 reward for the arrest and conviction of Miss De-Hart's assailant. While there had been an arrest, there could never be a conviction now, and Nunn was probably in no mood to reward the man who had helped spark the lynching he had tried to prevent. So the crowd pitched in instead, taking up what amounted to a thank offering to the anonymous stranger "who furnished proof of identification."[27]

Help from the governor never arrived. Culberson had responded to Taliaferro's telegram with one of his own, promising that "to the extent of my authority I will stand by you in any action you may take to protect your prisoner." But before Culberson could summon state aid, Taliaferro sent a second telegram, telling him "the mob had overpowered the sheriff and was in the process of hanging the prisoner." Culberson reportedly reacted to the news with anger, saying mob law "was a defilement to civilization, a disgrace to humanity and ruinous to any state in which it was practiced."[28]

A few voices, though not many, joined Culberson's denunciation. Significant condemnation of lynching in Texas was still several decades away. The few to weigh in against the lynching included the *Galveston Daily News,* which ran a front-page editorial blasting the mob: "The lynching at Bryan is another instance where popular fury disregarded even consideration of civilization and public order and wreaked its vengeance in a barbarous manner upon a helpless victim." The paper went on to urge lawmakers in Austin to pass anti-lynching legislation, arguing that "all thoughtful and judicious citizens are heartily sick of such exhibitions of savagery and it is to be hoped that on behalf of the good name of the state the governor will not dismiss the Bryan outrage with meaningless denunciation." Such pressure, along with the soaring numbers of lynchings elsewhere in the state, convinced the state legislature to pass its first-ever anti-lynching act that year that required prosecution of lynchers and the firing of sheriffs and other law officers who permitted lynchings. It is doubtful whether the law had much effect: Texans would go on to lynch more than 230 more victims in the next three decades, earning the state the number-three spot in the nation for mob-led killings.[29]

Washington's body was left dangling from the cottonwood tree on Main Street until the next morning, Sunday. The sight drew "a big crowd of people, including some ladies and children." Many of the onlookers likely were on their way to church services, as the Baptist, Methodist, Episcopal, and Catholic churches were all near Main Street. By 10:00 A.M., justice of the peace J. T. Closs decided the corpse had been displayed long enough, and ordered it to be taken down for an inquest. The verdict was standard issue: "the negro came to his death by hanging at the hands of an armed body of unknown men." Washington's body was then taken to his mother's home, where, curiously, Judge Harman paid a call "to see after funeral arrangements." Washington was buried that afternoon.[30]

With one exception, none of the elements of the Washington lynching was unique to Bryan. From the first accusation of rape to the final viewing of the body, the drama seemed to follow a standard script that newspapers repeated over and over again in every southern state. True, the mob apparently had not tortured, dismembered, or castrated Washington, nor had it subjected him to a slow, agonizing death by fire. Death-by-torture lynchings regularly occurred in Texas, most notably in the killing of Henry Smith in Paris, Texas, in 1893. In that lynching Smith, a black man, was coerced into confessing that he had raped and murdered a three-year-old white girl, and was slowly tortured and burned alive before a crowd of some 15,000 on a high platform built specifically for the event. Similarly, in Waco some years later, Jesse Washington was castrated and dismembered, then hanged over a fire beneath a tree limb, where he was burned to death in front of City Hall before a crowd of, again, about 15,000. His offense had been the alleged rape and murder of a white woman. A few years after the 1916 Waco lynching, another brutal spectacle erupted in Kirven, a small town to the east in Freestone County. There in 1922 three black men accused of raping and murdering a white teenaged girl were tied to a plow and burned alive in the middle of the town.[31]

None of the reported lynchings that occurred in Brazos County appears to have approached such levels of barbarity, probably because none of the rape cases after 1890 involved the additional accusation of murder, which likely would have enraged whites in Brazos County as much as those in Paris, Waco, or Kirven. However, accounts of the Brazos County lynchings were nonetheless typical, as if county residents—or the *Eagle*'s editor—were following a macabre lynching playbook. Standard elements of the script included bringing the accused black man to the alleged victim for positive identification, allowing the accused to pray and possibly confess before putting him to death, killing the accused in view of a large crowd, displaying the body publicly afterward, and concluding that the deed had been done "at the hands of persons unknown," or in this case, "by unknown men." But the lynching of Eugene Washington included one intriguing variation: the testimony of the anonymous Irishman.

The question was raised earlier of why the Irishman stepped forward. Why would a stranger who had already passed through town on his way to another destination go out of his way—in fact, return from that other destination—to condemn to death a man he had met randomly while walking along the railroad tracks? The newspapers, of course, offered no more clues to his motivation than they did to his identity, so any answer is speculative. It is worth noting that the first act of this lynching drama took place in Benchley—historically the home first of Irish slaveholders and farmers, then of Irish railroad workers. No one in Bryan seemed to know him, but possibly the Irishman had worked in Benchley some time earlier, or knew about the community through work connections on the railroad, and felt a tie to the area that he would not have felt for, say, Millican. Possibly after hearing about the rape, he viewed his walking companion as a genuine threat to the Benchley community.

Certainly it is fair to say that his low social status as a footloose Irishman would not have created any common bond with the equally low-status, footloose Washington, and would not have given him any reason to protect the African American. Historians have amply demonstrated the animosity many Irish in northern cities bore toward African Americans, particularly before and during the Civil War. The Irish in the South shared that animosity—and the attendant willingness to embrace the ideology of white supremacy as well. David Gleeson documented the strong support for slavery among Irish southerners, their enthusiastic embrace of the Confederacy, and their participation after the war in race riots and other campaigns to establish white supremacy. By denouncing Washington as a rapist, the Irishman was simply reflecting the actions of many of his compatriots across the South.[32]

Gleeson's major thesis was that such support of white supremacy enabled the Irish to become completely assimilated into southern culture by the end of Reconstruction and thus to become a "forgotten people" of the Old South as the nineteenth century drew to a close. But as late as the 1890s in Brazos County, the Irish were anything but forgotten. The popular Dunn & Daly Saloon on Main Street was heralded for its Irish heritage, and the chief means of identifying Mrs. Kelly, the massacred railroad laborers of Millican, and finally the anonymous witness in the Washington lynching was by their nationality—their Irishness. Nor were they completely assimilated—not yet. If Thomas Dunn and John Daly were highly respected members of the Bryan community, Mrs. Kelly and the Irish railroad laborers were considerably less so. And until he spoke up as a key witness providing the crucial testimony that helped spark mob violence, the Irishman of the Washington lynching had no standing in Brazos County whatsoever. Despite his lack of any other identity, the Irishman became a celebrated hero to the Bryan mob, the triumphant man of the hour, the antithesis of the black man dangling from the cottonwood tree. He was even sent on his way with a cash reward.

As Gleeson argued, such acts enabled the Irish eventually to blend seamlessly into southern culture. Complete assimilation did eventually happen in Brazos County, though it took place on a later timetable than Gleeson established elsewhere in the South. By the late 1890s the Irish of Brazos County were just on the verge of losing any lingering racial stigmas, and were ready to disappear into white, native-born southern society. But they were still visible; their Irish identity had not yet evaporated. Perhaps the willingness of the Irish witness to take part in a vicious demonstration of white supremacy—the strangled death of Eugene Washington—helped to erase the last vestiges of racial otherness that still clung to the local Irish community. Racial violence, after all, was one of the quickest and clearest ways to assert the racial dominance that whiteness conferred, though owning property and voting also helped considerably. Within a few years, participating in racial violence would not be necessary for Brazos County's Irish to be numbered among the county's whites. Wealth, social prestige, and long-term residence weighed heavily in the calculations of whiteness, as historians Stephanie Cole and Michael Phillips argued in their separate studies of the racial terrain of Dallas. In Bryan, when the Dunn & Daly Saloon closed in 1915 because of the illness of its surviving owner, John Daly, the *Eagle* ran a long story full of praise for the forty-year-old business and its owners. A similar story published twenty years earlier had made much of the Irish origins of the saloon keepers. But this time, not one word was written to suggest the owners ever had been anything but respectable white southerners. As Gleeson suggested, their Irishness was indeed forgotten.[33]

Only a few years after the Washington lynching, J. J. Cahill, a landowning farmer and the son of Irish-born parents, was elected to the county commissioners court from Justice Precinct 5. This is the precinct that comprised the northwestern portion of the county and included prime Brazos Bottom farmland, with the Brazos River running along its western edge. The area, which included Mudville and other small communities, had long had a sizeable African American majority, and was one of three areas in the county—the other two being Millican and Bryan—with a heavy concentration of black voters. Cahill had lived on a farm along Thompson Creek, an area closer to Bryan, since 1871.[34]

His mother, Mary Bowles Hannifin Cahill, had been born in Dublin and had emigrated to Texas by way of Galveston in 1859, having heard about the opportunities for a new life in America from two sisters who had left Ireland earlier. Married to a man named Michael Hannifin at the time, she moved to Millican, where her husband found work with the Houston & Texas Central Railroad. Hannifin was killed in Millican during the Civil War by an accidental explosion of some nearby Confederate ordnance, to which he had apparently contributed his own gunpowder. His widow, who had one son, subsequently married a railroad section foreman staying in her boardinghouse. His name was James Cahill, another Irishman. When the railroad completed the tracks to Bryan, the Cahills packed up and followed the crowd north to the new town. A few years later, in 1871, they bought a 377-acre farm west of Bryan. By that time, three more sons had been born, including Jerimiah Joseph Cahill, known simply as "J. J." Mary Cahill had also acquired a foster son, whose father, another Irish railroad worker, was unable to care for him.[35]

Her sons eventually acquired farms nearby, and by the turn of the twentieth century the Cahill presence in Precinct 5 was strong. By the 1890s Mary Cahill was known in the area as "Grandmother Cahill," and her sons were active in Democratic party politics. In May 1899 the county commissioners named J .J. Cahill as the Precinct 5 election official, and a year later his three brothers were elected delegates to the county Democratic convention. Such political participation paid off, especially for J. J. Cahill, who won a seat on the county commissioners court in 1904, taking the seat of the African American farmer Dennis Ballard, who had hung on to the post through most of the 1890s and had been reelected again in 1900. When he replaced Ballard in 1904, Cahill ended black representation on the Brazos County Court of Commissioners for the next six decades, and established an Irish political presence that by the early twentieth century no one in the county thought remarkable or even noticeable.[36] Before that happened, however, Dennis Ballard would be caught up in another episode of racial violence. This time the accusers were not Irish, but Bohemian, and the results would prove just as fatal as in the Eugene Washington lynching. As it turned out, the Bohemians had just as much to gain as the anonymous Irishman, and Ballard had a great deal to lose indeed.

Chapter 5

THE BOHEMIANS AND THE JEWS

We were much surprised at Nonie's announcement. The Bryanites are guessing whether he is a Jew or Bohemian. Suppose Grace knows who or what he is.

Letter from Mary Cavitt in Bryan
to her daughter in Houston, 30 July 1900

After the lynching of Eugene Washington in early 1897, mob violence in Brazos County quieted down for some time. That is not to say that the times were particularly peaceful, or that Sheriff Nunn had little to do. The usual assortment of feuds, murders, mysterious shootings, and arson attacks erupted regularly, but almost four years went by before Nunn had to face down another lynch mob. This next incident began late in 1900 with a double shooting and ended a year later with Bryan's first execution in at least twenty years. The shooting victims were Bohemian community leaders; the executed prisoner, a black man. The incident also involved Bryan's Jewish community in a brief but significant way. At one point in the story, the fate of the black prisoner was by no means certain, and some mysterious aspects of the case suggest this was similar to a "legal lynching"—that is, an execution held to prevent mob action. When it was all over, the Bohemians would find their racial status and social ranking enhanced; African Americans—especially African American men—would be branded once more as violent devils.

In the meantime, Nunn had his hands full trying to keep a precarious peace in a county where many people—white or black—tended to settle their differences with guns, knives, and torches. Millican's feuding families, of course, remained as feisty as ever. On the same day that Miss DeHart of Benchley sent word to Bryan that she had been raped, yet another shootout broke out on Millican's main street. "At Millican B. M. Curd and Ed Allen engaged in a little Winchester practice with each other as targets," reported the *Brenham Daily Banner* sardonically. "Allen had his horse killed from under him, and received two bullets in different parts of his body. He is not expected to live. Curd was shot in the calf of his right leg, the wound not being considered serious."[1]

But Millican by no means had a monopoly on the county's violence. The Millican method of settling quarrels had spread throughout the county by the end of the nineteenth century, and much of the violence now centered on Bryan. Shootouts occurred on Bryan's main street, though some of these were seemingly accidental, as in the case in February 1898 when merchant J. T. Hanway shot another merchant, H. Kernole, in the back because he thought he was a suspicious intruder. Kernole, wandering in the dark, had been too deaf to hear Hanway's warnings. A few months later the city attorney, A. G. Board, landed in jail briefly for starting a shootout in a saloon over differences with a political opponent. No one was hurt, but a considerable amount of glassware was broken. Possibly the incident enhanced Board's reputation, as he went on to win the election in the fall for county judge. More excitement occurred about a year and a half later, when Andrew Dozier, an African American, took an ax to his girlfriend, Anne Brigance, hacked her to death, then doused her dead body with oil and set it on fire. In the process of disposing of her body, Dozier also burned down the newly built home of the city postmaster, J. Allen Myers. Brigance had been the Myers family's cook and lived in a room in the back of their house, where the city marshal found her charred body amid the smoking ruins. Luckily for Dozier, the Myers family had not yet moved into the new house and thereby escaped injury. As it was, Dozier ended up getting twelve years in prison for arson, and another twenty-five for killing Brigance.[2]

African Americans provided the *Eagle* with a steady diet of crime news during these years. Most of the incidents involved the assault, rape, or killing of African Americans by other African Americans; in fact, nearly all violent crime committed by blacks involved black victims. During the interval between lynchings, from 1897 to 1901, the *Eagle* reported at least sixteen incidents in which African Americans were charged with murder; all the victims were black. Depending on the age, gender, and general reputation of the black victims among whites, sentences of the convicted criminals ranged from five years to life in the state penitentiary, which usually meant hard labor in a convict work camp. Much rarer were white victims of black crime. The only such incidents reported in the *Eagle* involved the theft of an animal such as a hog or a horse, or a house burglary.

One incident that made headlines in the *Eagle* was the shooting death of Bryan's long-standing African American policeman, Levi Neal. Neal had served as the city's sole night watchman, or policeman, off and on since about 1880, working as an assistant to the city marshal and deputy marshal. He seems to have been mostly employed at keeping the peace within the African American community, as Neal was often listed in the newspaper as the one making arrests of black suspects. Perhaps this caused resentment among some African Americans, or at least in one particular man whom he arrested one night in late February 1900. Neal had nabbed an ex-convict named Dennis Calhoun for some unnamed offense, and was on his way to the city jail with Calhoun in tow when Calhoun pulled out a pistol and shot Neal through the heart. He died immediately. Two other black men grabbed Calhoun before he could get away, and Calhoun was duly charged with murder and locked up. He was subsequently convicted and sentenced to life imprisonment, an indication of how highly Neal had been valued by Bryan's whites. As the *Eagle* noted patronizingly in his obituary, "Levi was a vigilant officer. He knew his duty and his place and kept within the bounds of both to an extent that was gratifying and helpful to the officers over him. His tragic and sudden death has been a matter of much regret."[3]

The *Eagle*'s ear was also closely tuned to whatever nefarious doings it could uncover in the Italian communities in town and in the Brazos Bottom, which obligingly provided another steady source of crime news. These incidents sounded more exotic, involving assassinations, poisonings, and knife fights. But here again, the victims were almost always other Italians, such as the case in February 1900, in which an Italian man, John Failla, was charged with killing two fellow Italians and wounding two others in a murderous rage. The "Tragedy at Mudville," as the *Eagle* labeled it, left Failla's wife and his wife's four-year-old niece dead, and his brother-in-law and an anonymous "old Italian woman" both wounded. Failla and his brother-in-law, Carlo Congelosi, lived near each other and had married sisters. Perhaps Failla had suspected an adulterous affair and was able to plead a classic defense, because he was acquitted of murdering the child, on a plea of insanity. The murder case involving his wife was thrown out of court.[4]

One immigrant group that rarely appeared in the newspaper in a crime context was the Bohemians. Usually the only news they generated was through the death of a respected member of the community, or the spectacular death of a burn victim or gruesome suicide. Occasionally the social doings of a group of Bohemians would be noted—such as the formation of a mutual aid society, or notice of an upcoming ball or barbecue. Such coverage was not much different from what was given to the activities of southern-born whites. The only noticeable difference was that, with a few exceptions, Bohemians were always identified by their nationality. Clearly the *Eagle* considered them different from American-born whites, but the degree of difference was unclear. Like the Italians, they seemed somewhat exotic, although less crime prone. At this point, they were still unknown and unassimilated, and lived largely outside white society. The *Eagle,* for example, failed to take note of the comings and goings of Bohemians at the train depot, a place that normally seemed to be a prime news generator for the local newspaper. Who went where—or who came from where—by train on any given day was always of interest to the *Eagle*. Either the newspaper's editor could see the depot platform from his office window, or he posted a correspondent at the depot to catch every incoming train in order to list the arrivals and departures of white citizens of note. Bohemians were not among them.

There is some evidence to suggest that Bohemians in Brazos County were not greeted with open arms. The derogatory nickname for someone of Bohemian origin, "bohunk," was already in circulation among southern-born whites in the county by the 1880s, and at least some newcomers experienced open prejudice from white neighbors as they struggled to learn the language and customs of their new home. But they were not entirely unwelcome, either. By the time the Bohemians began arriving in the county in the early 1870s, local whites had already recognized that European immigrants could be a valuable source of labor. There is no evidence that any Bohemian families stayed in the immigrant house that the town of Bryan had opened in the 1870s, but it is possible that some may have used it as a way station. Such welcome was generated partly by a desire common throughout the South at that time to find an alternative to what was perceived to be a recalcitrant and lazy black labor force, and was also no doubt spurred partly by earlier, positive encounters with northern Europeans such as German immigrants.

Most of Brazos County's Germans hailed from Prussia, and most had settled in the Kurten community (see chapter 2). A large number of Germans also had settled in the Wellborn and Rock Prairie areas south of Bryan. But many others lived in Bryan itself, where they prospered in a wide variety of occupations including physician, civil engineer, merchant, and carpenter. Some became active in the Democratic party, and were elected as delegates to various state and county conventions. By the time the Italians and Bohemians showed up en masse, the Germans had been thoroughly assimilated into the community life of Brazos County. The *Eagle* rarely, if ever, referred to prominent men—such as Henry Kurten or his neighbor, August Prinzel—as German, Prussian, or even as immigrants of any sort. Walter Wipprecht, the son of German immigrants, was a well-respected businessman who worked at one point in the highly visible job of manager of the Bryan cotton compress. He was frequently listed among the Democratic party leadership, served as the city's precinct chairman, and was elected a Bryan alderman in 1901. No mention was ever made in print referring to his foreign heritage.[5]

About the only references made to Germany were in connection with a Jewish furniture merchant, Samuel Levy, whose brother Julius returned to the fatherland in 1899 to pay a visit to their parents. The *Eagle* duly noted his international destination and—proudly, it seemed—announced the arrival of a "handsomely lithographed" postcard he had sent back to Bryan. If the Germans seemed to be held in high regard, so too were these Jewish residents of Bryan, many of whom also were German in origin, though again, the *Eagle* rarely noted it. The *Eagle* rarely noted the Jewish faith of these Bryanites, either, as if it were not a matter of any importance or news value. Occasionally a rabbi from Houston or Waco would visit Bryan to perform a circumcision, and every fall, the *Eagle* would inform the town that because of Yom Kippur, the Day of Atonement, Jewish businesses would be closed for the day.[6]

Jewish residents began arriving in Brazos County just after the Civil War, initially settling in Millican, where they established themselves mostly as merchants. The Sanger Brothers, a successful Jewish-run dry goods firm in north Texas, opened the first of a string of branch stores along the Houston & Texas Central Railroad in Millican in the mid-1860s, then moved on to Bryan and eventually to Dallas. By the early 1900s several dozen Jewish families were living in Bryan, where they earned their living as furniture merchants, grocers, liquor dealers, jewelers, and cotton merchants. The most prominent merchant was Samuel Levy, the furniture dealer, who frequently made news simply by leaving town or coming back by train. When he found a wife, "one the brightest and most wholesome girls" in Arkansas, in 1897, the *Eagle* highlighted the wedding announcement with the sort of gusto it reserved for Bryan's most elite families. Levy was later elected a city alderman in 1912, the same year he was also made a director of the First State Bank & Trust. Notable as his political achievement was, Levy was not the first Jewish resident of Bryan to be elected to the city council. In 1883 Marx Goldstein had won election to the same post.[7]

In the rest of the nation, especially in eastern cities, the Jewish population would substantially increase in the early twentieth century and would face an intense wave of anti-Semitism that had already begun to pick up strength in the last decades of the nineteenth century. Jews were a significant percentage of immigration in the late nineteenth and early twentieth centuries, but compared to the total U.S. population, their numbers were never great. In the South especially they were only a tiny percentage. From colonial times through the twentieth century, Jewish residents in the South made up less than 1 percent of the population. They were often highly visible in small towns as merchants and business owners, but their small numbers and their efforts to assimilate and win social acceptance largely kept anti-Semitism throughout the South at relatively low ebb, though there were some notable exceptions.

Historians have noted the prevailing tendency of southern Jews—both before and after the Civil War—to blend in with southern white society. Jewish southerners could be found among the ranks of slaveholders. They supported secession, the Confederacy, and the war, and they were on hand to help build the New South. Many even supported the regime of Jim Crow and its virulent racial segregation. "Southern Jews were rarely conspicuous—preferring to merge into the landscape, which their numbers made feasible," noted Stephen J. Whitfield. "They seemed to partake, generation after generation, of virtually the same values as their neighbors."[8]

The effort to keep a low profile was aided in no small way by white southerners' hostility toward African Americans, whose threatening and much larger presence helped to deflect criticism of Jews. As long as white southerners directed resentment and enmity toward the African Americans in their midst, Jewish residents were often able to escape blatant oppression. As southern newspaperman Hodding Carter observed much later in the twentieth century, "It takes perseverance to hate Jews and Negroes and Catholics all at the same time."[9]

In Bryan at the turn of the century, overt anti-Semitism is difficult to discern, at least in the pages of the newspaper. Like their counterparts elsewhere in the South, Jewish residents of Bryan were able to maintain a fairly low profile and may have been somewhat inconspicuous. But they were by no means invisible. They had not blended seamlessly into Brazos County's white society. A certain measure of ambivalence can be detected by the absence of Jewish residents in the lists of guests at prominent parties and social gatherings that were regularly highlighted in the *Eagle*. As historian Leonard Rogoff noted, Jews were tentatively accepted as white in the Jim Crow South, but their precise racial place was not fixed. They were too small a minority to present a political or cultural challenge, but they were nonetheless subject to discrimination, especially in social spheres. While they might be welcomed and respected as business owners, they were not likely to be included in whites' after-hours events and gatherings.[10]

As the twentieth century wore on, however, such "segregation at sundown," as one commentator described it, became more overt and vicious, especially in larger cities, such as Atlanta. One of the South's most infamous lynchings was the mob-led murder in Atlanta of Jewish factory manager Leo Frank in 1913. Frank had been accused of the rape and murder of a white teenaged girl who worked in his factory, and was convicted of the murder despite the possible involvement of a black janitor. But after a two-year-long appeal process, he succeeded in convincing the Georgia governor, John M. Slanton, to commute his sentence to life imprisonment. Less than two months later a mob kidnapped Frank from the prison farm and hanged him. Frank's lynching occurred only a few years after a North Carolina preacher published a book entitled *The Jew a Negro, Being a Study of the Jewish Ancestry from an Impartial Standpoint,* which joined growing speculation in the South about the racial status of Jews. The lynching brought home a terrible lesson about the unstable and precarious position of southern Jews in white society, and as historian Clive Webb noted, such acts of violence forced many Jewish southerners into "an even more passive acceptance of white supremacy."[11]

Like many of the European immigrants then arriving in Brazos County, the Jewish residents of Bryan were racial outsiders, not black, but inconclusively white—in other words, somewhere "in between." Such ambivalence can be seen in a curious statement in a letter written in 1900 by Mary Cavitt, one of Bryan's elite white women. Mrs. Cavitt, the wife of W. R. Cavitt, a respected doctor, dairy farmer, former state legislator, and former member of the A.& M. College board of directors, was passing along some local gossip to her daughter in Houston. She commented on what must have been an upcoming wedding: "We were much surprised at Nonie's announcement. The Bryanites are guessing whether he is a Jew or Bohemian. Suppose Grace knows who or what he is." Her use of "who or what" suggests that Nonie's intended did not meet with full approval by "the Bryanites," and even Mary Cavitt seemed not quite sure what to make of the news. Jews in Bryan may have penetrated the white economic and political arenas of the town, but their social standing remained ambiguous, as much as the Bohemians' standing.[12]

That such indeterminate, or in-between, status grew out of racial per-

Cavitt House, one of Bryan's oldest residences, built by the Cavitt family in 1875. Mary Cavitt was living here when she wrote her letter in 1901. Photo courtesy Carnegie Center of Brazos Valley History

ception rather than religious difference is evident by the marked absence of religious intolerance expressed in Bryan. The *Eagle* reported Jewish religious events and ceremonies with the same respectful tones it used for Methodist revivals, though the coverage was not as extensive. The overall lack of intolerance was especially noticeable in the fall of 1900, when a Roman Catholic order of nuns proposed building a convent and girls' school in Bryan. The Ursuline Convent in Galveston had been wiped out by the massive hurricane that year, and the sisters needed to relocate somewhere farther inland. They toured several prospective communities, and the *Eagle* excitedly listed the advantages of having the convent and its school in Bryan: "It would be a permanent institution and one that would provide splendid buildings and be of great benefit to the town."[13]

Accordingly, the business and civic leaders of the town made every effort to entice the nuns to move to Bryan, offering 50 acres of land on an attractive hill just to the east of town, and a start-up sum totaling $2,400. The sisters, headed by Mother Superior Mary Joseph, accepted the offer, and the *Eagle* spread the news with blaring headlines. "Upon this commanding eminence will be erected a magnificent three story brick edifice for the education of young ladies—a building of which the people of Bryan may feel justly proud and an institution which will add greatly to the fame of Bryan as an educational center," boasted the newspaper. When Mother Mary Joseph and members of her order visited Rome a few months later and had an audience with the pope, the *Eagle* again reported the news with pride. When the cornerstone was laid in March 1901, the city mayor and council, public school trustees, citizens' building committee, and a host of marching bands—including the A. and M. College Band—paraded through town to celebrate the event, all led by Brazos County's most respected Civil War veteran, Gen. H. B. Stoddard.[14]

What nobody seemed to notice—or voice any objection to—was that the new institution was Catholic. Such open welcome stood in sharp contrast to the rhetoric of nativist, anti-Catholic organizations and movements, such as the American Protective Association, which had swept over the Midwest earlier in the 1890s. Spurred by the economic depression that began in 1893 and by the arrival of hundreds of thousands of eastern and southern Europeans, most of whom were Catholic, the movement blamed most of the nation's problems on Rome and what it saw as the nefarious doings of an evil pope. Not so in Bryan. While zealous Baptists in town or in the county's outlying rural communities may have felt differently, especially those in the Baptist-dominated eastern uplands, Bryan's leaders of 1901 were enthusiastically welcoming anything and anyone who could expand the area's economic base and add to its prestige. Religious persuasion seemed to be irrelevant. One can argue, therefore, that the religious faith of Bryan's Jewish residents was not a contentious issue. Nor could the Roman Catholic faith of most Bohemians or Italians have posed much of a problem. The ambivalence with which southern-born whites in Brazos County viewed both Jews and Bohemians had little to do with religion, and everything to do with race.[15]

By the 1890s, when the Italians arrived en masse in Brazos County, the Bohemians had already begun to establish themselves as bonafide members of the Brazos County farming community. Bohemian communities had begun forming in Texas in the 1850s. By the end of the nineteenth century a large swath of central Texas, stretching west and south of Brazos County, was home to thousands of Czech-speakers. Unlike the Italians, who first appeared in Brazos County as town dwellers with various skills such as shoemaking and fruit vending, the Bohemians headed straight for the countryside, where most planted themselves in a clustered community west of Bryan. They arrived in small numbers at first. A few families crossed the Brazos River and moved over from neighboring Burleson County in the early 1870s, and by 1880 about six Bohemian families had settled near Bryan. The presence in Bryan of St. Joseph Catholic Church was a major draw, as there was no Catholic church at the time in Burleson County. About the same time, another group of Czech-speaking immigrants arrived in the county and settled south of Bryan, in the growing community of College Station. These other Czech-speakers were Moravians, and by 1880 about a dozen such families were living near the A.& M. College. While they were very similar culturally and linguistically to the Bohemians, and both would one day be known as Czechs, at this point in the nineteenth century they remained distinct, though such distinction seems to have been lost on most of the county's southern-born whites, who tended to refer to them all as Bohemians.[16]

By the late 1890s the community west of Bryan had its own post office and was known as Smetana, possibly named in honor of Bedrich Smetana, a musician in Prague who had died in the 1880s and was held in high regard for "opening the gates of Bohemian music to the world." Perhaps his performances had been attended by some of the Bohemians who later emigrated to Brazos County. Music, in any case, was an important element of Smetana's cultural life. The name also means "sweet cream" in Czech, and one story has it that the community was so named because its residents believed "the land was as good as cream." Just east of Mudville, Smetana was also east of the Brazos Bottoms, situated on prairie upland that rose from the fertile river bottomland that the Italians were in the process of claiming as their own. Most of the county's Italians lived in Mudville, and most of the Bohemians were in Smetana, although there were also some of each nationality in the other's stronghold.[17]

Both Mudville and Smetana were part of Brazos County Justice Precinct 5, which, as has been noted, was historically home to a large number of African Americans. Some of these African Americans had been living there since the earliest days of white settlement as slaves, and they had remained as laborers, sharecroppers and even property owners. Against all odds, African American residents of this part of Brazos County had managed to carve out a political stronghold that so far had survived the best efforts of white supremacists to squash it. From the 1880s onward, black voters had sent one of their own to the county court of commissioners and had elected a black justice of the peace and a black constable (see chapter 3). A few were also doing relatively well economically, having acquired their own land to grow cotton and corn. One well-documented African American farmer, Ned

Peterson, demonstrated that it was possible for black farmers in this part of the county to succeed as well as the average white farmer—with enough hard work and luck. Although Peterson's 150-acre farm was just south of Precinct 5, his situation was not unlike that of his black neighbors to the north, some of whom also had found white landowners willing to sell them land for their own farms on affordable terms.[18]

But white landowners seemed even more willing to sell land to newly arriving immigrants such as the Italians and the Bohemians, who frequently were in a better position financially to buy, and clearly did not pose the same kind of political and economic threat that black landowners might offer. While many of the Italians began their agricultural odyssey in Brazos County as lowly farm laborers, most of the Bohemians seem to have started closer to the top as renters. Probably many of them left their homeland with some financial resources, as most of those who emigrated to Texas in the latter half of the nineteenth century were "cottagers," or small landowners. Their plots of land in Bohemia and Moravia were not large enough to support their families, but could generate enough cash through sale to allow the cottagers to make a reasonably good start in Texas. As farm renters in Brazos County, Bohemian families could retain all of their profits from crop sales minus the cost of rent, unlike sharecroppers, who were forced into a sharecropping and crop lien system that substantially reduced or eliminated their capacity for profit. Many of the Bohemian renters began their farming career in Brazos County by leasing 25–30 acres. Within five to ten years, they were able not only to buy their own land, but to increase their holdings by two to five times the size of what they had originally rented. By 1900 close to 60 percent of Brazos County's Bohemian families were landowners, some with farms as large as 600 acres.[19]

One of the more successful members of the Bohemian community at Smetana was Jacob Shramek, who arrived in the United States in 1875 as an eleven-year-old. One of the few Moravians who lived in Smetana, Shramek married a Moravian-born woman named Victoria in 1887, and he first appeared on the Brazos County tax rolls in 1891 as the owner of 114 acres, a wagon, two horses, and eight cattle. By 1900 they had two daughters and two sons, and Shramek, now the postmaster of Smetana, was probably the most prominent Czech-speaker in the community. Likely he was proud of his eminence in the community, as he was the one who formally applied for the establishment of a post office in the community in 1896, asking that it be named Shramek. The post office was duly granted, but the name designated for it instead was Smetana. Jacob Shramek was also among the busiest members of the community. In addition to his farm and postal responsibilities, he ran a saloon in Smetana, which apparently was attached to or was part of his house.[20]

Another man living not far away in Precinct 5 was perhaps even more prominent in the community and was certainly better known county-wide. This was Dennis B. Ballard, a black farmer who owned 144 acres of fertile land along the Little Brazos River, a tributary of the Brazos, situated about halfway between Smetana and Mudville. Ballard, who lived about 5 miles west of Shramek's saloon, was born in Texas in 1845. Given the small numbers of free blacks in Texas before the war and the complete absence of free blacks in Brazos County, Ballard was most likely born a slave, though it is difficult to say for sure, or to know exactly where he was born and raised. At about age twenty, at the end of the Civil War, he married a woman named Emmeline, who had been born in what was known then as Indian Territory, which later became the state of Oklahoma. Family stories within the Czech community have it that Dennis Ballard served at one time as a "Buffalo Soldier"—that is, an African American soldier in a western U.S. cavalry unit—which, if true, would explain how he met his wife. The Ballards had a stepson, William Butler, and a son named Bob who was born about two years after they married.[21]

In 1877 Dennis Ballard began his career as a Brazos County landowner with 20 acres, which he slowly increased as the years passed. In 1880 he ran for a seat on the Brazos County Court of Commissioners and won. He kept on winning for the next six elections, surviving the 1890 "white man's campaign" that was waged to reduce black political power. Probably the campaign was aimed more at another black commissioner, Henry Maddox, and at the black state representative, Elias Mays, than at Ballard; newspaper rhetoric that railed against "black domination" referred specifically to Maddox and Mays but never mentioned Ballard. Ballard seems to have been well respected by whites, at least by the Bryan cotton buyers. He was a frequent winner of the premium offered each summer to the farmer who could get the first bale of cotton ginned, weighed, sold, and shipped out of Bryan. In 1897 the *Eagle* noted proudly that the "first bale" was brought in once more by a nearby resident. Not seeming to mind the winner's racial status, the *Eagle* reported: "It was brought in yesterday afternoon by Dennis Ballard, a prosperous colored farmer who brought in the first bale last year, and who lives nine miles from Bryan on the Little Brazos."[22]

The *Eagle* did not mention in that brief notice that Ballard also had been a long-time county commissioner. By 1897 Ballard had been out of office for three years, and perhaps the newspaper considered his fourteen-year tenure as a black political office holder worth forgetting, despite the respect suggested by the description "prosperous." In 1894 Ballard's string of elective victories was broken when he was defeated by Felix Phillips, who held on to the seat for two more terms. Phillips was probably white, but it is hard to determine his racial status because there were two F. Phillips listed in the county's 1900 manuscript census returns. One was white, one was black, and both lived in the same district Ballard had represented. To add to the muddle, there was a Felix Phillips who was an active leader in the county Republican party. While 90 percent of the Republicans in the county were black (according to the *Eagle*), several prominent party leaders, such as the alternating postmasters, J. Allen Myers and Tyler Haswell, were white. But since county histories list only two black commissioners for this era—Mattox and Ballard—it is likely that Ballard's rival was white, and may well have been the Republican Phillips.[23]

In any case, Phillips kept the seat until 1900, when Ballard won it back. It was a stunning political comeback after six years of being shut out of county politics, and it was especially remarkable in an era that saw black voters disenfranchised en masse across the South. Moreover, it was ten years after whites in Brazos County had launched a campaign to dismantle black voting power with a whites-only primary. And now, despite all that effort to wrest political power away from African Americans in Brazos County, Dennis Ballard had managed to find a way to get himself back into a seat of authority, where he would make decisions that would affect the entire county.

It was a remarkable achievement by any measure. But it was also a victory that would turn sour even as the votes were being counted and election results announced. Ballard's son, Bob, was now thirty-three years old. Census returns indicate that he lived at home with his parents. At one point he had apparently married but was now listed as a widower. He was a small man, weighing only 115 pounds, but somewhere along the way he had developed a fierce aggression. Seven years earlier, he had been in court for shooting and killing another black man, but was acquitted. Recently he had finished serving a three-year term on a county convict labor camp in Millican in the previous summer for the attempted murder of his uncle, Abe Batson. Soon thereafter he landed in the county road gang after pleading guilty to simple assault. Despite an attempt to escape the road gang, he spent the summer repairing county roads and bridges. There had been other shootings as well, as he later told a newspaper reporter.[24]

None of the short news accounts of his criminal career gave any hint as to the source of his explosive anger. But perhaps it is worth noting that he was born in 1868, the year of the Millican "race riot," when Texas, like the rest of the South, was in the throes of Reconstruction. Bob Ballard, who would have witnessed the promise and betrayal of black freedom as he grew up, might well have been what whites viewed as one of the angry and audacious "bad niggers" described by historian Leon Litwack. Perhaps he could be numbered among the "New Negroes," one who came of age well after slavery had ended and whose resentment against white oppression prevented him from ever acquiescing to the expectations of Brazos County's white society. If his father had been able to find a way to evade white displeasure while pursuing his own agenda, the younger Ballard could not. Of course, this is speculation, as neither of the Ballards left any records behind that reveal their attitudes toward white society. But it is speculation worth pondering because of the stark contrast between the father, who was among the county's most prominent and respected African American men, and the son, whose life would end in public humiliation and defeat.

Until the fall of 1900 Bob Ballard seemed to direct his anger only at other African Americans. The census taker of 1900 listed no occupation for him; perhaps he helped his father on his cotton farm when he was not serving time as a convict. By November 1900 he was a free man, but that would not last long. On November 7, the day after Election Day, he was out roaming around the Brazos Bottom and stopped in for a glass of beer at Jacob Shramek's saloon in Smetana.[25]

Shramek was no ordinary saloon keeper. As the local postmaster, he had also become something of a political figure in the Bohemian community by this time, serving as a link with the Democratic elite in Bryan. In June he was listed as a precinct delegate to the county Democratic convention, and about a month before the November election, Shramek had hosted a political rally and barbecue that attracted a "good sized crowd . . . many persons going out from town." He had served up all manner of meats, including beef, pork, and mutton, and brought in a band from College Station headed by Joe Holick, a fellow Moravian and leader of what would one day become the "Fightin' Texas Aggie Band" at the A. and M. College. "In the afternoon the candidates took advantage of the occasion to speak," reported the *Eagle,* "and at night a dance was given, which was attended by a large crowd." The *Eagle,* edited by a staunch member of the local Democratic party, made no mention of Republican sympathizers at this rally. Usually the newspaper made only the briefest mention of local Republican doings, while it described Democratic activities in great detail. So it seems safe to assume these were Democratic candidates, although Shramek as postmaster would have been a Republican appointee. Clearly Shramek, by now a naturalized citizen, knew where true power would soon lie in Brazos County, and it would not be with Republicans or, for that matter, with the African American voting bloc. It is also safe to assume that Dennis Ballard was not among the candidates who spoke at his barbecue.[26]

Inside Shramek's saloon after the election, an explosive argument ensued between Shramek and Bob Ballard. Newspaper reports never explained exactly what started it—the *Eagle* said it was "some trivial matter," while the *Dallas Morning News* reported the dispute was over the glass of beer. But the day itself seems highly significant: Ballard's father, Dennis, had stood for election again the day before, and early returns were showing that he had managed to pull off another victory, an act of racial defiance that may have inspired his son to display his own style of defiance. Possibly Ballard was boasting about his father; possibly Shramek took exception, and a fight started. Or perhaps Shramek—who maybe had backed Dennis Ballard's opponent—insulted the newly elected commissioner, and Bob Ballard took exception by responding with violence. Or maybe Shramek, who played host to a white Democratic political rally a month earlier, refused him service because he was black; Ballard insisted on a beer because of whose son he was. Who knows? In any case, Ballard pulled out a gun and fired away, shooting Shramek in the chest and leaving him for dead.[27]

Apparently still enraged, Ballard left the saloon, mounted his horse, and rode off. Four hundred yards along the road, he encountered a Moravian named Josef Blazek, or "Joe" Blazek, as the newspaper identified him, who was driving along in his wagon. According to newspaper accounts, Ballard overtook Blazek, rode around to the front of his wagon, and ordered him to halt and throw up his arms. "Ballard is then said to have taken his pocketbook from him and to have demanded that he give up other money which the negro insisted he had. Blazek protested that he had no more." Whereupon Ballard fired his pistol again, shooting Blazek twice "somewhere in the lower part of his body." Blazek fell back in his wagon, and Ballard rode off southward toward Batt's store—another local landmark in the Brazos Bottom—where witnesses later testified he was seen displaying the pistol and bragging about the shooting. It did not take Sheriff Nunn long to catch up with him. Before the day was over, Nunn—along with Bryan constable C. L. Baker, and the African American constable for Precinct 5, Powell Harvey—arrested him and brought him to the city jail.[28]

Both Shramek and Blazek initially survived the shooting. But the case soon turned serious. Blazek died of his wounds the next morning, and now Ballard was accused of murder. The news ignited Smetana. The Czech-speaking community had now lost a well-known and active civic leader. Blazek was a thirty-six-year-old farmer who had been in the United States since he was sixteen. His family—including both parents, two brothers, and two sisters—had moved directly to Texas from Moravia, and had settled immediately in College Station, just to the south of Bryan. Despite his youth, Blazek soon became deeply involved in community affairs, including an unsuccessful attempt to start a local chapter of the Czech fraternal organization, CSPS. Apparently having some musical ability, he also joined a brass band that regularly played at graduation ceremonies at the nearby A. and M. College and had even performed at Texas governor James Hogg's inauguration in Austin.[29]

Initially, farming prospects in College Station had turned out to be considerably less than what the Blazek family had hoped for. According to a memoir that Blazek's brother wrote in the 1920s, those early years were extremely difficult. "Illness among us all was very prevalent and extensive, and there were many shortages of such things as food, housing and clothing," Henry Blazek recalled. Racial prejudice was another major problem. Henry Blazek recorded that white neighbors turned out to be less than welcoming: "Worst of all the native Americans showed little patience with the 'bohunks' and were very openly hostile at times . . . we were destined to suffer all sorts of humiliations." But black farmers living nearby were no more helpful: "Our domicile was on the fringe of a black neighborhood, the inhabitants of which caused us no end of misery, particularly after they discovered that due to our language barrier we could neither communicate with them or with law enforcement agencies. Consequently there was little friendship and understanding between us. . . . Now all of this was our introduction to America."[30]

After a few years in College Station the family moved to Nebraska to recuperate from repeated bouts of malaria, but within a year they were back in Brazos County, probably in the College Station area, where they tried various farm rental arrangements. By then Josef Blazek had moved out on his own to a new home several counties west in La Grange, which was home to a large community of Bohemians. Blazek discovered several Czech

Josef Blazek. Blazek was one of Bob Ballard's shooting
victims in 1900. Blazek's death resulted in Ballard's "legal
lynching." Photo courtesy Ernie Wentrcek

newspapers there and decided to learn typesetting. Restless and ambitious,
he moved back to Brazos County at some point later, joining the Farmers' Alliance in College Station. He also either organized or took leadership
roles in several Czech fraternal organizations, schools, and reading societ-
ies. In 1893, now married, he had the money in hand to buy his own farm,
and subsequently established himself and his growing family as part of the
Smetana community near Bryan.

By now Blazek, like Shramek, was a naturalized citizen. Because of his
numerous civic activities, Blazek was probably as well known in the Czech-
speaking communities of Brazos County as was Jacob Shramek, though he
was undoubtedly more controversial. It is clear from a brief autobiography
that he wrote for a Czech newspaper in the 1890s that Blazek was something
of a maverick. Disillusioned with the sort of Catholicism he had seen back in

Josephine and Josef Blazek. After Josef Blazek's shooting death, his wife Josephine committed suicide in 1905. Photo courtesy Ernie Wentrcek

Moravia, he had decided as a teenager to be an atheist, and one of the many groups he joined in Brazos County was the Freethinker Society. Blazek apparently was not able to keep his views to himself, and was forced to leave one group he had led, the Plow and Book Society. As he wrote, "Having met with unfriendly sentiments from some of the members, mostly dyed-in-the-wool Catholics, I quit two years ago." At the end of his short memoir, Blazek added a brief statement that would prove to be highly ironic, in light of the circumstances of his death: "I seldom take part in political activities."

Given the combative and energetic personality his memoir presents, one might speculate just what actually occurred when Bob Ballard encountered Josef Blazek on the road outside Shramek's saloon and post office. As turn-of-the-century anti-lynching activist Ida B. Wells, and later, investigators working for the NAACP discovered, many news accounts of lynchings and African American crimes published in local southern newspapers embellished or outright fabricated details of the crimes to make them seem much worse than they were. Without any other contemporary account to use for comparison, it is impossible to say how truthful the *Eagle* was, and whether Ballard had indeed tried to rob Blazek. His brother Henry's account of the incident repeated the robbery story, but his memoir was written more than two decades later. Nonetheless, there is a hint of uncertainty in the news stories. Just as the *Eagle* had done in the description of Miss DeHart's attacker in the 1897 lynching story, newspapers also used that speculative phrase in describing the robbery scene: "said to have." Such a phrase could have its origins in the muddled memory of a bystander, or in the imaginative speculation rampant in any newsroom.[31]

Indeed, aspects of the story seem somewhat questionable, particularly the robbery attempt. Ballard's father was "a prosperous colored farmer," and his son evidently had enough money already in hand to buy a beer at Shramek's saloon. And having just left a deadly encounter that was probably sparked by a heated political argument, one might wonder whether robbery was the first thing that came to Ballard's mind when he saw Blazek. It seems more likely that Ballard, still brandishing his gun and still agitated over what had just taken place inside the saloon—and still insulted over what Shramek might have said to him—came across Blazek and began another argument. Blazek may not have been particularly cowed by the sight of an angry young black man on horseback. And given the hostility that apparently marked relations between immigrants such as the Blazek family and African Americans, as reflected in Henry Blazek's memoir, Josef Blazek could easily have fired a verbal volley at Ballard—resulting in another couple of rounds from Ballard's gun.

It is possible that all of Ballard's shootings that day were done in self-defense. It would not have been an uncommon scenario in that era, when African Americans could easily get caught up in bitter arguments with whites, be forced to defend themselves from serious physical threats, and then when the dust settled, find themselves charged with what authorities called unprovoked murder. Adding some credence to this theory is the report of another shooting not far away on the same day that the Bohemians were shot. An African American named Henry Johnson, who served as the mail carrier to the Brazos Bottom—a post whose high visibility might have caused considerable irritation among white residents—was shot twice through the chest. Johnson survived the attack, and there were no reports of any arrests for the crime. The *Eagle*'s description of the assailant, "a young man," without reference to race, implies that he was white. Moreover, this was the same election that produced the murderous campaign in Anderson, over in neighboring Grimes County, which culminated in a shootout at the courthouse. The wounded sheriff, Garrett Scott, a Populist who had hired black deputies, was run out of town by vengeful members of the White Man's Union. Racial tensions throughout the region were running high at that point, and if they reached flood stage in Grimes County, they doubtless did so as well in the Brazos Bottom.[32]

In any case, Blazek was dead. His widow, a fellow Moravian named Josephine, was now left with the care of six children, all born in Texas and ranging from one to eleven years old. The death of her husband was a terrible blow from which Josephine Blazek never recovered. Five years later, in ill health and despair, she would commit suicide by hanging herself in the family's smokehouse in Wheelock, another small community in northern Brazos County where she moved after her husband's death. Meanwhile, back in Smetana, her neighbors were no less distraught. The Bohemian community in Smetana was enraged by Blazek's murder and Shramek's shooting. Many of Shramek's and Blazek's Bohemian neighbors had been in Texas for about twenty years, which apparently was more than enough time to learn what a respectable southern white community should do in response to black atrocity. Evidently these Bohemians had learned southern white folkways quite well and avidly embraced them, because rumors soon spread into Bryan that a mob was forming among the Bohemians, and as the *Eagle* phrased it, "there was strong talk of summary vengeance."[33]

But this time Nunn—now the veteran of at least two lynchings, and who so far had been completely unsuccessful at stopping mob violence—acted quickly. By midday on the day Blazek died, possibly before his body was cold, Nunn ordered his deputies to get Ballard out of town. As the *Eagle* reported the next morning, "In order to prevent any trouble, the negro, Ballard, was taken out of jail by officers and spirited away to some other point, probably Franklin." In fact, Nunn took him down to Houston himself. The sheriff "spirited his prisoner away and brought him secretly to this city," reported the *Galveston Daily News* a day later, "where he is now safely located in a cell at the county jail." As it turned out, Nunn was not overreacting. The rumors proved true: that night, a mob of angry Bohemians marched to the door of the Bryan jail, demanding Ballard. To convince them that Ballard had gone, the jailer threw open the doors and let some of the crowd in for a tour to "satisfy themselves the prisoner was not there."[34]

At this point the Bohemians seem to have given up, or at least they were now content to wait until Ballard's trial, which would take place during the next session of the district court in the spring. Here is where the Bohemian community ceased to act like typical white southerners in other lynching sagas, in which angry mobs would pursue the train with the escaping prisoner, or intercept him before he could get to a safer place, or even storm the doors of the receiving jail. Instead, the Bohemians seem to have retreated peacefully to Smetana, where in the meantime Jacob Shramek was slowly recuperating from his chest wounds.

Having become so suddenly visible to the whites of Bryan, at least one of the Bohemians decided to keep their community in the public eye. Beginning in January, a correspondent named "Illuminator" began to publish a weekly news column in the *Eagle,* entitled "Smetana," which was similar to other columns about various small communities in Brazos County that the newspaper printed from time to time. Perhaps "Illuminator" thought that a column focusing on Smetana would give the Bohemians a veneer of respectability and legitimacy accorded to other communities, such as Kurten and Benchley, an impression that might prove important in Ballard's upcoming trial when the Bohemians would seek retribution for Blazek's death. Significantly, any Bohemians that "Illuminator" mentioned in the news from Smetana were very rarely identified as Bohemians. Updates on Jacob Shramek's health, for example, listed the postmaster simply by name, without any mention of his nationality. As if to emphasize the upright and law-abiding nature of those who lived in Smetana, one of the first things "Illuminator" reported in the first column was that Christmas had been "a time of quietness and good behavior." Moreover, Shramek was "tending to business again." The next week was similar: "All is peace and quietness at the time of this writing." A few weeks later, Illuminator reported that Shramek was doing so well that he "has been devoting some of his time to boring wells." In late February a woman in Smetana gave birth to underweight triplets, none of whom weighed more than 5 pounds. As the woman and her husband were poor, "having lost all in the storm and boll weevil district last year," Illuminator asked the wider Brazos community for help. These were not worthless beggars, Illuminator emphasized: "They are respectable Bohemians of this county, and their friends requested me to send the above to you."[35]

Curiously, the weekly Smetana news bulletins stopped in March—just about the time Ballard was due back in town for his trial. Perhaps Illuminator concluded that the columns had accomplished their mission of demonstrating that "respectable Bohemians" lived in Smetana, something that could be particularly important for any potential jury members who might be weighing the relative worth—either in class or in whiteness values— of Ballard's victims. Possibly some of the Bohemians, or at least the newspaper correspondent, may have realized that if they were unable to pull off a southern-style version of summary justice on the night after Blazek died, they still might ensure Ballard's death if they could present themselves as bonafide white victims of black violence. And judging from the curious turn the court case seems to have taken, such strategy—if it was so intentional—may have paid off.

The Bryan judiciary did not treat Ballard's case as a simple murder trial. First of all, authorities decided to try Ballard in two separate trials, on different days about a week apart. The first charge Ballard faced was assault with intent to murder—that is, the wounding of Jacob Shramek. The trial was set for March 18, 1901, and it seemed fairly straightforward. The *Eagle* gave the trial one paragraph in the next day's newspaper, reporting that Ballard had pled guilty and had been sentenced to seven years in the state penitentiary. This was more or less a standard sentence in Brazos County for an African American man who had assaulted a white victim. In similar cases, blacks assaulting whites had been sentenced to five or six years in prison; if blacks had assaulted blacks, of course, the sentence was much less, ranging from a $25 fine to three years in prison. Perhaps the seven years in Ballard's case indicated higher sympathy for Shramek—a good sign for the Bohemians who were nervously waiting for the next phase of the case. They poured into town in "large numbers" when the second trial began, showing "marked interest in all the details of the case." [36]

In the next trial on March 25, Ballard again pled guilty, this time to murdering Josef Blazek. The case immediately went to the jury, but then things stalled. The jury could not come to a decision. As Ballard had already pled guilty, the discussion was most likely over the sentencing. In most cases involving the murder of a white man by a black man, the sentence would have been death, without question. But the Bryan jury deliberated. And it continued to deliberate. Finally, the court adjourned for the day, and the newspaper reported that "a verdict is anxiously awaited." The "Hotel Arrivals" list that was also published in the *Eagle* named the guests at Bryan's two hotels. Among others staying at the Central Hotel were the "Bob Ballard jury," indicating that jury members had been sequestered until they could make up their minds what to do with the killer of Josef Blazek.

As it turned out, the jury foreman was Samuel Levy, the Jewish furniture merchant. Levy announced the jury's decision the next morning, on March 26. The *Eagle* blared the news the following day: "Bob Ballard To Hang: Will Expiate the Crime of Wanton Murder Upon the Gallows." The story began: "All will remember with horror the shooting of Jacob Shramek and especially the wanton killing of a defenseless Bohemian by a desperate negro near Smetana in this county some months ago." [37]

It is interesting to note that after the first stories in November, Blazek had become anonymous by the time of Ballard's trial, becoming an unnamed "defenseless Bohemian," while Shramek, the postmaster and Democratic political insider, retained his identity. Until Ballard was hanged a year

Central Hotel, Bryan. Around 1915 electric trolley cars provided transportation between Bryan and College Station. To the far right is the Central Hotel, where the jury for the Bob Ballard murder trial was sequestered while deliberating Ballard's sentence. The courthouse tower can seen in the background to the left. Photo courtesy Carnegie Center of Brazos Valley History

later, subsequent news stories about the case repeated those designations, indicating a certain measure of ambivalence about the social status of Bohemians. Shramek, who merely had been wounded and was up boring wells a few months later, was always named, while Blazek, the murder victim, became simply "another Bohemian."

The Bohemians who attended the trial were ecstatic when the verdict was announced, and they immediately sent a card of thanks to the jury and other authorities. The card, printed in the *Eagle* the next day, read as follows:

> We, the undersigned citizens of Brazos County, desire to express our heartfelt thanks to the jury, the officers and citizens who aided in bringing to conviction Bob Ballard; and especially do we desire to thank the jury who have beyond a doubt discharged their whole duty. (Signed) Jacob Shramek, Sam Luther, J. H. Wehrman and others.

It was clear from the phrasing just what the Bohemians were so grateful for: that the jury had done its "whole duty" by assessing the death penalty. Judging from the jury's delay and the Bohemian response, there undoubtedly had been some question whether Ballard would get death, life in prison, or even a lesser sentence of ten years in prison. The choice had enormous implications. Obviously it affected Ballard's life, but it would also determine the social ranking—and racial status—of Ballard's victims. Simply put, blacks who murdered blacks in Brazos County at the turn of the twentieth century never received the death penalty. Not even the killer of the respected African American policeman, Levi Neal, was sentenced to hang. Occasionally, as in the case of Neal's murderer, they were given life in prison if the black victim was deemed sufficiently respectable or vulnerable, but usually the sentences ranged from five to ten years.

If Ballard were given anything less than the death penalty, it would mean that the Brazos County jury—composed of certifiably white men, including the Jewish merchant Samuel Levy—considered the Bohemians to be less than white, somewhere above black but not quite white. A lesser sentence than death would convey considerably less honor, dignity, or worth than what would be accorded to the county's southern-born whites, and it would reinforce the in-between status that immigrants such as the Bohemians were trying so hard to overcome.

There is some evidence that the jury decided at first to award Ballard life imprisonment instead of death, but reversed its decision under pressure from a judge and others involved in the case. Evidence suggests that the judge refused to accept the initial verdict of life imprisonment and insisted that the jury hand down a death sentence. Several decades later, in the early 1930s, a University of Texas graduate student named Elmer Grady Marshall was researching the history of Brazos County for a master's thesis. He spent time talking with courthouse old-timers about lynchings of African Americans that had taken place in the county. One of Marshall's sources told him about a murder trial of a black man in which the outcome was rigged so that the man would hang. The trial may well have been Ballard's, although there was a curious change in the details of the 1930s story. As Marshall reported:

> A number of Negroes have been hanged legally; but, as in the case of mobs, their legal rights were not always observed. On one occasion a Negro was tried for murdering an Italian. Because of the intense dislike of Italians by the jury, the Negro was given life in the penitentiary instead of the usual death penalty. But the judge and prosecuting attorney had determined to hang the Negro. The sheriff, by some means, got possession of the verdict before the jury reported; and took it to the judge. The judge of the criminal court of appeals was in the courtroom, and his advice was sought. His methods of handling such cases were dictatorial. He said to the sheriff: "You go and tell the jury that the court cannot accept this verdict." The jury, after making an ineffectual attempt to erase its first decision, wrote one assessing the death penalty.[38]

Marshall then added the source of his information in a footnote:

> This story was given to the writer by a man who was a county official at the time of the trial. He requested that his name not be mentioned in connection

with the case. The writer had read the verdict. The words showing the first
decision of the jury are legible.

What gives this story some credence is the existence of the jury verdict of
Ballard's trial in the J. W. Batts Papers, which are archived in the Cushing
Library of Texas A&M University. Batts was the Brazos County district
clerk at the time of Ballard's trial and thus possibly was the "county official"
who talked to Marshall. For some unknown reason, Batts kept Ballard's verdict document himself instead of filing it in the courthouse, and it remained
among his personal papers. Most curious of all is the handwritten decision,
penned by Samuel Levy, which clearly shows an erasure and change. The decision now reads, "We the jury find the defendant guilty of murder in the first
degree and assess his punishment at death." However, just barely discernible
beneath the last phrase of the sentence is another phrase. It is very faded and
partially erased, but the words tentatively can be made out: " . . . and assess
his punishment by confinement in the State penitentiary for life." [39]

It is impossible to determine whether the mysterious change that was
made on Ballard's verdict is the same change referred to in the courthouse
story that Marshall heard more than thirty years later. But it likely is the
same, because there are no records of other executions happening at this
time, and Ballard's verdict document matches the description in Marshall's
story. If so, it makes an already interesting case even more intriguing. It
would show a considerable difference of opinion between members of the
jury and court officials over the severity of Ballard's crime. The jury, made
up of ordinary white citizens led by a Jewish merchant, may have regarded
the Bohemians with ambivalence and given Ballard the benefit of the
doubt—a doubt that was already evident by the length of their delibera-
tions. However, the judicial authorities, especially the visiting appeals judge
who was not part of the Bryan community, would have focused primarily
on Ballard. And what white authorities saw was a black repeat offender,
whose crimes had grown increasingly more violent, culminating in one of
the worst offenses a black could commit in the Jim Crow South: the attempted murder of a respected white public official. Moreover, Ballard was
also the son of a black political leader who had had the temerity to run for
office and win repeatedly, and was even then wielding public authority by
virtue of his role as county commissioner. Surely there could be no better
way of putting the commissioner in his place than by hanging his son.

The courthouse officials may also have focused on the Bohemian community and remembered the fierce anger that nearly led to another lynch-

ing. They may well have wanted to avoid community outrage—or at least the outrage of the Bohemian community—and the possibility of another jailhouse break-in by making sure that Ballard would die. According to Marshall's account, it was the sheriff who brought word of the jury's initial verdict to the judge. That sheriff, of course, was Sheriff Nunn, a man charged with keeping the peace but who already had been unable to prevent two lynchings in Bryan. Nunn clearly feared a third lynching, this time by the Bohemians. After all, they had already stormed the jail once before and might have lynched Ballard at that point if Nunn had not kept one step ahead of the mob by spiriting Ballard out of town. Nunn may have thought he could forestall another outbreak of mob violence by getting the verdict of life imprisonment changed to a death sentence. Thus, Ballard's execution bore the hallmarks of what historians term "legal lynching": an execution held "to prevent a lynching or to prevent further mob outbreaks after a lynching." As historian George C. Wright discovered in Kentucky, "countless numbers of black men were tried in hostile environments with judges and juries convinced of their guilt before hearing any evidence. . . . It is not difficult to imagine what would have happened to the members of the jury if they had returned a verdict of not guilty or had called for leniency."[40]

As for the jury in this case, Marshall's story would also demonstrate that Samuel Levy, whose own in-between status as a southern Jew was nearly as unresolved as that of the Bohemians and Italians, quickly backed down in the face of pressure from the courthouse establishment. As a member of the jury, and especially as its foreman, Levy evidently had far higher status than Bohemians and Italians, whose names at this point were not appearing on any jury lists. Jews of Bryan served on juries, held public office, and enjoyed favorable notice in the newspaper, all of which the southern and eastern Europeans were years away from achieving. But Levy was nonetheless a racial outsider. As a Jew and as a merchant, he would have been particularly dependent on the approval of Bryan's white elites. He was in no position to contest such a highly racialized judgment. And like many other Jews across the South, he may not even have felt any desire to challenge the authority of the town's white elite. It is impossible to know whether Levy's initial assessment of life imprisonment for Bob Ballard reflected an ambivalent view of the whiteness of Ballard's Bohemian victim or Levy's reluctance to impose a death sentence on a black man for a crime in which the circumstances may have been considerably more complex than what the newspaper presented.

The story is interesting on still another level. It shows a singular twist in the public memory of the case. Three decades later, Italians had been substituted for Bohemians in the courthouse story. The reason for the leniency of the life sentence, according to courthouse gossip, was that this ethnic group was so profoundly disliked. The Bohemians had been erased from the 1930s anecdote because by then they were nearly assimilated into the white culture of Brazos County. By the 1930s courthouse regulars could not remember that the Bohemians had once been outsiders, racially "in between," whose status was held in the balance by a white jury with a Jewish foreman. What lingered instead was the indeterminate status of another in-between group whose whiteness took somewhat longer to establish—that is, the Italians. Thus the Ballard story highlights the intricate racial hierarchy at play in Brazos County at the dawn of the twentieth century, wherein Jews, Italians, and Bohemians dwelled in a varying but indeterminate racial twilight. Each community was forced to struggle, sometimes at the others' expense, to affirm the possession of white skin.

Whatever took place in the jury room, the final decision was death. Ballard was led back to his jail cell to wait for the official sentencing, which by law could not take place until at least thirty days after the jury's decision. The next time the district court would meet would be in the fall, some six or seven months away. So Ballard had to wait in jail for the official sentence of death as well as for an execution date. In April he appealed the jury's decision, but the Texas Court of Criminal Appeals summarily affirmed the death sentence because Ballard had offered the court no evidence it could use to reverse the decision or even to remand the case for a new trial. "An appeal record in a criminal case containing no statement of facts and no motion for a new trial presents nothing for review, no exceptions having been reserved during the trial," read the court decision. It is doubtful that Ballard's lawyer even attended the appeal hearing, as no defense counsel was listed in the decision.[41]

Meanwhile, the Bohemians made no move to lynch him, as they were now well satisfied with the jury's verdict and evidently trusted the state to carry out the vengeance they had so eagerly sought. For his part, Dennis Ballard resumed his duties as county commissioner. In May county business included examining Sheriff Nunn's bill for $353.40 for feeding prisoners in the jail—which the court of commissioners, including Ballard, approved. Spring passed, and summer arrived. Dennis Ballard worked as hard as ever on his cotton farm, even without the occasional help of his son Bob. In late July Dennis Ballard ended up in a three-way tie for the first bale of cotton, having rushed to town so fast that none of the regular gins were ready to process the cotton. The three bales had to be taken over to the oil mill ginnery, which made sudden arrangements to "steam up" and begin the processing. The other two would-be first balers—one white, one black—were from Burleson County.[42]

By July Bob Ballard had been in the Bryan jail for eight months, and he was restless. One of his jailmates was an African American railroad section hand named Arthur Carter, who had been arrested for murdering another black railroad worker a few weeks before Ballard's violent encounter with the Bohemians. The two of them shared a cell, and they did not get along. A fight ensued, and Ballard got the worst of it, having been "considerably beaten about the head and face by Arthur Carter, who used the front leg of a chair." Carter claimed that Ballard had tried to kill him with a piece of iron and a wire handle. Jailers removed the weapons and other loose chains in the room and separated the men. Carter's trial took place in September, and the jury found him guilty of murder. In a typical sentence for murdering another black man, Carter was sent to prison for ten years.[43]

Two weeks later, District Court judge J. C. Scott officially sentenced Ballard to hang and set the execution date for Friday, November 22. With about six weeks left to live, Ballard apparently foreswore his violent ways and got religion. He met frequently with visiting pastors and read his Bible. People passing by the jail could hear his prayers and moans. Meanwhile, other residents of Bryan were following predictable seasonal routines, as well as witnessing new changes. While Ballard waited in jail for his execution, schools reopened and wealthy families returned from summer vacations. The town's population was growing: as schools opened again, officials reported an enrollment nearing 1,000 pupils, a 15 percent increase over last year's count. The enrollment was nearly evenly divided between white and black, though white students had a slight edge in numbers. The wealthier white students were drifting slowly back to school as their families returned to Texas. "The Bryan people are coming home from the north, east, south and west, where they have been spending the summer," noted the *Eagle*. "Mexico, Colorado, California, the Buffalo exposition, Niagara Falls and Canada were the principal attractions for those who went away for the heated term. . . . It is probable no town in the state the size of Bryan contributed so large a number of visitors to the Buffalo exposition."[44]

Some of the traveling Bryanites may have been on hand in Buffalo at the Pan-American Exposition when the anarchist Leon Czolgosz, a son of Polish immigrants, assassinated President William McKinley there in September. Like millions of others across the nation, Bryan residents held a mass meeting and then a memorial service at the opera house for the fallen president, with sermons and choirs and numerous speeches—some of which called for immigration restriction—while businesses closed and schools were dismissed.[45]

One of those in Bryan who had attended the Buffalo Exposition was a French-born dry goods merchant named M. Bonneville, who had been scouting out the latest styles and new trends, not only in fabric and clothing styles but also in transportation technology. In October his big purchase arrived by train: Bryan's very first automobile, a $750 steam-powered red Oldsmobile. Although the *Eagle* reported the new machine "shows up well when running," it could not have run very far or very well out of town. Bryan's Main Street was covered by then in a layer of crushed rock, but no other roads outside of town showed the remotest hint of any paving, and they would remain unpaved until the late 1920s. Nonetheless, Bonneville's purchase clearly was a harbinger of what was to come, and evidently others soon followed his lead. Five years later the city council felt obliged to institute an 8-mile-per-hour speed limit.[46]

The same month that Bonneville's new "Locomobile," as locals called it, arrived, the Ursuline sisters dedicated the "magnificent edifices" of their new convent and girls' school, which fronted what would soon be Ursuline Avenue, formerly known as the Bethel Road. The *Eagle* apparently had lost none of its earlier enthusiasm for the new institution, and seemed downright awed by the dedication rituals: "The dim religious light of the candles on the chapel altar, the sweet and soulful music, and the stately dignity of the ceremonies made a scene singularly impressive."[47]

October turned into November, and finally the day of Bob Ballard's execution arrived. It was "the first legal execution for many years in Brazos County." Ostensibly it was a private execution, but a crowd including five physicians, county officers, several undertakers, a selected number of unnamed citizens—possibly including some Bohemians—and five African American pastors were allowed to attend. Ballard seemed to be at peace with his fate. He told someone he was not afraid to die because "God had saved his soul and he was ready and willing to go." He was led from the jail without handcuffs, carrying his Bible. Then he mounted the steps of the scaffold where the black cap was put over his head and the rope around his neck. Either because he weighed so little or because the drop was too short, Ballard's neck was not broken when he fell through the trapdoor. And so he strangled. It took him thirteen minutes to die, though "with very few struggles," as the *Eagle* reported. The five physicians pronounced him dead. The undertakers placed his body in a coffin. In a last poignant detail, the *San*

In 1901 the Ursuline nuns in Galveston relocated their convent and school to Bryan after the hurricane of 1900 devastated their property. Their new central building, Villa Maria, was built just to the east of downtown and was heralded as a "magnificent edifice" by the *Eagle.* Photo courtesy Carnegie Center of Brazos Valley History

Antonio Express reported that his body was turned over to his father, Dennis Ballard, who took his son's remains to the Brazos Bottom for burial.[48]

Dennis Ballard remained on the county commissioners' court, taking care of county business as if he had the authority and power of a white man, though what it cost him to maintain such a posture can only be guessed. Three months later, in February 1902, Sheriff Nunn presented the commissioners with another jail bill, this time "for expenses incurred in hanging Bob Ballard." The commissioners—all of them—approved the bill. In July the cotton harvest was under way again, but this time Ballard was too slow to make first bale. He was beaten by a black sharecropper living nearby, Charles Odum. Ballard brought his bale in about a week later and tied for second place with another farmer. Curiously, the newspaper this time did not mention that Ballard was "colored," as it nearly always did in reference to African American newsmakers.[49]

That fall the indefatigable Ballard ran again for the commissioner's seat, and again he won. But this was to be Ballard's last term on the commissioners' court. That same year the Texas state legislature submitted to the Texas electorate a constitutional amendment that would institute a poll tax requirement for voting. It passed by a two-to-one margin in the state and by a similar margin in Brazos County, though significantly, it failed in the Brazos Bottom precincts. The following year the state legislature passed another election law requiring the poll tax to be paid between October and February preceding an election. The hope was that poor African Americans and Mexicans would not be able to pay so far in advance or would lose their receipts by election time. In Brazos County, as elsewhere in the state, the tactic worked extremely well. The county electorate was cut down to less than half of what it had been in previous years. The Brazos County tax collector reported in February 1903 that only 1,450 county residents had paid their poll tax, compared to a normal voting population of 3,500. It is fair to assume that of those who were able to pay and vote, the overwhelming majority were white, and they were not supporters of Dennis Ballard. For the next eight decades or so Brazos County became overwhelmingly Democratic, and all the rebellious political movements and Republican surges that had so vexed Democratic leaders in the late nineteenth century were finally and irrevocably squelched.[50]

In 1904 J. J. Cahill, the Texas-born son of Irish parents, was elected to the Brazos County Court of Commissioners from the Brazos Bottom. As described in chapter 4, Cahill had lived in the area since 1871. He had moved there when the area was still largely populated by African Americans, long before crowds of Czechs and Italians decided to settle there. Now these newcomers had moved onto land around him, surrounding him on all sides, and where he lived was now known as Smetana. Cahill lived about eight houses down from Jacob Shramek. By 1904 Cahill was about thirty-six years old and was married to a woman who was an Illinois-born daughter of Austrian parents. His Irish mother, locally known as "Grandmother Cahill," lived next door to him and was evidently a well-respected member of the community, as she had been mentioned with some concern by Illuminator in a "Smetana" column in the *Eagle* when she fell ill. J. J. Cahill served only one term, and was followed by a Texas-born son of German parents, J. C. Blume, who lived just outside the Smetana area, closer to Bryan. Blume served two terms, and was followed in turn by Cahill, and then by several Italians from Mudville.[51]

A final note of irony: in 1928, Fred A. Wehrman—the son of J. H Wehrman, who was Josef Blazek's brother-in-law and who had signed the thank-you note for the Bryan jury after Bob Ballard's death sentence—was elected the county commissioner for the Brazos Bottom. Fred Wehrman was Josef Blazek's nephew, and now occupied the commissioner's seat once held by the father of his uncle's killer. By the early twentieth century, a virtual parade of the children of European immigrants served as the Bottom's representatives in the Brazos County government. First Irish, then German, then Italian, and finally a Bohemian commissioner sat where Dennis Ballard had once served as the lone African American voice in local government.[52]

The Ballard era was over. One might argue that the prelude to its demise was the painful execution of a troubled African American man who could not live in peace in a white-dominated society. Bob Ballard had impotently vented his rage on the immigrant community that would one day supplant his father. Whatever had actually happened that day in the Smetana saloon, his crime and subsequent death sentence had helped to establish the whiteness of one of the immigrant communities, the Bohemians. And in the process, Ballard ironically had helped to end the visibility and the political strength of Brazos County's black community, even as he helped to elevate the Bohemians.

Chapter 6

CONCLUSION

*Texas House Speaker Gus Mutscher joined local government and busi-
ness leaders in expressing sorrow at the loss of Brazos A. Varisco, wealthy
Brazos County farmer and real estate investor, who died Saturday in a
Houston hospital. . . . District Judge W. C. Davis called Varisco "one of
the men who made this community. I don't know anyone who did more
for Bryan, College Station or Brazos County."*

BRYAN DAILY EAGLE, 26 July 1970

William Koppe, a young German immigrant, arrived in Bryan in 1868
with little to commend himself except a metalworking skill. But the town
was exploding with new businesses and booming with new growth, all of
it spawned by the arrival the year before of the Houston & Texas Central Railroad. Koppe quickly found a job with a man named Tom Burt,
who ran a hardware store. Within a few years, Koppe had managed to save
enough money to buy the business and run it himself. Koppe did so well
that he was able to invest further in a cotton plantation in the Brazos Bottom, where he also proved successful. Part of his success lay in his use of
black convict labor, which saved considerable expense in labor and enabled
him to raise the cotton that generated still more wealth, enough to build a
"handsome, three story building on Main Street" for his hardware business,
"which grew to mammoth proportions and required the services of a small
army of salesmen."[1]

But by 1895 he decided to give his full attention to what was now 7,000
acres of farmland along the Brazos River. He sold out to another up-and-
coming merchant, J. Allen Myers, the Republican postmaster and former
county clerk. Myers also did well, selling an assortment of plows, farm
tools, household items, and dry goods. But then in 1911 Myers, too, decided
he had had enough of the retail life, and sold the business—by then housed
in a new, sturdy, brick three-story building—for the tidy sum of $65,000.

J. Allen Myers's hardware store stood prominently on Main Street in Bryan, next to the Carnegie Library. Myers eventually sold his business to John K. Parker and John E. Astin, who renamed it Parker-Astin Hardware and moved it to a different location in town. Courtesy Carnegie Center of Brazos Valley History

The buyers were the scions of two of Bryan's most elite white families, the Parkers and the Astins, whose wealth also had been generated by cotton plantations in the Brazos Bottom. John K. Parker and John E. Astin bestowed their own monikers on the business, and it became known ever after as the Parker-Astin store. Eventually, it became the best known and most enduring establishment in Bryan, selling everything from wedding china to greeting cards to household appliances, and of course, hardware as well.[2]

Meanwhile, some of the Italians who had settled along the Brazos River west of Bryan and on the farmland east of town also were doing very well for themselves. One of these newcomers was a man named Brazos Varisco. He had arrived in Brazos County in 1907 as a five-year-old named Biaggio. His Italian nickname Brazi sounded so much like the name of the nearby river that friends began calling him Brazos, which he eventually adopted as his official name on his naturalization certificate in 1929. Thanks to the profits earned from his family's Brazos Bottom cotton fields, Varisco began acquiring valuable property in the 1930s, and by the 1940s his prosperity and business acumen qualified him to become the president of the Bryan Chamber of Commerce. The organization had begun in 1900 as the Bryan Business League, with membership restricted to "white male citizens of Bryan, of good moral character." Significantly, at that time no Italians were members, although they were among the city's successful businessmen.

By the time he died, Varisco was not only the city's most successful businessman, he also owned a substantial portion of the city itself. His holdings amounted to more than 3,000 acres of cotton-producing land in the Mudville area, a lumber company, two cotton gins, an airfield complete with aircraft, and substantial property in downtown Bryan that included the city's only high-rise retail and office building, known simply as the Varisco Building.[3]

One of Brazos Varisco's last acquisitions before he died in 1970 was the Parker-Astin store. Varisco kept the Parker-Astin name, probably because of its cachet. By the time he bought the store, most members of the Parker and Astin families were gone from Brazos County, but the family names were still held in high esteem and the store reflected the families' elite reputation. Varisco bought the store in 1966, and in some respects it was the culmination of a long climb from obscurity to high eminence. Although the purchase would prove to be a profitable transaction of enduring value, it also had profound symbolic value that could not have been lost on Varisco and his fellow Italian-born residents of Brazos County. It signified that Varisco, once an impoverished Sicilian newcomer whose family had arrived in Brazos County shortly after the turn of the century with little to call its own, was now among the county's most successful and prosperous citizens. Once of doubtful and ambiguous racial classification, Varisco was now at the helm of one of the city's most venerable businesses.

Beginning in the 1990s, Brazos Varisco's heirs began to sell off the various Varisco properties one by one. None of his descendants now lives in Brazos County. Instead, they are scattered in Houston and San Antonio, in Colorado and California, pursuing other interests and careers. None had any interest in maintaining the real estate empire that Brazos Varisco had built. One of the last properties to go was the Varisco Building, still the city's only high-rise office building, which stood as a bold symbol of its builder's prominence. The very last piece of Varisco's empire to be sold was the Parker-Astin store. The Parker-Astin store had survived into the twenty-first century. In 2005 the store changed hands once again. At the time of this writing, the current owners are Zane Anderson and Fred Forgey, developers specializing in historic buildings in Bryan. Many of Bryan's nineteenth-century buildings have been bought up in recent years, and redevelopment of the downtown has taken on vigorous new life, echoing, if faintly, the boom years of the city's birth. Like previous owners of the Parker-Astin store, neither of the current proprietors is native to Brazos County. And like Brazos Varisco, Anderson and Forgey retained the Parker-Astin name, recognizing the value of its lingering association with "Old Bryan," the prestigious and eminently respectable white southern families who can trace their lineage back many generations in Bryan's history.[4]

Occasional newspaper feature stories about the store, as well as the store's own publicity, describe it as beginning in 1911 with the investment of Parker and Astin. But its actual origins go back much further, to the very dawn of Bryan. The twists and turns of the store's history reflect many elements of Brazos County's history, including the boom and growth of Bryan as a new railroad town and trading center after the Civil War, the arrival and successful assimilation of German immigrants, the emergence of the Brazos Bottom as the county's cotton-producing region, the racial oppression and subjugation that convict labor signified, and now even the present-day resurgence of commercial life in downtown Bryan. The history of the store also reflects the ability of all manner of outsiders—a German immigrant, a Republican officeholder, an Italian sharecropper's son—to achieve the same status as wealthy, southern-born whites. It signifies that alien outsiders of nearly any sort could, and did, become respectable white citizens. The meteoric rise of the late owner of the store, Brazos Varisco, as well as of the immigrant community he represented, suggests that Brazos County was a place where nearly anyone, regardless of national origin, native language, or political affiliation, could thrive with enough initiative, hard work, and persistence.

Nearly anyone—but not quite everyone. Missing from the parade of the hardware store's owners were African Americans, who instead provided the labor that generated a substantial portion of the wealth necessary for the store's expansion and long-term success. African Americans were numbered among Bryan's business owners, but they were not many, and their businesses tended to involve manual labor, such as wagon hauling and laundry. There were black saloon keepers, barbers, schoolteachers, physicians, and even a newspaper publisher, but hired laborers and sharecroppers made up the dominant class of African American workers. Most lived in rural parts of the county, especially the Brazos Bottom, where convict labor camps and cotton plantations were located.[5]

The "Bottom," as locals still call it today, also reflects much of the county's history, especially the history of a black community that was once so populous and so strong politically that it could control the outcome of numerous county elections in the late nineteenth century. By the early twentieth century such strength had been vitiated, as evidenced by the removal from office of a long-standing county commissioner, the prosperous African

American farmer, Dennis Ballard. Much of the loss of political strength
was due to new state election laws that effectively disenfranchised most of
the county's black voters. But in Ballard's case, his loss was far deeper, more
painful, and personal. Before he lost his political office, he lost his only
child, a son, through racial confrontation, violence, and death.[6]

Violence, too, is an integral part of the county's history, as it was for
many communities across the South. While some of that violence consisted
of personal disputes and family feuds, a significant portion of it was racial.
Brazos County lies nearly dead center in the region of Texas in which the
state's heaviest concentration of lynchings took place: the counties along
the Brazos River from Waco to the Gulf of Mexico. Between the 1870s
and the 1930s, at least sixteen black men and youths—but probably many
more—lost their lives to lynch mobs in Brazos County. Such brutal deaths
provided an object lesson about white supremacy, and the inestimable value
of white skin compared to black. Among the last recorded lynchings in Brazos County were two that took place in 1922 and 1930, and originated in
the same areas as earlier episodes: Smetana, a community of Czechs in the
western section of the county, and Benchley, a historically Irish neighborhood north of Bryan.[7]

The 1922 lynching took place near Bryan, only a few weeks after the
gruesome burning of three black men in Kirven, not far away to the east in
Freestone County. Overall, it was a bad year for lynchings in Texas. The Ku
Klux Klan had revived, membership was soaring, and Klan chapters were
springing up in towns across Texas, including one in Brazos County. Across
the state, at least seventeen black and Hispanic men were hanged, shot, and
burned by mobs that year. Most of the lynch victims had been accused of
rape or murder, but what happened in Bryan showed that a man could be
killed for much less. On May 22 Colbert Wilson, an African American who
lived along Smetana Road, was whipped to death "by unmasked men" for
various offenses, including shooting a cow belonging to Roger Q. Astin, a
member of the wealthy Astin clan. Wilson had been jailed briefly on charges
of killing the cow, but he had been released because of insufficient evidence
against him. Wilson lived long enough after the whipping to tell police his
assailants had charged him with a long list of related offenses, including
shooting horses, poisoning hogs, burning barns, and even tearing up a pea
patch. The offenses apparently had been committed in the Smetana area, although he was found lying in a pasture near the Fin-Feather Lake in Bryan.
The *Eagle* reported that Wilson told police before he died that he could not

identify those who had attacked him, and no one was ever charged with his murder.[8]

Another lynching that had faint echoes of the 1897 episode took place in late June 1930, when a married woman in the Benchley area, Mrs. Henry Bowman, fled screaming from her house, claiming that a black man who worked for her husband had tried to attack her. The man was identified in the newspaper only as "Roan." Another account, published in Arthur Raper's classic 1933 study, *The Tragedy of Lynching,* listed him as Will Roan. He apparently was mentally disabled, and like countless African Americans a half-century earlier, he had moved to Brazos County from Louisiana some years earlier to work as a farm laborer. It was not clear how long he had been working for the Bowman family. Roan was "of the creole type with fair skin and light hair," and was considered by other black workers in the area to be a peaceful man who kept largely to himself. Other whites, including Brazos County sheriff Jim Reed, had a markedly different view. To them, he was "generally irresponsible." According to Raper's account, Roan's employer had beaten him severely the day before the alleged attack because Roan supposedly had been "sassy" with Mrs. Bowman. Mr. Bowman had taken Roan to his barn on Sunday, June 16, to strip him and whip him with a wet rope. The next afternoon Roan allegedly attacked Mrs. Bowman. Sheriff Reed refused to intervene at that point, apparently believing "that it was the white man's business to settle the affair with his hired hand." A later history of law enforcement in Brazos County acknowledged that Reed had a reputation of being "tough on blacks," and it is possible that Reed purposefully looked the other way in order to allow local whites "to settle the affair."[9]

The *Eagle* reported, "As quickly as word of the attempted attack spread through the community, a posse was formed and a search for the negro was made." Rumors had it that Roan had been caught and was being held on a farm in the Benchley area. Soon after, he was discovered lying dead in a nearby pasture in Benchley by two men who said they had happened to be out hunting, although they also gave other stories to explain their presence in the area. One of the discoverers had the very Irish name of John O'Conner. Law enforcement officials who were called to the scene told the newspaper they believed Roan had been taken from the farm to the field, and there shot dead "at the hands of persons unknown." Raper, quoting an unnamed black newspaper, wrote that Roan was also "found horribly mutilated." As the *Eagle* phrased it, it was a clear case of "vengeance at the hands of a posse of citizens of the Benchley area."

Raper, however, reported that African Americans in the area saw the incident as a clear case of white oppression: "They think rather that he and his employer got into some personal altercation and that the charge of attempted rape was trumped up as an excuse for getting rid of him." Perhaps it was also not coincidental that Roan died on the day before Juneteenth, and that the incident was reported in the newspaper on Juneteenth itself. Juneteenth—June 19—is the anniversary of the day Gen. Gordon Granger arrived in Galveston in 1865 to announce that the slaves in Texas were free. African Americans in Brazos County often celebrated the day with picnics and festivities, but in 1930, Juneteenth celebrations in Brazos County surely must have been dampened by the news of yet another lynching.[10]

These two incidents in 1922 and 1930 suggest the involvement in both cases of European immigrants—or more likely, their descendants. In the 1922 case the black victim, Colbert Wilson, lived in Smetana. In the 1930 episode Will Roan lived in Benchley and his body was "discovered" by a white man with an Irish-sounding name. But by the 1920s and 1930s, such identity in Brazos County had ceased to matter very greatly, and in neither account was there any mention of ethnicity among the aggrieved parties, or any reference to the immigrant character of the communities where the lynchings took place. The only identity that mattered then was that of the lynching victims, who were in both cases described as "Negro" men. No mention was made of the racial identity of anyone else involved in the stories, because the assumption was that they were all white.

The episodes were in marked contrast to those that occurred at the turn of the twentieth century, when Smetana was well known as a Bohemian settlement, and Benchley still had lingering associations with Irish settlers and railroad workers. As earlier chapters have shown, the racial status of many of the residents in these communities was highly ambiguous. Germans had been readily accepted in Brazos County as white people, but for others—including the Italians, the Irish, and the Bohemians—a question mark hung over their classification. The Bryan city sexton, for example, found himself adding new designations in the mid-1890s when he listed burials in the city cemetery. In addition to "white" and "colored," new arrivals in the cemetery were also "Italian" or "Bohemian," indicating they were neither "colored" nor "white," but somewhere "in between." As the nineteenth century drew to a close, Brazos County's whites struggled to determine just how to fit these newcomers into a racial hierarchy that had only two categories, black and white.

In the end, the immigrants settled the question themselves, by do-

ing what southern white people did, and in some ways, by doing it better. First of all, they bought property, and lots of it. By 1920, 30 percent
of the county's white farm owners were foreign-born, although they made
up only about 13 percent of the white population. They also topped native-
born whites when it came to the rate of farm ownership: more than half
(56 percent) of foreign-born farmers owned their land, compared to less
than half (49 percent) of native-born white farmers. Blacks were far below,
on the bottom tier with an 18 percent ownership rate. Investigators who visited the county for a U.S. congressional commission on immigration noted
that the Italians in particular had a reputation of being more productive
than other local farmers: "It is said that the Italians make a better crop than
many of the Americans or the Bohemians." But the Bohemians built tidier
looking farm buildings and homes that "seem to be better maintained than
those owned by the Italians." [11]

As more and more of the immigrants became naturalized citizens, they
and their children also began to exercise political rights by voting and holding office—activities that by the early twentieth century had become too
difficult and risky for the majority of the county's African Americans. By
then, political action was largely an activity reserved for whites. Before the
turn of the twentieth century, Dennis Ballard had represented Justice Precinct Number Five, an area of the county that once had a black majority, on
the county court of commissioners for nine two-year terms. But beginning
in 1904, he was replaced by a series of men whose parents had been Irish,
Italian, and Bohemian immigrants, whose votes filled the vacuum left by
the eroded black electorate. After Bob Ballard shot to death Joe Blazek,
Blazek's nephew went on to occupy Dennis Ballard's seat as county commissioner. And many, many years later, one of Blazek's direct descendants
achieved substantial political rank in Bryan: in 2004 Ernie Wentrcek,
Blazek's great-great-grandson, was elected mayor.

But effective as they were for establishing whiteness, property ownership
and voting took some time to achieve. There was a faster way, readily available, that had been in use since the county began as a white settlement in
the 1820s. That way was racial oppression. In three cases—a triple lynching
in 1896, a lynching on Bryan's Main Street in 1897, and a "legal lynching" in
1901—European immigrants were caught up in events that resulted in the
deaths of five black men. The first case began with an Italian who needed to
claim the identity of a frail and vulnerable white woman in order to get the
justice she sought in court. She may also have needed to vindicate herself
in the eyes of white residents of Bryan, who viewed her as less than white

because she was Italian, and who may have suspected her of engaging in an interracial affair. The second episode involved a nameless Irishman whose willingness to provide the testimony that a lynch mob craved helped to establish or solidify white credentials for other Irish living in Brazos County. The last incident caught up a group of Bohemians who recognized that their white identity depended on the public execution of their black assailant. In none of these cases was whiteness an explicitly articulated issue, but race nonetheless lay at the heart of all three episodes. European immigrants found themselves living in the midst of an intractable southern racial order in which privilege and power depended on the publicly acknowledged color of one's skin. Racial identity and the privileges of whiteness go far to explain the presence of these immigrants in each of the three stories. Historian Grace Elizabeth Hale has argued that violence—particularly against black men—was "a defining characteristic of whiteness" in the South. This was no less true in Brazos County, where violence helped to solve the puzzle of race and identity for thousands of foreign-born.[12]

It is worth noting the eventual outcome of the Italians' struggle to achieve the same status as the county's native-born whites. Of the three groups examined here—the Italians, the Irish, and the Bohemians—the Italians had the greatest difficulty in resolving their in-between racial status, and had to wait the longest to establish their whiteness. The triple lynching of 1896 may have vindicated Fannie Palazzo as a white woman, at least for that moment, but it would be some decades before the rest of the Italians in Brazos County would be fully accepted as white citizens.

After the lynching, Fannie Palazzo continued to farm her land east of Bryan and raise her children alone for at least the next fourteen years. Her husband, Charles Palazzo, evidently continued to suffer mental problems for some time, and he never lived in Brazos County again. The 1910 census listed him as an inmate in the State Lunatic Asylum in Austin, and he died that June, soon after the census was taken. His body was brought back to Bryan and buried in the Catholic cemetery, on the side reserved for Italians, an indication itself that ethnicity—and racial ambiguity—still mattered even in death. The other side of the cemetery was reserved for Czechs, Germans, Irish, and other Catholics.

Some time after Charles's death, Fannie Palazzo moved to Houston to live with her daughter, and she eventually died in Houston, where she is buried. Meanwhile, Joe Palazzo, Charles's brother, also continued to farm well into the twentieth century, prospering on his large acreage and eventually forsaking cotton farming for truck vegetables and cattle raising, like others in the area. He had the distinction of acquiring the first telephone in the neighborhood, making his home a sort of communications center for other Italians in that part of the county and further raising his status as a neighborhood leader. He died in 1923 and was buried near his younger brother. Fannie's son, also named Charles, who said he had witnessed the attack on his mother, continued to live on the family land and married another Italian-born woman, who was also named Frances. They eventually raised eight children, several of whom remained in the same area, on the same Palazzo land, to raise their own families. Much of the land remained in the hands of the Palazzo family down to the time of this writing. Sharecroppers and tenant farmers all are gone now, and there are no black families remaining in the neighborhood.[13]

As for the rest of the Brazos County Italian community, it continued to grow and thrive. The exact population is difficult to determine because of conflicting accounts. In 1911 the U.S. Immigration Commission reported the presence of some 350 Italian families, or 1,700 to 1,850 people, in Brazos County—a number more than twice what the U.S. Census Bureau reported for 1910. A brief account of the Brazos County Italian colony published in 1917 reported a burgeoning population of 3,000. Regardless of the exact numbers, it was clear by the first decade of the twentieth century that the Italians had settled permanently in the county, and in particular had claimed Mudville as their own. As the Immigration Commission investigator noticed in 1910, "The Italians occupy all the rich bottom land of the Brazos River." After the turn of the century, there were no more reported rapes or attacks of any sort on Italians by African Americans. Instead, in several instances, Italians shot and killed African Americans, and were exonerated in court.[14]

But they were not yet quite assimilated into Brazos County's white society. Immigration Commission investigators noticed clear social segregation between the Italians and other residents of the county, although they dismissed racism as a cause. "There is no race prejudice, but the Americans and the Bohemians have little to do with the Italians." But of course there was race prejudice: a few years earlier in neighboring Burleson County, Italians had been excluded from the white primary elections on the grounds of race, and were ranked instead with Mexicans and African Americans. Italians clearly had been excluded from the newly formed Bryan Business League. And Fannie Palazzo's credibility as a rape victim was weakened considerably because of her nationality—and her in-between racial status.

Fannie Palazzo's bid to be treated as a white woman was met initially with ambiguous response, before the lynching of her attacker helped to resolve her status. As for the rest of the Italian community, their in-between status was rapidly dissolving twenty years later in favor of whiteness. By World War I the Italians' landholdings had increased still further, and now they were voting. In competition with Bohemians, they replaced black officeholders by winning elected office at the justice of the peace and constable level. They put two of their own—Charles DiStefano followed by C. M. Degelia—on the county court of commissioners. By the 1930s many Italian-born residents, including Brazos Varisco, were on their way to becoming the county's most prominent citizens. By the time Varisco became the owner of the Parker-Astin store, there was no question of his credibility. He was the largest individual property owner in the county, and he paid the largest amount of taxes of any individual. One could argue that there was no more prominent person in Bryan or in the county than Brazos Varisco. Other families of Italian origin had also gone on to various high levels of economic, social, and political success, such as the Scarmados, the Ruffinos, the Lampos. Meanwhile, back in Mudville—also known as Steele's Store—the descendants of the Italians, who had cleared, planted, and finally claimed the area as their own, wanted recognition for their accomplishments, some sort of official statement of what they had achieved.

In 1992 they got their wish. A Texas historical marker was placed where the original store owned by Henry B. Steele had once stood. As is often the case with historical markers, the sign was as significant for what it left out as for what it included. The text of the marker reads:

> Anglo settlement in this area can be traced to 1851. Henry B. Steele built a general merchandise store in 1855 to serve residents of the rural community. Originally called Mudville because of frequent Brazos River floods, the store became the center of the community, and when a post office was established there in 1878 the settlement was renamed Steele's Store.
>
> Italian immigrants, primarily from the provinces of Trapani and Palermo, began settling here in the 1870s. Many of the families established large farms, and by the early 20th century the Italian community here was one of the largest in the United States. A one room schoolhouse built in 1889 was later replaced with larger structures as the population grew. The school eventually was consolidated with the Brazos County Independent School District.
>
> Predominantly Roman Catholic, the settlement was served by priests

from St. Anthony's Church in Bryan until 1903, when San Salvador Catholic Church was built. The church became the focal point of the community, with traditional Sicilian celebrations held each March to honor St. Joseph. Many descendants of the area's pioneer Italian families still reside in the vicinity.

Missing from the historical marker is any mention of the vibrant and politically active African American community that lived here long before the Italians arrived, or of the black farmers who worked the land with as much dedication as those who displaced them. When Henry B. Steele formally requested the establishment of a post office in 1878, on the eve of massive Italian immigration to the area, the community of Mudville was 75 percent black. In the following decades, the prosperous cotton farmer and county commissioner, Dennis Ballard; the justice of the peace, Matt Eaton; and the precinct constable, Powell Harvey, served as community leaders. It is interesting to note that of the three black leaders, Dennis Ballard's name lives on, though in a way that manages to be both prominent and obscure at the same time. When the 1892-era Brazos County Courthouse was demolished in the 1950s to make way for a new courthouse building, officials saved the granite cornerstone from the original building. It now rests outside the front entrance to the replacement courthouse, next to a historic cedar tree that also harkens back to earlier county courthouses. To commemorate the 1892 courthouse, county leaders later engraved on the granite stone a list of the names of the county judge and commissioners who were in office at the time that courthouse was built. As it happened, Dennis Ballard was one of those men, so the name "D. B. Ballard," among others, greets every visitor who enters or leaves the Brazos County Courthouse today. But there is no indication on the stone that Ballard was black, nor any mention of the tremendous odds he overcame to hold the position of county commissioner at a time when the political power of African Americans throughout the South had been virtually wiped out, nor any notice that he was one of the last African Americans in Texas who would serve in county leadership for a very long time.

The public memory of Dennis Ballard's life and work, and that of Matt Eaton and Powell Harvey, and especially of the community they served, is now gone, as evidenced by the historical marker in Steele's Store. What stands there instead is the record of a hard-working European immigrant community whose members assimilated into southern society and helped to develop the Texas county they adopted as their home. The Italians—like the German, Irish, and Bohemians—eventually achieved full whiteness, and the attendant insider status, as evidenced by the life of Brazos Antonio Varisco. But such status came at a cost, though not to them. Erased from the public memory of Steele's Store were those who were outsiders from the beginning, and who would remain outsiders—Brazos County's African Americans.[15]

NOTES

INTRODUCTION

1. The tally of lynch victims in Brazos County is drawn from newspaper reports compiled in Page, "African Americans in Brazos County: A Partial Bibliography," in *Brazos County Notebooks.*

2. For southern violence, see Ayers, *Vengeance and Justice.* For Brazos County violence, see Brundidge, ed., *Brazos County History,* 92–98, 267–83; Page, "African-Americans in Brazos County." For lynching in Texas, see "Lynching," in *The New Handbook of Texas,* ed. Tyler; Chapman, "Lynching in Texas"; Buenger, *Path to a Modern South,* 19–26; Carrigan, *Making of a Lynching Culture.* For case studies of Texas lynchings, see SoRelle, "'Waco Horror,'" 517–37; Akers, *Flames after Midnight;* Bernstein, *First Waco Horror.*

3. Barr, *Black Texans,* 84–85.

4. A substantial number of works about lynching have been published in recent decades, and the following is only a sampling of some of the most important studies. Among the first historians to focus on lynching is Jacquelyn Dowd Hall, whose *Revolt against Chivalry: Jessie Daniel Ames and the Women's Campaign Against Lynching* provided a gendered analysis of racial violence. Innovative psychological perspective can be found in Williamson, *Crucible of Race.* For comparative political and social analysis, see Brundage, *Lynching in the New South.* For an economic explanation of lynching that ties mob violence to the rise and fall of cotton prices, see Tolnay and Beck, *Festival of Violence.* Hale, *Making Whiteness,* offers a cultural theory that links lynching to a new consumerism. For analysis that probes the connection between lynching and southern evangelical religion, see Mathews, "Southern Rite of Human Sacrifice," and Patterson, *Rituals of Blood.* Feimster, "Ladies and Lynching," offers further perspective on the influence of gender in lynching. For an exploration of the historical use and meaning of the word *lynching,* see Waldrep, *Many Faces of Judge Lynch.* Pfeifer, *Rough Justice,* examines lynching in the Midwest and West, as well as in the South, and argues that lynching was an aspect of a larger cultural war between supporters of mob violence and the advocates of due process. Carrigan's *Making of a Lynching Culture* is part of a growing body of scholarship that examines the role of historical memory in forming the context of lynching. In regard to how lynchings are remembered, thought-provoking commentary on historians' perceptions of lynching can be found in Williamson, "Wounds, Not Scars." For a nonacademic overview of lynching in America, see Dray, *At the Hands of Persons Unknown.*

5. Berlin and Gutman, "Natives and Immigrants, Free Men and Slaves."

6. Rousey, "Aliens in the WASP Nest," 162; Fleming, "Immigration to the Southern States"; Woodward, *Origins of the New South;* Ayers, *Promise of the New South.*

7. Cunningham, "The Italian, a Hindrance to White Solidarity in Louisiana, 1890–1898"; Ingalls, "Lynching and Establishment Violence in Tampa, 1858–1935"; Foley, *White Scourge.*

8. Foley, *White Scourge,* 5, 211.

9. Kolchin, "Whiteness Studies."

10. Cole, "Finding Race in Turn-of-the-Century Dallas," in *Beyond Black and White: Race, Ethnicity, and Gender in the U.S. South and Southwest,* ed. Cole and Parker, 75–91; Phillips, *White Metropolis.*

11. The term *in-between* is borrowed from Barrett and Roediger, "Inbetween Peoples"; and Orsi, "Religious Boundaries of an Inbetween People."

12. Higham, *Strangers in the Land,* chap. 4; Jacobson, *Whiteness of a Different Color,* chap. 2.

13. For a comparative analysis of the racial violence and lynching directed at Mexican Americans and African Americans, see Carrigan and Webb, "*Muerto por Unos Desconocidos* (Killed by Persons Unknown)," in *Beyond Black and White,* ed. Cole and Parker.

14. Charles L. Flynn, Jr., *White Land, Black Labor: Caste and Class in Late Nineteenth Century Georgia* (Baton Rouge: Louisiana State University Press, 1982), 8, 27; quoted in Mancini, *One Dies, Get Another,* 21.

CHAPTER 1

1. The *Daily State Journal* reference in the epigraph to this chapter was quoted in Brundidge, ed., *Brazos County History,* 100; Dodson's letter is published in Foster, ed., *Bryan Legends and Legacies,* 26–31.

2. Carrigan, *Making of a Lynching Culture,* 187.

3. "Brazos County," in *New Handbook of Texas,* ed. Tyler, 1:712–14.

4. Brundidge, ed., *Brazos County History,* 1; "Robert Hemphill Millican," in *Handbook of Texas,* 4:746; Marshall, "History of Brazos County, Texas," 17.

5. Brundidge, ed., *Brazos County History,* 27–29, 85; "Millican," in *Handbook of Texas,* 4:747; Campbell, *Gone to Texas,* 306.

6. Brundidge, ed., *Brazos County History,* 27–29.

7. Ibid.

8. "Brazos County," in *Handbook of Texas;* Brundidge, ed., *Brazos County History,* 49, 65–77; Marshall, "History of Brazos County, Texas," 1.

9. "Boonville," in *Handbook of Texas,* 1:641; Brundidge, ed., *Brazos County History,* 23.

10. U.S. Congress, Department of the Census, *Seventh Census of the United States, 1850. Population.*

11. *Seventh Census of the United States* (1850); Slave and Free Population Schedules of the Seventh Census of the United States (1850), Texas, Brazos County; Brundidge, ed., *Brazos County History,* 8–15; "Brazos County," in *Handbook of Texas.*

12. *Eighth Census of the United States* (1860); Slave and Free Population Schedules of the Eighth Census of the United States (1860), Texas, Brazos County.

13. Brundidge, ed., *Brazos County History,* 8–9.

14. For an analysis of lower South influence on antebellum Texas and the assimilation of German immigrants, see Buenger, *Secession and the Union in Texas,* 10, 80–84.

15. Brundidge, ed., *Brazos County History,* 27, 237–39; Brazos County Tax Rolls, 1866; Population Schedules of the Ninth and Tenth Census of the U.S. (1870, 1880), Texas, Brazos County; U.S. Department of Commerce, Bureau of the Census, *Tenth Census of the United States, 1880. Population.* Slave and Free Population Schedules of the Eighth Census of the United States (1860), Texas, Brazos County.

16. Kingston, Attlesey and Crawford, *Texas Almanac's Political History of Texas,* 50–54.

17. Brundidge, ed., *Brazos County History,* 85–86; Brazos County Probate Minutes, Vol. E, 344 (microfilm reel #1020030). I am indebted to Bill Page of Texas A&M University Libraries Humanities and Social Science Reference Services for information regarding Brazos County's Civil War combat fatalities.

18. Page, "Millican, Texas," 116; *Galveston Daily News,* 2 October 1867; Brundidge, ed., *Brazos County History,* 3–4.

19. Bumstead, "Recollections of a Western Volunteer." Again, I am indebted to Bill Page for calling my attention to this article.

20. Ibid. Page, "Millican, Texas," 116; *Galveston Daily News,* 2 October 1867; Brundidge, ed., *Brazos County History,* 3–4. The discussion in the following paragraphs is drawn from these sources.

21. Campbell, *Gone to Texas,* 274–80; Barr, *Reconstruction to Reform,* 3–9; Brundidge, ed., *Brazos County History,* 97; Texas Election Registers, 1838–1972 (1869–1873), Brazos County.

22. Ibid. For a comprehensive overview of Reconstruction in Texas, see also Moneyhon, *Texas after the Civil War.*

23. Campbell, *Gone to Texas,* 279. The following account of the Millican "riot" is based on information in Crouch, *Freedman's Bureau and Black Texans,* chap. 5; Brundidge, ed., *Brazos County History,* 95–98; Page, "Millican, Texas, 1821–1889: A Sourcebook," in *Brazos County Notebooks,* 124–30; Moneyhon, *Texas after the Civil War,* 95.

24. George Hamilton, "Lawmen and Outlaws," in *Brazos County History,* ed. Brundidge, 269; Page, "Millican, Texas," 221; *Houston Daily Post,* 1 March 1887.

25. Page, "Millican, Texas," 3; Grimes County Historical Comission, *History of Grimes County,* 56.

26. Campbell, *Gone to Texas,* 282–85; Brundidge, ed., *Brazos County History,* 332.

27. Brundidge, ed., *Brazos County History,* 98.

28. Myers, *Life of Joseph Allen,* 5–9.

29. Ibid.

30. Brundidge, ed., *Brazos County History,* 98; Page, "Millican, Texas," 154–77; *Galveston Daily News,* 22 July 1870.

31. Brundidge, ed., *Brazos County History,* 98; Page, "Millican, Texas," 154–77; *Galveston Daily News,* 22 July 1870.

32. Brundidge, ed., *Brazos County History,* 98; Page, "Millican, Texas," 157; *Galveston Daily News,* 8 August 1875; *Bryan Eagle,* 12 September 1895.

33. Brundidge, ed., *Brazos County History,* 98; Page, "Millican, Texas," 157; *Galveston Daily News,* 8 August 1875; *Bryan Eagle,* 12 September 1895.

34. Texas Election Registers, 1838–1972 (1886, 1888), Brazos County.

35. U.S. Congress, Department of the Census, *Ninth Census of the United States, 1870. Population.*

36. Foster, *Bryan Legends,* 26–30.

37. Slave and Free Population Schedules (1850, 1860).

38. Page, "Brazos County Postal History, 1841–1900"; Brazos County Tax Rolls, 1880; Population Schedule, Tenth Census (1880); Brundidge, ed., *Brazos County History,* 37.

39. Page, "African-Americans in Brazos County," in *Brazos County Notebooks,* 2.

40. Hamilton, "Lawmen and Outlaws," in *Brazos County History,* ed. Brundidge, 270–73.

41. Population Schedule, Twelfth Census of the United States (1900), Texas, Brazos County.

42. *Bryan Eagle,* 26 June 1890.

43. Guterl, *The Color of Race in America,* 5–6.

CHAPTER 2

1. For example, "Bryan is a white man's town," *Bryan Eagle,* 26 September 1895.

2. *Bryan Eagle,* 9 March, 10 June, 12 June, 20 June 1896.

3. *Bryan Eagle,* 14 June 1896.

4. *Bryan Eagle,* 4 September 1890, 22 February 1896.

5. *Bryan Eagle,* 3 July 1890, 4 April 1895, 25 July 1895.

6. *Bryan Eagle,* 25 September 1890.

7. *Bryan Eagle,* 24 June 1897; U.S. Department of Commerce, Bureau of the Census, *Twelfth Census of the United States, 1900. Agriculture, Part I.*

8. Ibid.

9. *Bryan Eagle,* 9 June 1896.

10. The following account of the 1896 Bryan lynching is based on news reports in the *Bryan Eagle,* 10–12 June 1896, and in George Hamilton, "Lawmen and Outlaws," in *Brazos County History,* ed. Brundidge, 270–73.

11. *Bryan Eagle,* 18 June 1896; Hamilton, "Lawmen and Outlaws," in *Brazos County History,* ed. Brundidge, 278.

12. *Bryan Eagle,* 21 June 1896.

13. *Bryan Eagle,* 23 June 1896; Brazos County Criminal Court Records, 1896, Book IV.

14. Brundidge, ed., *Brazos County History,* 259.

15. Marshall, "History of Brazos County, Texas," 199; Brundidge, ed., *Brazos County History,* 65. For a vivid overview of rural life in central Texas in the early twentieth century, see Sitton and Utley, *From Can See to Can't.*

16. *Bryan Eagle,* 25 April 1895. The literature on the Farmer's Alliance and the growth and decline of Populism is vast and covers many different aspects and arguments about its development. For a historiographical analysis of works published from the 1960s through the 1980s, see Holmes, "Populism: In Search of Context." Book-length studies include Goodwyn, *Democratic Promise;* Hahn, *Roots of Southern Populism;* McMath, *Populist Vanguard;* McMath, *American Populism.* For studies of Populism in Texas, see Cantrell, *Kenneth and John B. Raynor and the Limits of Southern Dissent;* Goodwyn, "Populist Dreams and Negro Rights," 1435–56.

17. *Bryan Eagle,* 29 July, 11 August 1898.

18. *Brenham Banner,* 6 August 1874, quoted in Kelley, "Plantation Frontiers," 392. Kelley's dissertation provides an extended discussion of the German communities in Washington and other counties in the nineteenth century. For Germans in Texas, see Jordan, *German Seed in Texas Soil.*

19. Brundidge, ed., *Brazos County History,* 237–39.

20. Myers, *Life of Joseph Allen Myers,* 29.

21. *Bryan Eagle,* 7 August 1890, 10 May 1898.

22. *Bryan Eagle,* 22 June 1899; 25 April, 2 May, 7 November 1895.

23. *Bryan Eagle,* 7 August 1890, 14 June 1900, 29 June 1933.

24. For an extended discussion of fractious politics in Texas at the county level dur-

ing this time period, see Buenger, *Path to a Modern South,* chap. 1; Kingston, Attlesey, and Crawford, *Texas Almanac's Political History of Texas,* 58, 62.

25. Kingston, Attlesey, and Crawford, *Texas Almanac's Political History of Texas,* 76, 80; *Galveston Daily News,* 14 November 1888; *Bryan Eagle,* 13 March 1890.

26. Nieman, "Black Political Power and Criminal Justice"; Cantrell, *Kenneth and John B. Raynor and the Limits of Southern Dissent,* 238–40; Goodwyn, "Populist Dreams and Negro Rights."

27. Kamphoefner, "New Perspectives on Texas Germans and the Confederacy," 453.

28. Cantrell, *Kenneth and John B. Raynor,* 239–40, 326.

29. Goodwyn, "Populist Dreams," 1439–46.

30. *Bryan Eagle,* 8, 11, 14 November 1900.

31. While Steele's Store is listed as the community's name on a historical marker in the area, Mudville remained the name used on county maps, including a map published in 2002 by the Bryan–College Station Chamber of Commerce. Given a choice, therefore, I have preferred Mudville. Additional evidence in favor of Mudville was the *Eagle*'s use of the name in publishing election returns during the 1890s.

32. Pitre, *Through Many Dangers, Toils, and Snares,* 58, 117; *Bryan Eagle,* 22 November 1894; Texas Election Registers (1880–1916), Brazos County.

33. Barr, *Reconstruction to Reform,* 43–48; Texas Election Registers (1878), Brazos County.

34. *Galveston Daily News,* 12 November 1878, cited in Page, "African Americans in Brazos County: Politics," in *Brazos County Notebooks,* 6.

35. *Brenham Banner,* 27 July 1880, cited in Page, "African Americans in Brazos County: Politics," in *Brazos County Notebooks,* 7.

36. Texas Election Registers (1880–1916), Brazos County.

37. Perman, *Struggle for Mastery,* 9–36, 270–81; Barr, *Reconstruction to Reform,* chap. 13; *Bryan Eagle,* 24 July 1890.

38. *Bryan Eagle,* 3 February 1890.

39. U.S. Department of Commerce, Bureau of the Census, *Eleventh Census of the United States, 1890. Population;* U.S. Department of Commerce, Bureau of the Census, *Tenth Census of the United States, 1880, Population;* U.S. Department of Commerce, Bureau of the Census, *Thirteenth Census of the United States, 1900.*

40. *Bryan Eagle,* 19 December 1889.

41. Marshall, "History of Brazos County, Texas," 168–71; Page, "Millican, Texas"; Page, "Dark Deeds and Desperadoes: Newspaper Accounts of Crimes and Criminals, 1853–1889," in *Brazos County Notebooks.*

42. Ayers, *Vengeance and Justice,* chap. 6; Mancini, *One Dies, Get Another,* 178.

43. Walker, *Penology for Profit;* Population Schedule, Tenth Census of the United States (1880), Texas, Brazos County; *Bryan Eagle,* 11 March 1897.

44. U.S. Department of Commerce, Bureau of the Census, *Eleventh Census of the United States, 1890. Population;* U.S. Department of Commerce, Bureau of the Census, *Tenth Census of the United States, 1880, Population;* U.S. Department of Commerce, Bureau of the Census, *Thirteenth Census of the United States, 1900.*

45. Brundage, *Lynching in the New South,* 114–15, 120–24; Buenger, *Path to a Modern South,* 22; Tolnay and Beck, *Festival of Violence,* 38–39, 81–82. For an analysis of other factors leading to lynching, such as the historical memory and culture of violence that evolved through frontier settlement and racial slavery, African American resistance to white oppression, and tacit approval from political and legal authorities, see Carrigan, *Making of a Lynching Culture.*

46. *Bryan Eagle,* 6 March 1890.

47. *Bryan Eagle,* 24 July 1890.

48. *Bryan Eagle,* 11 September 1890.

49. Barr, *Black Texans,* 72–76; Campbell, *Gone to Texas,* 316; Rice, *Negro in Texas,* 34–52; Texas Election Registers, 1838–1972, Brazos County, 1890–1914.

50. *Bryan Eagle,* 25 July 1890.

51. *Bryan Eagle,* 24 April 1890, 22 April 1897.

52. Population Schedule of the Eighth Census of the U.S. (1860), Alabama, Clarke County; Population Schedule of the Ninth Census of the U.S. (1870), Texas, Burleson County; Population Schedule of the Tenth and Twelfth Census of the U.S. (1880, 1900), Texas, Brazos County; Brazos County Tax Rolls, 1879, 1885, 1890; Hamilton, "Lawmen and Outlaws," in *Brazos County History,* ed. Brundidge, 268.

53. Population Schedule of the Eighth Census of the U.S. (1860), Texas, Washington County; *Bryan Eagle,* 24 April, 19 June 1890; 12 September 1895.

54. *Bryan Eagle,* 22 May 1890, 25 July 1890; Texas Election Registers, (1890–1902), Brazos County.

55. Campbell, *Gone to Texas,* 321; Marshall, "History of Brazos County, Texas," 199.

56. For a similar analysis of northeastern Texas and the influence of the prohibition campaign on racial attitudes, see Buenger, *Path to a Modern South,* chap. 1, especially 24–26.

57. *Bryan Eagle,* 18 June 1896.

58. Hamilton, "Lawmen and Outlaws," in *Brazos County History,* ed. Brundidge, 278. The family connection between W. N. Smith and D. D. Dawson is shown in an obituary of Smith's brother, R. H. Smith, which was published in the *Bryan Eagle,* 8 May 1902.

59. Hamilton, "Lawmen and Outlaws," in *Brazos County History,* ed. Brundidge, 278; Page, "Brazos County Residents," in *Brazos County Notebooks; Bryan Eagle,* 11 November 1898, 14 November 1900.

CHAPTER 3

1. *Bryan Eagle,* 11 June 1896.

2. For a brief sampling of lynching studies, see introduction, note 4, above.

3. *Navasota Daily Examiner,* 4 April 1900, quoted in Goodwyn, "Populist Dreams and Negro Rights," 1439.

4. *Bryan Eagle,* 18 September 1890.

5. For photographs of numerous homes and buildings in Bryan around the turn of the twentieth century, see Brundidge, ed., *Brazos County History,* 357–90.

6. Ibid., 438; *Bryan Eagle,* 9 January 1890.

7. Brundidge, ed., *Brazos County History,* 362; *Bryan Eagle,* 18 July, 8 August, 7 November 1895; 27 May, 2 June, 9 June 1897.

8. *Bryan Eagle,* 11 June 1896.

9. Ibid.; *Navasota Tablet,* January 1878, cited in Brundidge, ed., *Brazos County History,* 29, 280.

10. *Bryan Eagle,* 11 June 1896.

11. *Bryan Eagle,* 6 December 1894; Brundidge, ed., *Brazos County History,* 58–59; Hall, *Revolt against Chivalry,* 145–49; Brundage, *Lynching in the New South,* 58–68.

12. *Bryan Eagle,* 6 December 1894.

13. *Bryan Eagle,* 4 April 1895, 10–12 June 1896; "Reddick v. State," 274.

14. For lynching statistics for Texas, see Chapman, "Lynching in Texas," 94–96; and Williams, "Lynching Records at Tuskegee Institute," 8. However, as noted in the text, caution must be used when examining sources such as the Tuskegee Institute or the *Chicago Tribune* as they have been found to be unreliable. When historians conducted their own research into local newspaper records, they discovered these lists to have significantly underreported the true level of violence. In the case of Brazos County, newspaper records indicate that at least sixteen lynchings occurred there, whereas official tallies have included only eight. See also, for example, Wright, *Racial Violence in Kentucky,* 4–10; Waldrep, *Many Faces of Judge Lynch,* 9, 12, 112–16, 132. See also Carrigan, *Making of a Lynching Culture,* 133, 252–53.

15. Chapman, "Lynching in Texas," 94–96; Williams, "Lynching Records at Tuskegee Institute," 8; Hale, *Making Whiteness,* 201. For a "taxonomy" of mob violence as it related to southern lynching and the prevalence of mass mobs, see Brundage, *Lynching in the New South,* 36–45.

16. Tolnay and Beck, *Festival of Violence,* 92; Brundage, *Lynching in the New South,* 68–69; McMurray, *To Keep the Waters Troubled.*

17. This quotation can be found in many studies of Ida B. Wells. See, for example, McMurray, *To Keep the Waters Troubled,* 145–47. One of the first historians to raise the question of gender was Jacquelyn Dowd Hall, whose biography of Jessie Daniel Ames, the head of the 1930s-era Association of Southern Women for the Prevention of Lynching, explored a new way to look at the impact of lynching on southern society—specifically how lynching affected the lives of white women. Hall concluded—and argued that Ames had discovered—that lynching was a tool used by white men to control not only blacks, but white women as well. By reiterating the justification for lynching over and over again—that is, the idea that lynching was necessary to protect white women from the ravages of lustful black men, known as black beast rapists—white men created a culture of fear and dependency for both black and white southerners, especially for white southern women. Hall's analysis, rooted as it was in 1970s feminist thinking, portrayed white women largely as victims of white male oppression. See Hall, *Revolt against Chivalry.*

18. Hodes, *White Women, Black Men,* 207, 202.

19. Feimster, "'Ladies and Lynching,'" 117.

20. Dorr, "Seeking Shelter under the Cloak of Chivalry." See also Dorr, *White Women, Rape, and the Power of Race in Virginia.*

21. Population Schedule, Ninth Census of the United States (1870), Texas, Brazos County.

22. Brundidge, ed., *Brazos County History,* 5; Marshall, "History of Brazos County, Texas," 106–8. For analysis of other efforts in the South to attract European immigrants, see Fleming, "Immigration to the Southern States"; Berthoff, "Southern Attitudes toward Immigration, 1865–1914"; Brandfon, "End of Immigration to the Cotton Fields."

23. Population Schedule, Tenth Census of the United States (1880), Texas, Brazos County; Brundidge, ed., *Brazos County History,* 273.

24. U.S. Department of Commerce, Bureau of the Census, *Eleventh Census of the United States, 1890. Population;* Brazos County Tax Rolls, 1887; *Bryan Eagle,* 13 May 1897; Boykin, *Italians of Steele's Store, Texas,* 26; Belfiglio, *Italian Experience in Texas,* 104–17.

25. *Bryan Eagle,* 13 May 1897; Rolle, *Westward the Immigrants,* 226; Belfiglio, *Italian Experience in Texas,* 107; Boykin, *Italians of Steele's Store, Texas,* 39.

26. U.S. Department of Commerce, *Eleventh Census, 1890. Population;* Population Schedule, Tenth Census of the United States (1880), Texas, Brazos County.

27. Brazos County Tax Rolls, 1876, 1886; Population Schedule, Tenth Census of the United States (1880), Texas, Brazos County.

28. *Bryan Eagle,* 30 April, 15 September 1898, 26 February 1902.

29. Bryan Cemetery Register, Book 3, 1868–1912; Brazos County Inquest Records, 1898–1911.

30. *Bryan Eagle,* 8 September, 15 December 1898.

31. *Bryan Eagle,* 24 July 1890.

32. *Bryan Eagle,* 24 March, 24 September 1901; 27 March 1902. Population Schedule of the Twelfth Census of the U.S. (1900), Texas, Brazos County; Brazos County tax rolls, 1900.

33. Friedman, *Crime and Punishment in American History,* 217–20.

34. U.S. Congress, U.S. Immigration Commission, "Recent Immigrants in Agriculture," in Part 24 of *Reports of the Immigration Commission: Immigrants in Industries,* 1:349–52; *Bryan Daily Eagle,* 15 May 1966.

35. *Washington Post,* 20 July 1899. Many thanks to Bill Page for locating this citation and calling my attention to it.

36. *New York Times,* 12 April 1904. Again, I am grateful to Bill Page for locating this citation. Jacobson, *Whiteness of a Different Color,* 57.

37. Scarpaci, "Immigrants in the New South."

38. Webb, "Lynching of Sicilian Immigrants in the American South, 1886–1910," 57.

39. Scarpaci, "Tale of Selective Accommodation," 44–45.

40. Brazos County Tax Rolls, 1887, 1900, 1904; Ramirez and Palazzo Sr. interview.

41. *Bryan Eagle,* 6 December 1894.

42. Hamilton, "Lawmen and Outlaws," in *Brazos County History,* ed. Brundidge, 276.

43. Ibid.; Population Schedule of the Twelfth Census of the U.S. (1900), Texas, Brazos County.

44. *Bryan Eagle,* 6 December 1894.

45. Hamilton, "Lawmen and Outlaws," in *Brazos County History,* ed. Brundidge, 276–78.

46. *Southwestern Reporter,* 274.

47. *Bryan Eagle,* 10 June 1896.

48. *Bryan Eagle,* 12, 18 June 1896.

49. *Southwestern Reporter,* 274.

50. *Bryan Eagle,* 11 June 1896.

CHAPTER 4

1. The following account of the attack on Miss DeHart and the capture and lynching of Eugene Washington is based on news accounts published in the *Bryan Eagle,* 22–28 January 1897; *San Antonio Daily Express,* 22–24 January 1897; *Galveston Daily News,* 22–25 January 1897; *Austin Daily Statesman,* 24 January 1897; and *Marshall Messenger,* 25 January 1897.

2. Information about Bryan's black neighborhoods in the 1890s was gleaned from the pages of the *Eagle,* which occasionally mentioned black residents of Bryan, and from the manuscript census returns for the Population Schedule for the Twelfth Census of the United States (1900), Texas, Brazos County. For a personal memoir of life in the Candy

Hill neighborhood, which developed later in the twentieth century, see Nash, *Bigmama Didn't Shop at Woolworth's*.

3. McMurray, *To Keep the Waters Troubled;* Hodes, *White Women, Black Men*.

4. *Bryan Eagle*, 28 January 1897.

5. For a vivid analysis of male culture and recreation in rural southern towns, see Ownby, *Subduing Satan*, especially chap. 2, "The Town: Main Street."

6. Gleeson, *The Irish in the South, 1815–1877*, 1–73; Roediger, *Wages of Whiteness*.

7. Flannery, *Irish Texans*, 31–58; "Irish," in *New Handbook of Texas*, 3:870; Gleeson, *Irish in the South*, 31–37; Nance, *Early History of Bryan and the Surrounding Area*, 3.

8. Gleeson, *Irish in the South*, 27, 75, 122–23, 132–36; Slave and Free Population Schedules of the Seventh and Eighth Census of the U.S. (1850, 1860), Texas, Brazos County.

9. U.S. Congress, Bureau of the Census, *Ninth Census of the United States, 1870, Population;* U.S. Congress, Bureau of the Census, *Tenth Census of the United States, 1880, Population*.

10. *Bryan Eagle*, 12 September 1895, 18 March 1896.

11. Page, "Millican, Texas, 1821–1889: A Sourcebook," in *Brazos County Notebooks*, 227; *Brenham Daily Banner*, 3 May 1889.

12. Population Schedule of the Ninth Census of the U.S. (1870), Texas, Brazos County; Brundidge, ed., *Brazos County History*, 95–96.

13. Page, "Millican, Texas," 197; *Galveston Daily News*, 7 September 1880.

14. Page, "Millican, Texas," 227; *Galveston Daily News*, 21 May 1889.

15. Myers, *Life of Joseph Allen Myers*.

16. Population Schedule of the Tenth and Twelfth Census of the U.S. (1880, 1900), Texas, Brazos County; *Bryan Eagle*, 7 February 1895. The narration of events in the following paragraphs is based on this newspaper story.

17. *Galveston Daily News*, 31 January through 2 February 1895; *Bryan Eagle*, 7 February 1895. The latter source is the basis for the quotations and further narration of events in the following paragraphs.

18. Plea bargaining became more evident in court cases as the nineteenth century drew to a close, and became widely pervasive in the twentieth century. See Friedman, *Crime and Punishment in American History*, 250–52.

19. *Bryan Eagle*, 18 April 1895.

20. *Bryan Eagle*, 25 April 1895.

21. *Bryan Eagle*, 18 April, 3 October 1895; 8 October 1901. Litwack, *Trouble in Mind*, 253.

22. *Bryan Eagle*, 18 September 1902, 11 December 1902, 16 April 1903, 4 June 1903.

23. *Bryan Eagle*, 29 January 1897.

24. Ibid.

25. *San Antonio Daily Express*, 24 January 1897; *Galveston Daily News*, 24 January 1897.

26. *Bryan Eagle*, 28 January 1897.

27. Ibid.

28. *San Antonio Daily Express*, 24 January 1897.

29. *Galveston Daily News*, 24 January 1897; Barr, *Black Texans*, 85.

30. *Bryan Eagle*, 28 January 1897.

31. For an analysis of the standard format given to lynching reportage and the set protocol it implied, see Waldrep, *Many Faces of Judge Lynch*, 87. For an account of the Henry Smith lynching, see Buenger, *Path to a Modern South*, 3–4, 19–25. For accounts of the Jesse Washington lynching, see Bernstein, *First Waco Horror;* Carrigan, *Making of*

a Lynching Culture, 1–7, 189–206; SoRelle, "'Waco Horror.'" For the Kirven episode, see Akers, *Flames after Midnight.*

32. Gleeson, *Irish in the South,* 121–86.

33. Cole, "Finding Race in Turn-of-the-Century Dallas," in *Beyond Black and White,* ed. Cole and Parker; Phillips, *White Metropolis; Bryan Eagle,* 8 July 1915.

34. Brundidge, ed., *Brazos County History,* 197.

35. Ibid.

36. Texas Election Register (1904), Brazos County; Population Schedule for the Twelfth Census of the United States (1900), Texas, Brazos County; *Bryan Eagle,* 18 May 1899, 14 June 1900.

CHAPTER 5

1. *Brenham Daily Banner,* 23 January 1897.

2. *Bryan Eagle,* 3 February 1898, 8 June 1898, 22 June 1899.

3. *Bryan Eagle,* 1 March 1900.

4. *Bryan Eagle,* 15 February 1900, 5 April 1900, 18 October 1900.

5. Population Schedule of the Tenth and Twelfth Census of the U.S. (1880, 1900), Texas, Brazos County; *Bryan Eagle,* 9 August 1900, 4 April 1901, 25 December 1902.

6. *Bryan Eagle,* 15 June 1899, 17 September 1895, 2 November 1897, 3 March 1898.

7. Page, "Before Temple Freda: Jewish Residents of Brazos County, Texas, 1865–1913," in *Brazos County Notebooks;* "Sanger Brothers," in *New Handbook of Texas; Bryan Eagle,* 16 June 1897, 18 January and 29 February 1912; *Galveston Daily News,* 3 January 1883. See also Rosenberg, *Sangers'.*

8. Webb, *Fight against Fear,* chap. 1; Whitfield, "Jews and Other Southerners," 88–89.

9. Webb, *Fight against Fear* 16; Hodding Carter, *Where Main Street Meets the River* (New York: Rinehart, 1953,), 185–86, quoted in Whitfield, "Jews and Other Southerners," 86.

10. Rogoff, "Is the Jew White?" 195, 209.

11. Harry Golden, "Jew and Gentile in the New South: Segregation at Sundown," *Commentary* 20 (November 1955): 403, quoted in Rogoff, "Is the Jew White?" 212; Dinnerstein, *Anti-Semitism in America,* chap. 3; Jacobson, *Whiteness of a Different Color,* 62–66; Webb, *Fight against Fear,* 17–18. See also Dinnerstein, *Leo Frank Case.*

12. Cavitt Collection, Correspondence, Box/Binder 2, letter no. 6.

13. *Bryan Eagle,* 18 October 1900.

14. *Bryan Eagle,* 6 November, 6 December 1900; 31 January, 19 March 1901.

15. Archdeacon, *Becoming American,* 150–51; Higham, *Strangers in the Land,* 80–87.

16. U.S. Congress, U.S. Immigration Commission, "Recent Immigrants in Agriculture," in Part 24 of *Reports of the Immigration Commission: Immigrants in Industries,* 391–92; Population Schedule of the Tenth Census of the U.S. (1880), Texas, Brazos County; Machann and Mendl, eds., *Czech Voices,* 113–19. Because much of the Bob Ballard story is based on news accounts that reflected the common usage at the time of *Bohemian* for all Czech-speakers, I will follow suit to avoid confusion.

17. *Bryan Eagle,* 11 October 1900; *Guide to Historic Brazos County,* 14.

18. Texas Election Registers, 1838–1972 (1880–1914), Brazos County; Carlson, ed., *African-American Lifeways in East-Central Texas,* 23–62.

19. Machann and Mendl, *Krasna Amerika*, 7–67; U.S. Congress, *Reports of the Immigration Commission*, 391–92.

20. Population Schedule of the Twelfth Census of the U.S. (1900), Texas, Brazos County; Brazos County Tax Rolls, 1891; *Bryan Eagle*, 7 November 1901; Page, "Brazos County Postal History, 1841–1900."

21. Population Schedule of the Twelfth Census of the U.S. (1900), Texas, Brazos County; Brazos County Tax Rolls, 1901; Wentrcek interview.

22. Brazos County Tax Rolls, 1877; *Bryan Eagle*, 3 April 1890, 6 March 1890, 22 July 1897.

23. Population Schedule of the Twelfth Census of the U.S. (1900), Texas, Brazos County; Texas Election Registers (1894–1900), Brazos County.

24. *Bryan Eagle*, 4–25 March 1897, 5 April 1900, 28 November 1901.

25. Population Schedule of the Twelfth Census of the U.S. (1900), Texas, Brazos County; Litwack, *Trouble in Mind*, 437–44.

26. *Bryan Eagle*, 14 June, 11 October 1900.

27. *Bryan Eagle*, 7 November 1900; *Dallas Morning News*, 23 November 1901.

28. *Galveston Daily News*, 8 November 1900; *San Antonio Daily Express*, 23 November 1901.

29. Machann, *Czech Voices*, 95–99; Wentrcek interview.

30. Henry Blazek, "The Dry Summer of 1925," *Hospodar* (November 1925), translated and reprinted in *Vestnik*, 13 December 1978. Vestnik is a weekly newspaper published in Temple, Texas, for Czech families and their descendants. I am grateful to Ernie Wentrcek for calling my attention to this article. The information on the Blazek family in the following paragraphs is drawn from Machann, *Czech Voices*, 95–99.

31. *Bryan Eagle*, 11 November 1900.

32. See Litwack, *Trouble in Mind*; *Bryan Eagle*, 8 November 1900.

33. *Bryan Eagle*, 9, 11 November 1900; Population Schedule of the Twelfth Census of the U.S. (1900), Texas, Brazos County. Josephine Blazek's suicide was reported in the *Eagle*, 13 May 1905. Again, I am grateful to Ernie Wentrcek for calling my attention to her death.

34. *Bryan Eagle*, 9, 11 November 1900; *Galveston Daily News*, 10 November 1900.

35. *Bryan Eagle*, 10, 17, 31 January, 21, 28 February 1901.

36. *Bryan Eagle*, 19, 26 March 1901.

37. *Bryan Eagle*, 27 March 1901.

38. Marshall, "History of Brazos County, Texas," 71–72.

39. "Ballard File," Batts Papers, Cushing Library, Texas A&M University Library, College Station.

40. Wright, *Racial Violence in Kentucky*, 1865–1940, 12.

41. "Ballard v. State," *Southwestern Reporter* 62 (1901): 1061.

42. *Bryan Eagle*, 23 May, 1 August 1901.

43. *Bryan Eagle*, 18 October 1900; 25 July, 26 September 1901.

44. *Bryan Eagle*, 1 September, 10, 22 October 1901.

45. *Bryan Eagle*, 18, 20 September 1901.

46. *Bryan Eagle*, 8 October 1901; Brundidge, ed., *Brazos County History*, 30, 421; Marshall, "History of Brazos County, Texas," 206–8.

47. *Bryan Eagle*, 22 October 1901.

48. *Bryan Eagle*, 28 November 1901; *San Antonio Daily Express*, 23 November 1901.

49. *Bryan Eagle*, 20 February, 31 July 1902.

50. Texas Election Registers, 1838–1972 (1902), Brazos County; Barr, *Reconstruction to*

Reform, 206–7; Kingston, Attlesey and Crawford, eds., *Texas Almanac's Political History of Texas,* 58, 62, 72, 76, 272; *Bryan Eagle,* 6 November 1902, 5 February 1903.

51. Texas Election Registers, 1838–1972 (1904–1922), Brazos County; *Bryan Eagle,* 28 February 1901.

52. Texas Election Registers.

CHAPTER 6

1. *Bryan Daily Eagle,* 10 January 1895, 27 November 1902.

2. Myers, "Life of Joseph Allen Myers," 32.

3. Ibid.; *Houston Post,* 15 September 1969, sec. 5, 3; Brazos County, Naturalization Service Petitions and Records, vol. 3, petition no. 158; *Bryan Daily Eagle,* 9 August 1949.

4. Page, "Who's Who in Brazos County," in *Brazos County Notebooks; Bryan Daily Eagle,* 15 May 1966; *Bryan–College Station Eagle,* 13 October 2002; Anderson interview; Guido interview.

5. Brundidge, ed., *Brazos County History,* 11.

6. Page, "African-Americans in Brazos County," in *Brazos County Notebooks.*

7. The tally of lynch victims in Brazos County is drawn from newspaper reports compiled in Page, "African Americans in Brazos County," in *Brazos County Notebooks.*

8. *Bryan Eagle,* 23 May 1922.

9. *Bryan Eagle,* 19 June 1930; Raper, *Tragedy of,* 125–29; Hamilton, "Lawmen and Outlaws," in *Brazos County History,* ed. Brundidge, 291.

10. *Bryan Eagle,* 19 June 1930; Raper, *Tragedy of Lynching,* 126.

11. U.S. Department of Commerce, Bureau of the Census, *Fourteenth Census of the United States, 1920. Agriculture;* U.S. Congress, U.S. Immigration Commission, "Recent Immigrants in Agriculture," in Part 24 of *Reports of the Immigration Commission: Immigrants in Industries,* 2:391, 1:351.

12. Hale, "Without Sanctuary."

13. Ramirez and Palazzo Sr. interview; Brazos County Tax Rolls, 1904; Population Schedules of the Thirteenth Census of the U.S. (1910), Texas, Brazos County; Population Schedule of the Fourteenth Census of the U.S. (1920), Texas, Brazos County; Brazos County Criminal Court Minutes, 1896, Book IV.

14. *Reports of the Immigration Commission,* 349; Antonio Mangano, *Sons of Italy: A Social and Religious Study of the Italians in America* (New York: Missionary Education Movement of the United States and Canada, 1917), 9, quoted in Rolle, *Westward the Immigrants,* 229–30; *Bryan Eagle,* 17 January 1901, 6 June 1906; Brazos County Criminal Court Minutes, 1900–1906.

15. Page, "Brazos County Postal History, 1841–1900."

BIBLIOGRAPHY

PRIMARY SOURCES

Newspapers and Journals

Bryan Eagle. 1889–1970.
Galveston Daily News. 1867–1910.
San Antonio Express. 1895–1901.
Southwestern Reporter. 1896, 1901.

Brazos County Documents

Bryan Cemetery Register, Book Three. 1868–1912.
District Court Criminal Records. 1894–1910.
Inquest Records. 1898–1911.
Marriage Records. 1887–1891.
Tax Rolls. 1880–1910.

Census Documents and Publications

Population Schedules (Free and Slave) of the Seventh and Eighth Censuses of the U.S., 1850, 1860, Texas, Brazos County.
U.S. Congress, U.S. Immigration Commission. "Recent Immigrants in Agriculture." In Part 24 of *Reports of the Immigration Commission: Immigrants in Industries.* Vol. 83, Sen. Doc. 633, 61st Cong., 2d sess. Washington, D.C.: Government Printing Office, 1911. Vols. 1 and 2.
U.S. Department of Commerce, Bureau of the Census. *Eighth Census of the United States, 1860. Population.* Washington, D.C.: Government Printing Office, 1864.
———. *Ninth Census of the United States, 1870. Population.* Washington, D.C.: Government Printing Office, 1872.
———. *Tenth Census of the United States, 1880. Population.* Washington, D.C.: Government Printing Office, 1883.
———. *Eleventh Census of the United States, 1890. Population.* Washington, D.C.: Government Printing Office, 1895.
———. *Twelfth Census of the United States, 1900. Population.* Washington, D.C.: Government Printing Office, 1902.
———. *Thirteenth Census of the United States, 1910. Population.* Washington, D.C.: Government Printing Office, 1913.
———. *Fourteenth Census of the United States, 1920. Population.* Washington, D.C.: Government Printing Office, 1921.

Archival and Manuscript Collections, and Memoirs

Batt Papers, Cushing Library, Texas A&M University, College Station.

Cavitt Collection, Carnegie Center of Brazos Valley History, Bryan, Texas.

Myers, J. Allen. "Life of Joseph Allen Myers, Written in the Month of November, 1927." Unpublished memoir, Carnegie Center of Brazos Valley History, Bryan, Texas.

Oral Interviews

Anderson, Zane, by Cynthia Nevels, 2 June 2006, Parker-Astin Store, Bryan, Texas.

Guido, Cosmo and Antoinette, by Cynthia Nevels, 5 June 2006, telephone interview.

Palazzo, Vincent J., Sr., Andrew C. Ramirez, Vincent J. Palazzo, Jr., and David Wayne Marino, by Cynthia Nevels, 17 May 2004, Mount Calvary Cemetery, Bryan, Texas.

Wentrcek, Ernie, by Cynthia Nevels, 1 June 2006, Bryan Municipal Building, Bryan, Texas.

SECONDARY SOURCES

Akers, Monte. *Flames after Midnight: Murder, Vengeance, and the Desolation of a Texas Community.* Austin: University of Texas Press, 1999.

Alba, Richard D. *Italian Americans: Into the Twilight of Ethnicity.* Englewood Cliffs, N.J.: Prentice-Hall, Inc., 1985.

Archdeacon, Thomas J. *Becoming American: An Ethnic History.* New York: Free Press, 1983.

Ayers, Edward. *The Promise of the New South: Life after Reconstruction.* New York: Oxford University Press, 1992.

———— *Vengeance and Justice: Crime and Punishment in the Nineteenth-Century American South.* New York: Oxford University Press, 1984.

Barr, Alwyn. *Black Texans: A History of African Americans in Texas, 1528–1995.* 2d ed. Norman: University of Oklahoma Press, 1996.

————. *Reconstruction to Reform: Texas Politics, 1876–1906.* Austin: University of Texas Press, 1971.

Barrett, James R., and David Roediger. "Inbetween Peoples: Race, Nationality and the 'New Immigrant' Working Class." *Journal of American Ethnic History* 16 (Spring 1997): 3–44.

Belfiglio, Cav. Valentine J. *The Italian Experience in Texas.* Austin: Eakin Press, 1983.

Berlin, Ira, and Herbert G. Gutman. "Natives and Immigrants, Free Men and Slaves: Urban Workingmen in the Antebellum American South." *American Historical Review* 88 (December 1983): 1175–1200.

Bernstein, Patricia. *The First Waco Horror: The Lynching of Jesse Washington and the Rise of the NAACP.* College Station: Texas A&M University Press, 2005.

Berthoff, Rowland T. "Southern Attitudes toward Immigration, 1865–1914." *Journal of Southern History* 17 (August 1951): 328–60.

Blee, Kathleen M. *Women of the Klan: Racism and Gender in the 1920s.* Berkeley: University of California Press, 1991.

Boykin, Rosemary DePasquale. *The Italians of Steele's Store, Texas.* Nacogdoches, Texas: Ericson Books, 1993.

Brandfon, Robert L. "The End of Immigration to the Cotton Fields." *Mississippi Valley Historical Review* 50 (March 1964): 591–611.

Brundage, Fitzhugh. *Lynching in the New South: Georgia and Virginia, 1880–1930.* Urbana: University of Illinois Press, 1993.

Brundidge, Glenna Fourman, ed. *Brazos County History: Rich Past—Bright Future.* Bryan, Texas: Family History Foundation, 1986.

Buenger, Walter L. *Secession and the Union in Texas.* Austin: University of Texas Press, 1984.

———. *The Path to a Modern South: Northeast Texas between Reconstruction and the Great Depression.* Austin: University of Texas Press, 2001.

Bumstead, S. J. "Recollections of a Western Volunteer." *United Service: A Quarterly Review of Military and Naval Affairs* (April 1886): 14.

Campbell, Randolph B. *Gone to Texas: A History of the Lone Star State.* New York: Oxford University Press, 2003.

Cantrell, Gregg. *Kenneth and John B. Raynor and the Limits of Southern Dissent.* Urbana: University of Illinois Press, 1993.

Carlson, Shawn Bonath, ed. *African American Lifeways in East-Central Texas: The Ned Peterson Farmstead (41BZ115), Brazos County, Texas.* College Station: Center for Environmental Archaeology, Texas A&M University, 1995.

Carrigan, William D. *The Making of a Lynching Culture: Violence and Vigilantism in Central Texas, 1836–1916.* Urbana: University of Illinois Press, 2004.

Carrigan, William D., and Clive Webb. "*Muerto por Unos Desconocidos* (Killed by Persons Unknown): Mob Violence against Blacks and Mexicans." In *Beyond Black and White: Race, Ethnicity, and Gender in the U.S. South and Southwest,* ed. Stephanie Cole and Alison M. Parker, 35–74. College Station: Texas A&M University Press for the University of Texas at Arlington, 2004.

Chapman, David. L. "Lynching in Texas." Master's thesis, Texas Tech University, 1973.

Cole, Stephanie. "Finding Race in Turn-of-the-Century Dallas." In *Beyond Black and White: Race, Ethnicity, and Gender in the U.S. South and Southwest,* ed. Stephanie Cole and Alison M. Parker, 75–96. College Station: Texas A&M University Press for the University of Texas at Arlington, 2004.

Crouch, Barry A. *The Freedman's Bureau and Black Texans.* Austin: University of Texas Press, 1992.

Cunningham, George E. "The Italian, a Hindrance to White Solidarity in Louisiana, 1890–1898." *Journal of Negro History* 50 (January 1965): 22–36.

Daniels, Roger. *Coming to America: A History of Immigration and Ethnicity in American Life.* New York: HarperCollins, 1990.

Dinnerstein, Leonard. *Anti-Semitism in America.* New York: Oxford University Press, 1994.

———. *The Leo Frank Case.* Athens: University of Georgia Press, 1987 [1968].

Dinnerstein, Leonard, and Mary Palsson, eds. *Jews in the South.* Baton Rouge: Louisiana State University Press, 1973.

Dorr, Lisa Lindquist. "Seeking Shelter under the Cloak of Chivalry: White Women, Rape, and the Limits of Protection in Twentieth-Century Virginia." Presented at Southern Historical Association annual conference, New Orleans, 2001.

———. *White Women, Rape, and the Power of Race in Virginia: 1900–1960.* Chapel Hill: University of North Carolina Press, 2004.

Dray, Phillip. *At the Hands of Persons Unknown: The Lynching of Black America.* New York: Random House, 2002.

Feimster, Crystal Nicole. "Ladies and Lynching: The Gendered Discourse of Mob Violence in the New South, 1880–1930." Ph.D. diss., Princeton University, 2000.

Flannery, John Brendan. *The Irish Texans.* San Antonio: University of Texas Institute of Texas Cultures at San Antonio, 1980.

Fleming, Walter. "Immigration to the Southern States." *Political Science Quarterly* 20 (1905): 276–97.

Foley, Neil. *White Scourge: Mexicans, Blacks and Poor Whites in Texas Cotton Culture.* Berkeley: University of California Press, 1997.

Foster, Betty Clements, ed. *Bryan Legends and Legacies.* Bryan, Texas: City of Bryan, 1996.

Friedman, Lawrence M. *Crime and Punishment in American History.* New York: Basic Books, 1993.

Gleeson, David T. *The Irish in the South, 1815–1877.* Chapel Hill: University of North Carolina Press, 2001.

Goodwyn, Lawrence C. *Democratic Promise: The Populist Movement in America.* New York: Oxford University Press, 1976.

———. "Populist Dreams and Negro Rights: East Texas as a Case Study." *American Historical Review* 76 (December 1971): 1435–56.

Gossett, Thomas F. *Race: The History of an Idea in America.* New York: Oxford University Press, 1963; reprint, 1997.

A Guide to Historic Brazos County. Bryan: Brazos Heritage Society, 2003.

Guterl, Matthew Pratt. *The Color of Race in America, 1900–1940.* Cambridge, Mass.: Harvard University Press, 2001.

Hahn, Steven. *The Roots of Southern Populism: Yeoman Farmers and the Transformation of the Georgia Upcountry, 1850–1890.* New York: Oxford University Press, 1980.

Hale, Grace Elizabeth. *Making Whiteness: The Culture of Segregation in the South, 1890–1940.* New York: Pantheon Books, 1998.

———. "Without Sanctuary: Lynching Photography in America." Exhibition review. *Journal of American History* 89 (December 2002): 989–94.

Hall, Jacquelyn Dowd. *Revolt against Chivalry: Jessie Daniel Ames and the Women's Campaign against Lynching.* Rev. ed. New York: Columbia University Press, 1993.

Hamilton, George. "Lawmen and Outlaws." In *Brazos County History: Rich Past—Bright Future,* ed. Glenna Fourman Brundidge, 267–301. Bryan, Texas: Family History Foundation, 1986.

Hewitt, William Phillip. "The Czechs in Texas: A Study of the Immigration and the Development of Czech Ethnicity, 1850–1920." Ph.D. diss., University of Texas at Austin, 1978.

Higham, John. *Strangers in the Land: Patterns of American Nativism, 1860–1925.* New Brunswick, N.J.: Rutgers University Press, 1955.

Hodes, Martha. *White Women, Black Men: Illicit Sex in the Nineteenth Century South.* New Haven: Yale University Press, 1998.

Holmes, William F. "Populism: In Search of Context." *Agricultural History* 68 (1990): 26–58.

Ingalls, Robert P. "Lynching and Establishment Violence in Tampa, 1858–1935." *Journal of Southern History* 53 (November 1987): 613–44.

Jacobson, Matthew Frye. *Whiteness of a Different Color: European Immigrants and the Alchemy of Race.* Cambridge, Mass.: Harvard University Press, 1999.

Jordan, Terry G. *German Seed in Texas Soil: Immigrant Farmers in Nineteenth Century Texas.* Austin: University of Texas Press, 1966.

Kaganoff, Nathan M., and Melvin I. Urofsky, eds. *"Turn to the South": Essays on Southern Jewry.* Charlottesville: University Press of Virginia, 1979.

Kamphoefner, Walter. "New Perspectives on Texas Germans and the Confederacy." *Southwestern Historical Quarterly* 102 (April 1999): 441–51.

Kelley, Sean Michael. "Plantation Frontiers: Race, Ethnicity, and Family along the Brazos River of Texas, 1821–1886." Ph.D. diss., University of Texas, 2000.

Kingston, Mike, Sam Attlesey, and Mary G. Crawford. *Texas Almanac's Political History of Texas.* Austin: Eakin Press, 1992.

Kolchin, Peter. "Whiteness Studies: The New History of Race in America." *Journal of American History* 89, no. 1 (June 2002). Available online at: http://www.historycooperative .org/journals/jah.89.1/kolchin.htm

Kraut, Alan M. *The Huddled Masses: The Immigrant in American Society, 1880–1921.* American History Series. Arlington Heights, Ill.: Harlan-Davidson, 1982.

Litwack, Leon F. *Trouble in Mind: Black Southerners in the Age of Jim Crow.* New York: Vintage Books, 1998.

Machann, Clinton, and James W. Mendl. *Krasna Amerika: A Study of the Texas Czech, 1851–1939.* Austin: Eakin Press, 1983.

Machann, Clinton, and James W. Mendl, eds. *Czech Voices: Stories from Texas in the Amerikan Narodni Kalendar.* College Station: Texas A&M University Press, 1991.

Mancini, Matthew J. *One Dies, Get Another: Convict Leasing in the American South, 1866–1928.* Columbia: University of South Carolina Press, 1996.

Marshall, Elmer Grady. "The History of Brazos County, Texas." Master's thesis, University of Texas at Austin, 1937.

Mathews, Donald. "The Southern Rite of Human Sacrifice." *Journal of Southern Religion* (2000): 4. Avaailable online at: http://jsr.as.wvu.edu/mathews2.htm

McMath, Robert. *American Populism: A Social History, 1877–1898.* New York: Hill and Wang, 1992.

———. *Populist Vanguard: A History of the Southern Farmer's Alliance.* Chapel Hill: University of North Carolina Press, 1975.

McMurray, Linda O. *To Keep the Waters Troubled: The Life of Ida B. Wells.* New York: Oxford University Press, 1998.

Moneyhon, Carl. *Texas after the Civil War: The Struggle of Reconstruction.* College Station: Texas A&M University Press, 2004.

Nance, Joseph Milton. *The Early History of Bryan and Surrounding Area.* Bryan: Hood's Brigade–Bryan Centennial Committee, 1962.

Nash, Sunny. *Bigmama Didn't Shop at Woolworth's.* College Station: Texas A&M University Press, 1996.

Nieman, Donald G. "Black Political Power and Criminal Justice: Washington County, Texas, 1868–1884." *Journal of Southern History* 55 (August 1989): 391–420.

Orsi, Robert. "The Religious Boundaries of an Inbetween People: Street Feste and the Problem of the Dark-Skinned Other in Italian Harlem, 1920–1990." *American Quarterly* 44 (September 1992): 313–47.

Ownby, Ted. Ownby, *Subduing Satan: Religion, Recreation, and Manhood in the Rural South, 1865–1920.* Chapel Hill: University of North Carolina Press, 1990.

Page, Bill. *Brazos County Notebooks.* College Station: Humanities and Social Sciences Reference Services, Texas A&M University, 1999.

Patterson, Orlando. *Rituals of Blood: Consequences of Slavery in Two American Centuries.* Washington, D.C.: Civitas, 1999.

Perman, Michael. *Struggle for Mastery: Disenfranchisement in the South, 1888–1908.* Chapel Hill: University of North Carolina Press, 2001.

Pfeiffer, Michael J. *Rough Justice: Lynching and American Society, 1874–1947.* Urbana: University of Illinois Press, 2004.

Phillips, Michael. *White Metropolis: Race, Ethnicity, and Religion in Dallas, 1841–2001.* Austin: University of Texas Press, 2006.

Pitre, Merline. *Through Many Dangers, Toils, and Snares: The Black Leadership of Texas, 1868–1900.* Austin: Eakin Press, 1985.

Raper, Arthur. *The Tragedy of Lynching.* Chapel Hill: University of North Carolina Press, 1933. Reprint, New York: Negro Universities Press, 1969.

Rice, Lawrence D. *The Negro in Texas: 1874–1900.* Baton Rouge: Louisiana State University Press, 1971.

Roediger, David R. *The Wages of Whiteness: Race and the Making of the American Working Class,* rev. ed. London: Verso, 1999.

Rogoff, Leonard. "Is the Jew White?: The Racial Place of the Southern Jew." *American Jewish History* 85, no. 3 (1997): 195–230.

Rolle, Andrew. *Westward the Immigrants: Italian Adventurers and Colonists in Expanding America.* Niwot: University of Colorado Press, 1999.

Rosenberg, Leon Joseph. *Sangers': Pioneer Texas Merchants.* Austin: Texas State Historical Association, 1978.

Rousey, Dennis C. "Aliens in the WASP Nest: Ethnocultural Diversity in the Antebellum American South." *Journal of American History* 79 (June 1992): 152–64.

Scarpaci, Jean. "Immigrants in the New South: Italians in Louisiana's Sugar Parishes, 1880–1910." *Labor History* 16 (Spring 1975): 165–83.

———. "A Tale of Selective Accommodation: Sicilians and Native Whites in Louisiana." *Journal of Ethnic Studies* 5 (1977): 37–50.

Sitton, Thad, and Dan K. Utley. *From Can See to Can't: Texas Cotton Farmers in the Southern Prairies.* Austin: University of Texas Press, 1997.

Skrabanek, Robert L. *We're Czechs.* Centennial Series of the Association of Former Students, Texas A&M University, no. 25. College Station: Texas A&M University Press, 1988.

SoRelle, James. "'The Waco Horror': The Lynching of Jesse Washington." *Southwestern Historical Quarterly* 86 (April 1983): 517–36.

Tindall, George Brown. *Natives and Newcomers: Ethnic Southerners and Southern Ethnics.* Jack N. and Addie D. Averitt Lecture Series, no. 3. Athens: University of Georgia Press, 1995.s

Tolnay, Stewart E., and E. M. Beck. *A Festival of Violence: An Analysis of Southern Lynchings, 1882–1930.* Urbana: University of Illinois Press, 1995.

Tyler, Ron, ed. *The New Handbook of Texas.* Austin: Texas State Historical Association, 1996.

Waldrep, Christopher. *The Many Faces of Judge Lynch: Extralegal Violence and Punishment in America.* New York: Palgrave Macmillan, 2002.

Walker, Donald R. *Penology for Profit: A History of the Texas Prison System, 1867–1912.* College Station: Texas A&M University Press, 1988.

Webb, Clive. *Fight against Fear: Southern Jews and Black Civil Rights.* Athens: University of Georgia Press, 2003.

———. "Lynching of Sicilian Immigrants in the American South, 1886–1910." *American Nineteenth Century History* vol. 3, no. 1 (Spring 2002): 45–76.

Whitfield, Stephen J. "Jews and Other Southerners: Counterpoint and Paradox." In *"Turn to the South": Essays on Southern Jewry,* ed. Nathan M. Kaganoff and Melvin I. Urofsky. 88–89. Charlottesville: University Press of Virginia, 1979.

Williams, Daniel T. "The Lynching Records at Tuskegee Institute." In *Eight Negro Bibliographies.* New York: Kraus Reprint Co, 1970.

Williamson, Joel. *The Crucible of Race: Black/White Relations in the American South since Emancipation.* New York: Oxford University Press, 1984.

———. "Wounds, Not Scars: Lynching, the National Conscience, and the American Historian." *Journal of American History* 83, no. 4 (March 1997): 1217–72.

Woodward, C. Vann. *Origins of the New South, 1877–1913.* Baton Rouge: Louisiana State University Press, 1951.

Wright, George C. *Racial Violence in Kentucky, 1865–1940: Lynchings, Mob Rule, and "Legal Lynchings."* Baton Rouge: Louisiana State University Press, 1990.

INDEX

Abercrombie, G. B., 47

African Americans: black militia in Millican, 20–21; black-on-black crime, 28, 119; Brazos County presence of, 2, 15, 26–28, 51–53; as business owners, 97, 153; churches as political centers for, 19–20; criminalization of, 52, 67, 119; and emancipation, 17; as focus of white anxieties, 10, 20, 52, 71, 74; and immigrants, 85, 114–15, 127; invisibility to history, 161; and Jim Crow segregation, 66, 123; lack of social mobility, 4; as landowners, 128, 129–30; and newspaper's focus on crime, 119–20; political influence of, 19–20, 22, 39, 45, 48–56, 65, 117, 129–30, 144–45, 147, 161; political manipulation of, 19, 20, 29, 46–47, 50, 65, 66–67, 147–48; post-Civil War community in Mudville, 26–28; repression of, 52, 153, 157; residential patterns in Bryan, 96–97; social isolation of, 78; support for Myers, 24; unequal justice for, 88–89, 92–93, 109–10, 136, 140–41. *See also* Republicans; slavery

agriculture, 13, 14, 18, 40. *See also* cotton production; labor

alcoholic beverages, prohibition on, 43, 60

Allen, Ed, 118–19

American Indians, 10, 14, 29

American Protective Association, 126

Anderson, Zane, 152

anti-lynching legislation, 113

anti-Semitism, 123

Asberry, Alexander, 47

Asberry, Texana, 88

assimilation: immigrants' successful, 5, 32, 79–81, 115–16, 121–22, 148–53, 156–62; and Jewish presence in South, 123. *See also* whiteness

Astin, John E., 151

Astin, Roger Q., 154

Austin, Stephen F., 10, 11, 102

Ayers, Edward, 4

Baker, C. L., 133

Ballard, Bob, 129, 130–31, 132–33, 135–45, 146–47

Ballard, Dennis, 55, 117, 129–30, 144–45, 147, 161

Ballard, Emmeline, 129

Baptists, 43, 60, 126

Barron, J. W., 22

Barson, Abe, 130

Benchley, Texas, 96, 98, 102, 114, 155

Berlin, Ira, 3

Blackland Prairie, 12

black militia in Millican, 20–21

blacks. *See* African Americans

black women, and witness credibility, 88–89, 92–93

Blazek, Henry, 133

Blazek, Josef, 132–35, 139

Blazek, Josephine, *135*, 137

Blume, J. C., 148

Board, A. G., 110, 119

Bohemian Czechs: assimilation of, 148–49; and Ballard's execution, 132–44; influx of, 28; as landowners, 127–29; low profile of, 120–21; origins in Brazos County, 126–27; racial identity for, 121, 133, 138–44; settlement patterns, 77–78. *See also* Moravian Czechs

Boldridge, Nonnie, 24

Bonneville, M., 146

Boonville, Texas, 13, 18

Bowman, Mrs. Henry, 155

Bradley, Ezekiel, 28

Brandon, T. L. D., 78

Brazoria County, 52–53

Brazos Bottom: black majority in, 153–54; and black political clout, 45; Bohemian political influence in, 148–49; and culture of violence, 120; economic importance of, 12; Italian prosperity in, 83. *See also* Mudville, Texas

Brazos County: African-American presence, 2, 15, 26–28, 51–53; binary racial division, 5–6, 29–30; during Civil War, 16–18; culture of violence in, 9–10, 12, 18–28, 118–19, 120,

ISBN-13: 978-1-58544-589-9
ISBN-10: 1-58544-589-4